The New Parliaments of Central and Eastern Europe

Edited by
DAVID M. OLSON and PHILIP NORTON

FRANK CASS
LONDON • PORTLAND, OR.

First published in 1996 in **Great** *Britain by*
FRANK CASS AND COMPANY LIMITED
Crown House, 47 Chase Side, Southgate, London N14 5BP, England

and in the United States of America by
FRANK CASS
c/o International Specialized Book Services, Inc.
5824 N.E. Hassalo Street, Portland, Oregon 927213-3640

Reprinted 2001

British Library Cataloguing in Publication Data

The new parliaments of Central and Eastern Europe
1. Legislative bodies – Europe, Central   2. Legislative bodies
– Europe, Eastern
I. Olson, David M.   II. Norton, Philip
328.3'0943

ISBN 0 7146 4715 2 (hardback)
ISBN 0 7146 4261 4 (paperback)

Library of Congress Cataloging-in-Publication Data

The new parliaments of Central and Eastern Europe / edited by David M.
   Olson and Philip Norton.
      p. cm.
   "This group of studies first appeared in a Special issue of the
Journal of legislative studies, vol. 2, no. 1 (Spring 1996) "--CIP's
pub. info.
   Includes bibliographical references and index.
   ISBN 0-7146-4715-2 (hb). -- ISBN 0-7146-4261-4 (pb)
   1. Legislative bodies--Europe, Eastern. 2. Legislative bodies-
-Former Soviet republics. 3. Europe, Eastern--Politics and
government--1989- 4. Former Soviet republics--Politics and
government. I. Olson, David M. II. Norton, Philip.
JN96.A71N49 1996   95-53926
306.2'3'09491717--dc20   CIP

This group of studies first appeared in a Special Issue of *The Journal of Legislative Studies*, Vol.2, No.1 (Spring 1996), [The New Parliaments of Central and Eastern Europe].

Printed & bound by Antony Rowe Ltd, Eastbourne

Contents

Legislatures in Democratic Transition

DAVID M. OLSON and PHILIP NORTON

Legislatures are ubiquitous and have consequences for political systems. The focus of analysis has typically been the role of the legislature in affecting policy outcomes in an established polity. Opportunities for analysing the role of legislatures in regime transitions have been limited. The transition from Communist regimes to new democracies in central and eastern Europe provides a rich field for analysis. This paper provides the framework for analysis, identifying two key variables in constitution making – the specific experiences of a nation and borrowing from foreign practice – and three sets of variables in determining legislative activity: the external environment, internal characteristics, and policy attributes.

Legislatures are remarkable institutions. They are pervasive. Relatively few countries are without one. Federal nations typically have several. They are a core feature of democratic states. They have also been a feature of many Communist and one-party states. Their consequences for their respective political systems have varied enormously,[1] but all have fulfilled a core legitimising function.[2]

Given their constitutional status as core state institutions, their number and, in some cases, their longevity – the Icelandic *Althingi* and the British Parliament dating back several centuries – it is not surprising that literature on legislatures is extensive. Yet the literature is notable for its gaps as much as for its quantity. We know a great deal about individual legislatures, most notably the US Congress, but relatively little about legislatures as a particular species of institution. The obstacles to comparative analysis have been several and substantial.[3]

Where legislatures have been analysed in some detail it has typically been in terms of their role in an established, though not necessarily stable, polity. Their powers and their relationship to other state institutions have been defined by constitutions, and study has focused on those relationships and the capacity of the legislature to influence or determine public policy. Malcolm Shaw, in his study of legislative committees, quotes approvingly the definition of Edelman and Zelniker: 'Parliamentary strength or weakness we consider as an institution's command of political resources for

David M. Olson is Professor of Political Science, University of North Carolina-Greensboro, USA. Philip Norton is Professor of Government at the University of Hull, UK.

The research making this volume possible was supported in part by grants from the International Research and Exchanges Board, and the National Science Foundation Grant #9312375. Their joint assistance was essential in making it possible for the contributors to meet.

the purpose of influencing public policy'.[4] Few attempts have been made to consider the role of legislatures in regime transition. What role do legislatures play in the change from one political system to another? Are they important actors, serving to shape a new constitution and give it life? Or are they peripheral and dependent, the product of forces upon which they then exert no reciprocal influence?

One reason for the limited attempt at answering such questions is limited resources. The field of comparative legislative study is not a crowded one and scholars are not necessarily in a position to study at close quarters some of the transitions that take place. Another reason is limited opportunity. Though the century has been littered with countries moving from one political system to another – dictatorship to democracy, one-party state to multi-party state, democracy to military dictatorship – there have been relatively few cases in recent history where several countries with one particular type of regime have moved over to another type at the same time. The basis for systematic comparative analysis has been limited.

Latin America has provided a rare case of regime changes occurring at once among many countries in a region, and has generated an important literature.[5] Europe now offers three other examples. Three countries of southern Europe have witnessed the transition from authoritarian regimes to new democracies.[6] In western Europe, a category encompassing the preceding three countries, the development of the European Union has created a new constitutional environment for parliaments of the Member States.[7] In central and eastern Europe, the collapse of the Soviet regime has led to the emergence of new post-Communist regimes. For legislative scholars, events in Europe in recent years thus provide a rich field of study.

It is the events in central and eastern Europe that form the focus of this volume. The fall of Communism throughout central and eastern Europe created opportunities that seemed unimaginable less than ten years before. The old regimes collapsed. One disappeared with the reunification of Germany. The other newly liberated nations each had the opportunity to forge a new democratic constitution.

In analysing the period of transition, there are two common features. One is the time period. The newly emerging democratic nations were undergoing their transition at the same time. The other is the creation of a legislature. As in other countries, though going by different names – for convenience, referred to here as parliaments – legislatures were transformed in each country.

We thus have the basis for a systematic analysis of the role of parliaments in the transition from non-democratic to democratic regimes. That analysis is of countries that differ remarkably. The countries of the Soviet bloc were under the same yoke but beyond that often had little in common. Soviet domination did not so much transform the societies that existed but rather held them in check. Once the Soviet yoke was removed there was, in Enoch Powell's words, a reversion to type.[8]

The 'type' varies considerably. Some of the countries have some pre-Communist experience of democratic structures and practices; others have none. Some, notably Poland with the Roman Catholic Church, have a unifying social force; others have none. Some are ethnically homogeneous; others are not, displaying at times serious ethnic tensions. Some appear to have an entrepreneurial culture, or at least exhibit an entrepreneurial tendency; some appear to have a culture of dependency, which the Soviet years reinforced rather than erased. To refer to 'central and eastern Europe' is to refer to a geographical entity and a collection of countries that endured the same domination for a part of the twentieth century, and are having to come to terms with the consequences of the end of that domination, but beyond that is a term with limited utility.

The shared experience of these countries in terms of Soviet hegemony provides us, then, with the focus of our enquiry but we proceed on the basis that they are very different in their social, economic and political needs and orientations. We would hypothesise therefore that parliaments in these countries will develop in different ways. The extent of differences, and similarities, will form the core of our enquiry.

The potential for different responses by legislatures is facilitated by the nature of the new environment in which they are created. The transition from Communist to post-Communist regimes has been a paradigmatic one. The nature of the change and the nature of Communist rule combine to create a situation in which parliaments operate in a relatively uncrowded political space.

Whereas parliaments in established democratic regimes are typically constrained by organised interests external to the legislature – notably mass-membership political parties and pressure groups, with a party or parties dominating the executive – such influences are limited or inchoate in the new democracies, parties and pressure groups having in most cases to be formed from scratch. Under the old regime, the dominant and usually the only external source of control was the Communist Party. With its demise, there is no single body to replace it and in most cases no developed organisations capable of stepping in. Where parties and pressure groups are created quickly, and take root, the parliament may develop links with them or may be constrained by their activities. Where no such development occurs, or takes place in a limited or fragmented way, there is the potential for parliaments to exercise powers largely unrestrained by such external influences.

Given the newness of parties, there is no experience of being held responsible, through parties, to electors. Party organisation inside and outside parliament is typically rudimentary, with little or no linkage between the party outside and the party inside the parliament. Within the institution, the new members have not had time to develop the complicated internal structures of political parties and committees. The institution itself is likely to have a poorly developed infrastructure and few resources. Where new parties establish themselves and attract mass support, the links with party members in parliament may develop and lead to some degree of party cohesion. Where parties are poorly organised or fragmented, there is the possibility that members' actions may be shaped by individual preferences or perceptions of mass demands.

We thus have the basis for a fascinating study of legislative development in regime formation and in the early years of the new regimes. Our analytic concern is two-fold. First, to see how parliaments have emerged and responded in the initial stages of regime formation. Second, to locate their place in the polity today. Have they been central actors in the development of a new polity, and what place do they now occupy in that polity?

NEW CONSTITUTIONS

Legislatures do not exist in a vacuum. The very existence of a legislature derives from a constitution and that constitution not only determines its existence but stipulates its basic powers and its relationship to other state organs and to the citizen. This is as much a feature of the United Kingdom, with its 'unwritten' constitution as it is of countries with constitutions codified in a single document.

Yet constitutions themselves do not suddenly appear from nowhere. As John Stuart Mill observed, they 'are the work of men.... Men did not wake up on a summer morning and find them sprung up'.[9] Constitutions are man-made constructs. With the fall of the old regimes, the new polities of central and eastern Europe had to establish new constitutions. We are concerned here not only with who was given responsibility for drawing up the new constitutions, but where they drew their inspiration from. What were the principal influences in drawing up the provisions of each new constitution?

There are several potential influences on the constitution makers, but the two most likely influences are, we assume, foreign experience and the political culture and practice of the country. Have the constitution makers tried to make a complete break with past practice, drawing on a study of Western and other legislatures, or have they drawn on their own past national experience?

We know that Western regimes have been keen to offer the benefit of their knowledge and experience to the newly emerging democracies. Various countries have established funds to pass on such knowledge. The National Endowment for Democracy in the USA has been especially active. In 1990 the House of Representatives established a Task Force on the

Development of Parliamentary Institutions in Eastern Europe. The Republican and Democrat parties have promoted the dissemination of knowledge through their own related bodies. An East–West Parliamentary Practice Project, funded in part by the Ford Foundation and drawing on a range of Western participants, was also established. A range of bodies was set up by western European governments: in the United Kingdom, for example, a Know How Fund was set up and the Westminster Foundation for Democracy established. The European Commission in 1992 launched the PHARE Democracy Programme as part of its programme to assist economic and political reform in central and eastern Europe.[10]

Not only was aid and expertise offered and dispatched to the newly emerging democracies, but parliamentarians and parliamentary officials were invited to visit Western legislatures for discussions and briefings. Visiting delegations from the new parliaments became – and continue to be – a regular sight in west European parliaments. The result, as Michael Lee noted, was that 'the national assembly presidents and the new parliamentarians in the East had a plethora of choice, with Western embassies in Eastern capitals subject to barrages of requests'.[11]

Yet the constitution makers have been able not only to look across borders at experience elsewhere but also to look at their own history. Each country had a parliament under the old regime. Though falling within the same category of legislature, there were variations in activity and effect. 'In a few communist states, constituency services by deputies to communist legislatures are quite real.... A related function involves the communication of citizen needs to higher authorities, primarily state bureaucracies.'[12] The Polish *Sejm* achieved some limited degree of administrative oversight.[13] This experience may have served to influence the form in which the new legislature was drawn. The more active the old legislature was, the more we would expect past experience to influence the drafters of the new constitution.

The fact that most constitution makers would have little or no experience of a legislature other than their own would, in any event, seem likely to colour their perspective. Furthermore, though the old regime may have been repudiated, the services of officials and even some politicians of the old regime may have been needed in order to get the new system working, and thus some of the culture of the old regime may have carried over. Where politicians of the old regime were involved in the constitution-making process, then we would expect the impact of the culture to be most marked.

LEGISLATIVE IMPACT

What, then, determines the effect of the legislature in a new democracy? We structure our analysis on the basis of three sets of variables. They derive from certain assumptions about change, and to that extent we are testing working hypotheses. Our principal assumptions are that variables external to the legislature will largely determine its capacity to exercise an independent influence in regime development and policy making and that variables internal to it – along with the nature of policy brought before it – will, at most, reinforce but not determine that capacity.

The three sets of variables are those of the external environment, internal characteristics, and policy attributes. Each includes several specific indicators.[14] These are listed in Table 1.

TABLE 1

THE POLITICAL ACTIVITY OF PARLIAMENTS: KEY VARIABLES AND INDICATORS

A. **EXTERNAL ENVIRONMENT**
    1.   constitutional structure:
        presidential, parliamentary and variations

    2.   administrative structure:
        decentralised and open, or centralised and closed

    3.   party and electoral system:
        party system; organisation of parties; party activity in
        candidate nomination and election campaigns

    4.   interest groups:
        numerous, specialised, conflicts, relationships with
        administrative agencies

B. **INTERNAL CHARACTERISTICS**
    5.   the members:
        professional background; political experience and
        aspirations; degree of interest in the legislature

    6.   parliamentary parties:
        party system in the legislature; internal organisation and
        decision making; factionalism; relations among parties

    7.   committees:
        number and size; permanence of jurisdiction and
        membership; relations to administrative agencies; autonomy

    8.   The chamber:
        length of sessions; autonomy in setting agenda; resources
        for chamber, parties, committees and members

    9.   constituency relations:
        electoral and legislative involvement of citizens,
        constituency groups in member and legislative activities

C. **ATTRIBUTES OF POLICY**
    10. content and dynamics of public policies:
        substantive content; dynamics as new or settled issues;
        stability of participants and their interactions

External Environment

The Constitutional Structure

Fundamental to determining the legislature's role in a democratic polity is the type of political system stipulated by the constitution. Is it a presidential, parliamentary or hybrid system? In a presidential system there is a separation of powers and personnel; in a parliamentary system, there is no such separation, with the government being chosen through the legislature and not independently of it.[15] A hybrid system, by definition, is something of a cross-breed of the two, typically having an elected president but a government drawn from the parliament.

Presidential systems tend to predominate in the Americas, especially Latin and South America, but also – most visibly – in the USA. parliamentary systems predominate in western Europe and Commonwealth countries. However, there are differences in type within this category. Westminster systems of parliamentary government, with typically a single-party executive and chamber-oriented legislature, predominate in Commonwealth countries, notably the UK, but also Canada, India, Australia and New Zealand. The Republic of Ireland also falls within this category. Continental parliamentary systems, with a greater emphasis on coalition and consensus-building, especially in committees, predominate on the mainland of western Europe, the exemplar being Germany. The hybrid model is represented by France.

Empirical studies of legislatures suggest that the independent political activity and influence of legislatures is greater in presidential systems than parliamentary systems and that within the latter category continental parliamentary models tend to be more active than Westminster models. The experience of France, the hybrid model, suggests a particularly weak legislature.

The constitution provides the formal and fundamental framework for legislatures. But it is only a starting point in determining the relationship between the executive and the legislature. In most cases, the 90 per cent rule applies, with 90 per cent of legislative activity being initiated by the executive, which gets 90 per cent of what it wants.[16] Yet a number of countries with parliamentary forms of government have legislatures that have very differing impacts on public policy. With some, something closer to a 100 per cent rule applies. The British and Irish parliaments, for example, have acted with far less freedom than, say, the Italian, Swedish or Dutch parliaments.[17] We thus have to look at external variables beyond types of constitutions.

The Administrative Structure

The organisation of ministries, and the manner of their decision making, vary in extent and openness and decentralisation,[18] which in turn can have an impact on the activity of legislatures in the policy process. The more open the process and decentralised the locus of decisions, the greater the opportunity for legislative activity. Though sufficient evidence on this indicator is hard to obtain, it would appear that the French and German parliaments have less impact, at least on monetary policy, than do the legislatures of Britain and the USA, in part because of how their executive agencies function.[19] Swedish parliamentarians are engaged in the advisory commissions that are a feature of the decentralised and accessible Swedish administration.

Party System and Election Campaign Structure

The number and internal structures of political parties vary among democracies. There are two-party, multi-party, and dominant-party systems, with many variations in each of these categories. Some parties are highly organised and disciplined, others loosely organised with little internal discipline. In parliaments where one party has an absolute majority, and where that party is highly disciplined, we expect the parliament to have less scope for independent action than in systems where no one party dominates and/or weak party discipline prevails. In some parliaments, sanctions against members breaking party discipline are draconian. In India it entails expulsion from the parliament. In others, such as the US Congress, sanctions are weak or ineffective.

The electoral system is also an important variable, facilitating or limiting the entry of parties to the legislature. The plurality, or first-past-the-post, system – as employed in the United States and Britain – is seen to favour two principal parties. Systems of proportional representation are seen to favour parties beyond the two largest, though the extent to which they do so varies. Threshold requirements limit parties with a small fraction of the vote from gaining parliamentary representation. Types of electoral systems may also facilitate control of the central party over nominations. Some list systems of proportional representation are viewed as strengthening the hold of the central party. Other systems give greater choice to local parties or to electors.

Electoral systems are a key variable in determining the type of party system. Also important in some systems are the legal constraints on party formation. Laws are variously passed that affect parties, such as those regulating the financing of election campaigns. A number of countries also have laws dealing exclusively with political parties.[20] These typically affirm the right of parties to form but also impose some degree of regulation through, for example, criteria to be met for registering as a party. Particularly relevant in the context of the present study is the finding by Avnon, in a review of such laws in democratic countries, that those who chose to legislate a parties law, with the exception of Finland and Israel, had previously experienced a collapse of their democratic systems. 'In the process of reforming their democratic structures, the legislatures in these polities enacted parties laws that would ensure that political parties perform functions commensurate with the goals and practices of modern democracies.'[21] It would seem plausible to hypothesise that newly democratising regimes would tread a similar route.

Interest Groups

Private organisations of persons, communities or businesses often attempt to influence the decisions of government, and when they do they are termed interest groups.[22] In all systems, interest groups would rather accomplish their objectives with administrative agencies; failing that, they turn to the legislature. Even under a semi-military government, the dissatisfaction of the computer industry with administrative decisions led to increased policy activism by the Brazilian Congress.[23] We would expect parliamentary activity to increase as interest groups become more numerous, functionally specialised and homogeneous in composition, and as they disagree with one another and with operating bureaus.[24] In the absence of agreement between groups, and between groups and the relevant agency or department, the more likely groups are to seek allies in the legislature. Certain internal characteristics of the legislature, such as a specialised and active committee system, may further encourage groups to seek to encourage and influence parliamentary activity.

Internal Characteristics

The extent to which a legislature is well organised and well equipped can affect its ability to participate in the policy process. If a parliament is closely controlled externally, it makes little difference how it is organised internally. But if it has some latitude for independent thought and action, its ability to take advantage of those opportunities is affected by the extent to which it is internally organised.

The main means by which legislatures are internally organised are political parties and committees. Parties in democratic legislatures are usually few in number, large in size, and relatively 'strong', while committees tend to be more numerous, smaller in size and 'weak'. Parties tend to concentrate on the organisation of power, while committees work more with the substance of issues. In externally controlled legislatures, few committees are permitted, and their actions are limited. In the most inert of legislatures, even political parties are prohibited. The Polish Parliament of the early 1950s, for example, in which even the Communist Party was not permitted to be organised, was referred to as the 'Silent Parliament'.[25]

In democratic parliaments, the place and importance of committees and political parties tend to vary inversely with each other. In the British Parliament, the committees are subordinate to party leaders. The US Congress illustrates the opposite extreme, in which committees are largely autonomous from parties. It is this contrast that makes the British Parliament and the American Congress the prime examples of opposite ways by which democracies typically structure their national legislatures. The critical importance of committees in the autonomous functioning of parliament is well illustrated by the long and difficult process, largely opposed by the government of the day, to develop the departmental select committees in the British House of Commons in the 1970s.[26] Yet the continental parliaments have evolved a structure which combines political parties – which do select prime ministers and support cabinets – with active and important committees. The committees have delayed, amended and defeated government legislation. How these committees function in practice varies in part with the party system and with the majority–minority base of the cabinet.[27]

Political Parties

Democratic parliamentary parties differ in the degree of their internal organisation and centralisation. Parties in the US Congress are neither disciplined nor highly organised. Parliamentary parties in west European legislatures are more disciplined and organised. Both Swedish and German parliamentary parties, for example, have an extensive network of internal party committees. For parties in government, committees provide a means of communication with and protest against the decisions of their own party's government. For the opposition, they provide a means of developing policy preferences to pit against those of the government. Committee leaders from both sides may be able to negotiate with each other to explore compromise solutions.[28]

If one party has a majority, as in Britain and the USA, and if both parties have a weak internal structure, decision making will flow elsewhere in the system. Opportunities for legislative decision making are increased either by numerous parties and a consequent lack of a single majority party, or by weakly organised parties with little discipline. On the other hand, too many parties, and too little organisation, would fragment the legislature, depriving it of any internal ability to organise itself.[29] Given the conditions created by the collapse of the Soviet regime, creating opportunities for new parties in a competitive and politically muddled environment, we would expect the prospect of too many parties with underdeveloped infrastructures to be a very real one.

Chamber Committees

Committees vary greatly, with two attributes defining their ability to function in the policy process. Committees which are permanent rather than temporary, and committees which parallel rather than cross-cut the administrative structure, have an increased ability to both know and act in the policy process independently of the executive.[30] Committees can also facilitate greater independence in that partisanship can be relaxed. The lack of publicity, relative to the chamber, may permit greater candour in voice and vote, personal friendships may form across party lines and working together over time may encourage a common view to develop. Such committees can also become the means by which parties negotiate with one another.[31] This is especially so where party leaders are placed on chamber committees. Leaders and experts from different parties are thus able to interact. The personal offices of these members, and other places of personal meeting, become the places for cross-party agreements to be explored.

The expertise of committees may be increased by their powers to hear and receive evidence from external sources. Some committees, such as the *ad hoc* standing committees in the British House of Commons, have no power to take evidence. Other committees, such as the departmental select committees in the British House, do have evidence-taking powers, albeit limited. Some committees in other legislatures have virtually unlimited powers to take evidence.

The composition of the membership of committees is another independent variable. Members may be chosen because of their knowledge of the sector covered by the committee. They may be chosen because of their seniority in the chamber or parliamentary party. Where committees are permanent, continuing service by incumbents may build up both a collective expertise and a more independent ethos. The absence of such characteristics may limit the capacity of committees to operate independently. Committees in new legislatures will have had no opportunity to develop a collective ethos.

Chamber

Characteristics of the chamber itself affect the capacity of a legislature to shape public policy. Some legislatures have carved out some capacity for agenda setting, even in strong party systems. The British Parliament, for example, protects a portion of the legislative timetable for private members' bills; several significant social reforms have been enacted through such legislation.[32]

Another chamber variable is that of resources for both the chamber and its individual members. While no legislature can match the US Congress in staff support, the resources available to other legislatures vary widely. Some, such as the Canadian House of Commons, provide substantial research and support staff for committees, while others – such as the Irish Parliament – have been notable for their parsimony in the provision of resources. Some legislatures have increased resources in recent years, though substantial resources do not by themselves lead to increased parliamentary activity and independence of the executive.[33]

Legislator–Citizen Relations

Contact between legislators and citizens may be an important variable influencing the activity of parliaments on public policy. How open and direct are the links? Are citizens able to exert influence on particular legislators? Is there an emphasis on localism, as in Ireland, the USA and, to a lesser extent, the United Kingdom, or is there a notable divorce between parliamentary activity and both individual citizens and local interests? In some systems, the links are well developed. In the newly emerging democracies, we would expect the absence of a culture of making demands on legislators to militate against such links. Conversely, we would expect a counter-pressure in the need for legislators to build support in what may be politically turbulent conditions, with parties not necessarily establishing a solid and continuing base of support. Legislators may thus seek to bolster support through developing their links with citizens and local interests.

Policy Attributes

The way in which the executive and the legislature work on issues varies in part with the type of issue. The distinction between foreign and domestic policy is a broad example. It may also be that the substantive content of policy imposes a commonality across national boundaries and even across political systems: housing and airports as issues, for example, may share more similarities across countries than with each other within any single country.

Policy Content

While there are many categorisations of types of public issues, it would appear that legislatures are more active on issues affecting the distribution of benefits, and on the propagation of values, but less active on issues of either security (foreign or internal) or macro-economic policy. The French constitution allocates policy sectors to different government officials.

Policy Circumstances

Issues also differ in the circumstances in which they come to governmental attention. Some issues are highly visible and important to a wide public, while others are less visible and recognised. Some issues stimulate a wide variety of contentious interest groups, while others do not. Legislatures tend to be more active on newer and more controversial issues, and on those which arouse disagreement among interest groups, and less active on older and less controversial issues.

Policy Stages

Policy proposals are frequently prepared within administrative agencies and/or by outside advisory commissions. Involvement by legislatures is after their preparation, though the participation by some legislators (as in Sweden) in the commissions may provide some parliamentary input at the formulation stage. If a measure is brought before parliament enjoying the support of all those affected by it, then the parliament may have little option but to accept it. When it is implemented, parliamentary activity may increase. Individual legislators may seek to gain benefits for those within their constituencies. Committees may review how the policy has been implemented. Governments may regard such review as less threatening than review at earlier stages, since there may be little that the legislature can do in a definitive sense.

It may be that the unusual policy demands on the new democracies – illustrated by, but not limited to, the creation of a whole new economic system – place most of their issues in the new and unsettled category, thus creating unusual opportunities for these new legislatures to act.

CONCLUSION

The set of factors we have outlined combine to shape the ability of legislatures to function actively and autonomously in the policy formation process of their respective democratic political systems. The generalisations, derived from the experience of established democracies, suggest a way of examining the parliaments of the new democracies. The contributors to this volume undertake such an examination. In each case, they explore the genesis of the new parliament and how it is now operating in the polity. Their findings allow us to address the questions posed earlier. What have been the primary influences on parliament-building in the new democracies? And what determines the affect of the legislatures in policy making?

NOTES

1. See R. Packenham, 'Legislatures and Political Development', in A. Kornberg and L.D. Musolf (eds.), *Legislatures in Developmental Perspective* (Durham NC: Duke University Press, 1970), pp.521–37.
2. P. Norton (ed.), *Legislatures* (Oxford: Oxford University Press, 1990), p.1.
3. See Norton, *Legislatures*, pp.3–9.
4. M. Shaw, 'Conclusions', in J.D. Lees and M. Shaw (eds.), *Committees in Legislatures* (Durham NC: Duke University Press, 1979).
5. G. O'Donnell and P.C. Schmitter, 'Tentative Conclusions about Uncertain Democracies', in G. O'Donnell and P.C. Schmitter (eds.), *Transitions from Authoritarian Rule: Prospects for Democracy* (Baltimore MD: Johns Hopkins University Press, 1986).
6. U. Liebert and M. Cotta (eds.), *Parliament and Democratic Consolidation in Southern Europe* (London: Pinter, 1990).
7. P. Norton (ed.), *National Parliaments and the European Union* (London: Frank Cass, 1996).
8. E. Powell, 'Parliamentary Sovereignty in the 1990s', in P. Norton (ed.), *New Directions in British Politics?* (Aldershot: Edward Elgar, 1991), p.143.
9. J.S. Mill, *Representative Government* (London: Everyman Library ed., 1968), p.177.
10. See D. Blackman, 'The European Parliament's Aid Initiatives in Support of Democratic Development in Central and Eastern Europe', *The Journal of Legislative Studies*, 1, 2 (1995), pp.301–14.
11. J.M. Lee, 'British Aid to Parliaments Overseas', *The Journal of Legislative Studies*, 1, 1 (1995), p.126.
12. D. Nelson, 'Communist Legislatures and Communist Politics', in D. Nelson and S. White (eds.), *Communist Legislatures in Comparative Perspective* (London: Macmillan, 1982), p.8.
13. See D.M. Olson and M.D. Simon, 'The Institutional Development of a Minimal Parliament: The Case of the Polish Sejm', in D. Nelson and S. White (eds.), *Communist Legislatures in Comparative Perspective* (London: Macmillan, 1982), pp.47–84.
14. These derive from D.M. Olson and M.L. Mezey, *Legislatures in the Policy Process* (Cambridge: Cambridge University Press, 1991).
15. For these and other distinguishing attributes of the two types, see D.V. Verney, 'Parliamentary Government and Presidential Government', in A. Lijphart (ed.), *Parliamentary Versus Presidential Government* (Oxford: Oxford University Press, 1992).
16. D.M. Olson, *The Legislative Process: A Comparative Approach* (New York: Harper & Row, 1980), p.174; R.J. Dalton, *Politics in West Germany* (Glenview IL: Scott, Foresman, 1989), p.313.
17. See, for example, P. Norton, 'The Legislative Powers of Parliament', in C. Flinterman, A.W. Heringa and L. Waddington (eds.), *The Evolving Role of Parliaments in Europe* (Antwerp: MAKLU, 1994), pp.15–32.
18. C. Campbell and T. Garrand, 'Bureaucracy and Legislative Democracy in Canada, the U.K., the U.S. and Switzerland: From Turtle Syndrome to Collegiality', paper presented at the annual meeting of the American Political Science Association, New York, 1981.
19. L.T. LeLoup and J.T. Woolley, 'Legislative Oversight of Monetary Policy in France, Germany, Great Britain, and the United States', in Olson and Mezey (eds.), *Legislatures in the Policy Process*.
20. See D. Avnon, 'Parties Laws in Democratic Systems of Government', *The Journal of Legislative Studies*, 1, 2 (1995), pp.283–300.
21. Avnon, p.296.
22. D.B. Truman, *The Governmental Process* (New York: Knopf, 1951).
23. A.I. Baaklini and A.C. Pjo do Rego, 'Congress and the Development of a Computer Industry Policy in Brazil', in Olson and Mezey (eds.), *Legislatures in the Policy Process*.
24. D.M. Olson and M.L. Mezey, 'Parliaments and Public Policy', in Olson and Mezey (eds), *Legislatures in the Policy Process*, pp.11–12.
25. A. Burda, *Parliament of the Polish People's Republic* (Warsaw: Ossolineum, 1978), p.163.
26. M. Jogerst, *Reform in the House of Commons* (Lexington KY: University Press of Kentucky, 1993); P. Norton, *The Commons in Perspective* (Oxford: Martin Robertson, 1981), pp.231–2.

27. U. Liebert and M. Cotta (eds.), *Parliament and Democratic Consolidation in Southern Europe* (London: Pinter, 1990).
28. L.T. LeLoup and J.T. Woolley, 'Legislative Oversight of Monetary Policy in France, Germany, Great Britain, and the United States', in Olson and Mezey (eds.), *Legislatures in the Policy Process*, p.51; G. Loewenberg, *Parliament in the German Political System* (Ithaca NY: Cornell, 1967); M. Isberg, *The First Decade of the Unicameral Riksdag: The Role of the Swedish Parliament in the 1970s* (Stockholm: Statsvetenskapliga Institutionen, Stockholms Universitet, 1982); D. Arter, 'The Swedish Riksdag: The Case of a Strong Policy-Influencing Assembly', in Norton (ed), *Parliaments in Western Europe*.
29. M.L. Mezey, 'Parliaments and Public Policy: An Assessment', in Olson and Mezey (eds.), *Legislatures in the Policy Process*, p.207.
30. J.D. Lees and M. Shaw, *Committees in Legislatures: A Comparative Analysis* (Durham NC: Duke University Press, 1979); D.M. Olson and M.L. Mezey, 'Parliaments and Public Policy', in Olson and Mezey (eds.), *Legislatures in the Policy Process*, pp.14–15.
31. W. Steffani, 'Parties (Parliamentary Groups), and Committees in the Bundestag', in U. Thaysen *et al.* (eds.), *The U.S. Congress and the German Bundestag: Comparisons of Democratic Processes* (Boulder CO: Westview, 1990).
32. See P.G. Richards, *Parliament and Conscience* (London: George Allen & Unwin, 1970); D. Marsh and M. Read, *Private Members' Bills* (Cambridge: Cambridge University Press, 1988); P. Norton, *Does Parliament Matter?* (Hemel Hempstead: Harvester Wheatsheaf, 1993).
33. P. Norton, 'The Legislative Powers of Parliament', in C. Flinterman, A.W. Heringa and L. Waddington (eds.), *The Evolving Role of Parliaments in Europe* (Antwerp: MAKLU, 1994).

Democratic Parliamentarism in Hungary: The First Parliament (1990–94) and the Entry of the Second Parliament

ATTILA ÁGH

The First Parliament – the first democratically elected parliament in Hungary after the collapse of state socialism – covered its full parliamentary cycle (1990–94). This is unique in central and eastern Europe and gives also a unique opportunity for analysis in this four-year cycle. The new election in 1994 changed the ruling coalition but the same six parties were elected to the Second Parliament, so the political learning process of parties as major actors of transition can be continued in the Hungarian Parliament. This paper analyses, with data and documentation, all major aspects of the activities of the First Parliament.

There has been a strong tradition of parliamentarism and constitutionalism in Hungary since the mid-nineteenth century which has been revived during the scattered periods of re-democratisation. In 1989 there was a general agreement among political actors that Hungary had to become a 'parliamentary' democracy with a relatively weak president, that is, a parliamentary system as opposed to a presidential one. The debate is still going on concerning the appropriate relationships between the prime minister, parliament and president; however, nobody has questioned the basic consensus over the need for a 'parliamentary' system in Hungary. The parliament inherited from the era of state socialism was unicameral, but discussions on the necessity of a bicameral parliament have returned from time to time.

The Hungarian parliamentary and electoral system was gradually reformed in the 1980s (*well before* the actual 'system change', unlike in the other state socialist countries of eastern Europe). Consequently, several features of a democratic parliamentary system were in evidence even before the first, 'founding' election. Thus it can be firmly stated that the last parliament of the former 'state socialist' system also played a positive role in handling its initial crisis and in engineering the first phases of democratic transition. The state socialist system was changed step-by-step through the introduction of reform-legislation; in addition to these important measures, in 1989 some new, opposition MPs were elected in by-elections. Although

Attila Ágh is Professor of Political Science at Budapest University of Economic Sciences and Director of the Hungarian Centre for Democracy.

the turning point between the old and new parliament in 1990 was very important for Hungary, the contrast between those parliaments at the time of the change was relatively small compared to the changes going on throughout the entire east-central European region (ECE).

Between 1990 and 1994 – over the whole four-year cycle – the same parliament and government was in power in Hungary; this is a unique record when considered in the light of events across the whole of the ECE. Thus the first democratically elected Hungarian Parliament was the longest serving one in the ECE, and this is why it is suitable for a 'longitudinal' analysis. *My basic hypothesis is that both the positive and negative features of the ECE parliaments have appeared in Hungary in the most marked way*: the biggest achievements in legislation and constitution-making appear alongside the most significant setbacks in the new democratic system (collectively, the latter can be referred to as 'Authoritarian Renewal').[1]

THE INSTITUTIONAL STRUCTURE OF THE FIRST PARLIAMENT

Constitutional Arrangements

The 1990 Constitution laid down the principles of the Hungarian parliamentary system in the following way: Article 19 (1) 'The supreme organ of state power and popular representation of the Republic of Hungary shall be the National Assembly.' (2) 'The National Assembly exercising its rights deriving from popular sovereignty, shall guarantee the constitutional order of society and shall determine the structure, orientation and conditions of the government.'[2]

At the same time, this constitution introduced the German structure of the positive non-confidence vote, and by this action has created a very strong prime ministerial post. Only the prime minister has responsibility before parliament for the whole government – the traditional ministerial responsibility has been discontinued – and the prime minister can be removed only by electing a new one; what this actually means is that the post of prime minister is secure for the whole parliamentary cycle. Basically, the prime minister is not just the head of government, but all the ministers are only members of his government; the prime minister can dismiss ministers at his own discretion, and such dismissals are not dependent on parliament. The constitution orders that:

> Article 39/A (1) A motion of non-confidence may be submitted in writing against the Prime Minister, with the indication of the person nominated for the office of Prime Minister. This shall be agreed upon by at least one-fifth of the representatives. A motion of non-

confidence submitted against the Prime Minister shall be considered as a motion of non-confidence against the Government. If, in consequence of the motion, the majority of the National Assembly express their non-confidence, the person nominated for the office of Prime Minister shall be considered to have been elected.[3]

This motion of non-confidence – usually referred to as a positive non-confidence vote – has produced a very strong executive. The executive is led by the prime minister through his extended office, which in turn is headed by state secretaries. Alongside the strong executive is a rather weak parliament, because the means by which parliament can control the government have been significantly reduced (for example, interpellations cannot lead to the dismissal of ministers and so on).

The constitution provided, however, some checks and balances against the overwhelming power of a too stable and strong prime minister: these 'watchdog' instruments are the President of the Republic and the Constitutional Court. The president has substantial 'negative' or controlling rights *vis à vis* the domination of parliament by the government – namely, in the nominations for certain leading posts his counter-signature is needed; in addition, in the legislative process he is not obliged to sign new bills and can send them back to committee or parliament itself for further discussions and/or send them to the Constitutional Court. This control or 'watchdog' function of the president has been generalised in the constitution into a very powerful position; in the event of serious conflicts the president is provided with rights to protect the democratic institutions from abuse and degeneration.

Article 29 (1) of the constitution orders that 'The head of state of Hungary shall be the President of the Republic who represents the unity of the nation and safeguards the democratic functioning of the State organizations'.

The president has proved to be the protector of democratic institutions *vis à vis* the apparently overwhelming power of the (Antall, then Boross) national-conservative government and in this position has been supported by the Constitutional Court. The latter has also been very important as a balancing power between parliament and an overbearing government. The Constitutional Court has wide powers and it is probably the most powerful of its kind in the world. Although an analysis of this point is not our concern now, it is, nevertheless, very important to mention here its role in controlling and cancelling the voluntaristic decisions of the (first) parliament.

Article 32/A of the constitution rules that (1) 'The Constitutional Court shall review the constitutionality of laws and statutes and shall perform the tasks assigned to it by law.' (2) 'In the case of determining unconstitutionality, the Constitutional Court shall annul the laws and other statutes.' (3) 'The proceedings of the Constitutional Court in cases determined by law may be initiated by anyone.'[4]

The Constitutional Court has been acting since 1 January 1990 and it has been one of the major institutions of the 'checks and balances' system. The Constitutional Court received in the 1990–94 parliamentary cycle 260 decisions to investigate (including 21 acts of parliament and 12 decrees of government) and it declared 80 of them (31 per cent) unconstitutional. The President of the Republic on his part sent seven laws passed by the parliament to the Constitutional Court to investigate and the Constitutional Court annulled six of them. These laws were politically very important prestige issues for the Antall–Boross Government, for example, the Compensation Act, the Trade Union Act and the Act on the retrospective punishment for those politically active in the former regime.

Administrative or 'Intergovernmental' Relations

From the very beginning of systemic change it has been emphasised by the new political forces that the overconcentrated administrative structure (in which local administrative bodies serve merely as local representatives of the centralised state) has to be removed and replaced by a democratic administrative structure. The latter should be based on the substantial autonomy of local governments in their dealings with central government. The constitution formulates this principle as follows:

> Article 42: The communities of the electors in communities, towns, in the capital city and its districts as well as in the counties, shall have the powers of local self-government. The exercise of the powers of local self-government shall be an independent, democratic administration of local public affairs concerning the community of the electors and the exercise of local public authority in the interest of the population.

The First Parliament passed the act on local governments as one of the first laws of the new political system. The regulation of local self-governments – as well as their relations with local 'parliaments' – is dealt with in detail in Acts LXIV and LXV 1990. A certain degree of urgency was involved in this situation because of the need to complete the constitutional structure in time for the local government elections (that were scheduled for September and October 1990). Unlike the national elections in spring 1990, however, the local government elections were not won by the governing national-conservatives (involving, at the outset, a three-party coalition) but by the liberal parties (primarily the Alliance of Free Democrats, and also the

Alliance of Young Democrats). Thus a 'dual power' emerged for four years: the conservatives ruling the centre, and the liberals ruling the local governments. This led to a situation in which there was an 'overpoliticisation' of issues concerning intergovernmental relations.

In autumn 1990 a highly contradictory constitutional and political situation emerged. The central government succeeded, in the political bargaining process over local self-government, in establishing a system of 'commissioners of the republic'. The role of these senior civil servants was to oversee a given number of counties in Hungary in order to ensure the maintenance of correct legal procedures in the local self-government in these counties. However, the situation which actually emerged was one in which the government-appointed 'supervisors' tried to exercise political control over local governments on behalf of the central government. Thus there was, to some extent, a return to the former system of the centralised administrative state, and consequently this mechanism did not solve the real problems of the 'missing middle' in the administrative structure between central and local government. This missing middle thus was vulnerable to invasion by some governmental agencies, the latter having attempted to fill the administrative gap. Yet despite this state of affairs, it was also true that some local governments were unable to function properly without the instructions of the paternalistic state.

Party System and Electoral Law

In the recent re-democratisation process, the rise of the multiparty system began very early in Hungary. The formative phase was under way in 1987–88 and by late 1989 all the parties which were subsequently to play an important role in the political life, had already organised themselves such that they were 'ready' for the spring 1990 election. This election represented a kind of 'natural selection' in the 'hundred party system' (that is, the hundred parties which initially set out on the first election campaign). In the competition which took place only six parties survived (and, indeed, it is these same parties which were re-elected in the spring 1994 election). Although the Hungarian parliamentary party system has experienced some fragmentation, it has avoided the unworkability of some other ECE parliaments. This is not only because of the relatively early rise and long organisation processes which the main parties underwent, but also due to the electoral law which set a four per cent (in 1994 five per cent) threshold for the parliamentary parties.[5]

Hungary can be regarded as a classic example of the application of the south European thesis in central Europe, in that parliaments have been the central site and parties the chief actors of systemic change. The Hungarian Parliament was the first and the fundamental political institution to be reorganised in a democratic way; the parties themselves, having been the chief actors of the democratisation process, also experienced a parliamentarisation phase in their own internal democratisation and transformation. The first period, however, can be characterised as one dominated by *overparliamentarisation* and *overparticisation* – that is, both parliament and parties have had an exaggerated role, being almost the only influential institutions. The reason for this is simply that the other actors one would expect to find on the political scene had not yet made their entry. The task for the rest of the 1990s is to ensure that the whole democratic institutional structure is set up. Once this is done, parliament and parties will still have their central roles, but these roles will have been divested of their 'monopolistic' character, and thus they will be able to function more appropriately and hence more effectively in the political system.

Compared to the other ECE countries, the Hungarian parliamentary parties are rather well developed and organised in that they have a clear political profile and, relatively, more solid voting bases. This has been proved by the second free elections in 1994. However, taken by themselves, the contrast between the political and social existence of the parties is considerable, since these parties are politically very strong (as the only actual political actors), but at the same time socially weak, having small memberships and sparse national organisational structures. Therefore, the Hungarian parties primarily exist as 'parliamentary' parties, that is, through and in the parliament. Almost exclusively, it is their parliamentary activities which are transmitted through the media to the public (and that includes their own party memberships). There has been a big political and social distance between the (parliamentary) party leaderships and the rank and file members – the ordinary members of the parties. It has been obvious that this distance is much bigger than in west European countries. Moreover, It Is clear that this distance is even greater between the (parliamentary) political elite and the population, and this is at least a partial explanation for the low – and, as it turned out, continuously decreasing – popularity of the First Parliament and the political parties in Hungary.[6]

The Hungarian electoral system is a combination of individual constituencies and party lists. There are 386 seats in the Hungarian Parliament; 176 (45 per cent) are elected from the single member individual constituencies (in two rounds) and 210 (55 per cent) on party lists. There are two lists: the first is the territorial list (Hungary has 20 territorial units and people cast their votes for these territorial party lists). The second one is the national list, which to some extent compensates the losers of the individual constituences in order to make the system more proportional and it also cumulates the remaining votes after the distribution of seats on the territorial lists to give seats for them on the national level. As two elections have proved so far, this system is not too complicated, and it seems that voters have understood it and been able to 'use' it efficiently. In its essence it is certainly not a proportional representation (PR) system, since it gives more seats to the winning party than it would under a PR system. The electoral law has been designed on purpose to produce an easily identifiable winner, so that a solid majority can be created for a stable government. Given the fact that all the other ECE countries have had frequent changes of government since their own respective systemic changes, this electoral law can be considered successful. With the apparently close correlation between the consolidated party system and the electoral law, the First Parliament has thus found it unnecessary to make significant changes to the latter.[7]

The Political Meso-System: The Organised Interests

The constitutional place of the political meso-system has not yet been arranged – it has been only half made and in a very contradictory way. It has been one of the biggest problems of the Hungarian democratic transformation, and has been the major reason for overparliamentarisation and overparticisation. At the national Round Table talks the issue of a social pact was raised (as in Spain); however, this was in vain for in the event only a political pact was concluded. Since then the issue of the social pact has been raised several times, but the national-conservative government refused to consider it. The social pact, as it is known in Spain, Italy and Austria, is about the legal arrangements for the organised interests in the political or policy-making system on one side, and about the austerity measures to cope with the economic crisis on the other. Thus it has become yet another major task for the new government. In late 1995, a consensus emerged on the necessity of a social pact. If this consensus unfolds in the way it initially appeared to be doing, the national Interest Concertation Council could be changed from a quasi-symbolic institution and mere meeting place, into a meaningful part or stage in the policy-making process. The necessary connections between parliament and organised interests have to be created as well, including the extension of the range of socio-political actors and the incorporation of their elites.

The concept of negotiated democracy as a synthesis, an organic integration of the negotiated economy on the meso-level with macro-politics does not necessitate a second chamber based on the functional representation in Hungary, but it presupposes the following institutionalisation: (1) The participation of organised interests in parliamentary commissions and at committee public hearings, and their role as consultants for different state agencies. (2) The regular consultation of parliamentary parties with the representatives of organised interests in matters of vital concern *before* the fundamental socio-economic decisions are made. (3) There should be preliminary consultations on draft laws – before they are submitted to parliament – involving experts and leaders of organised interests; also, their participation in the implementation of those laws should be encouraged. And (4) various individual and personal contacts among MPs, heads of state agencies and leaders of organised interests should be maintained in order to strengthen the informational network.[8]

The chances of the social pact and the constitutional arrangements for the political meso-system looked very good at the beginning of the new cycle in Hungary – that is, at the start of the Second Parliament. One would hope that there will be integration of the decision-making processes on the meso- and micro-levels, this being brought about by the insertion of intermediary bodies into the parliamentary legislative process. This integration would make the legislative process and the activities of parliament and parliamentary parties not only more democratic and legitimate for the public, but also much more effective and efficient in legislation, and efficacious in the implementation of that legislation, since the First Parliament experienced many weaknesses in this field.[9]

Parliamentary Parties

The First Parliament was composed of six parties and some independents (see Table 1). Three parties (Hungarian Democratic Forum – HDF, Independent Smallholders Party – ISP and Christian Democratic People's Party – CDPP) formed the ruling centre-right coalition with an almost 60 per cent majority; three other parties (Alliance of Free Democrats – AFD, Hungarian Socialist Party – HSP, and Alliance of Young Democrats – AYD) were in opposition. This structure remained basically unchanged between the three governmental and three oppositional parties, although the governing coalition was eroded to a great extent, because the biggest governmental party suffered a series of splits which produced a series of successor parties, and the ISP as a party left the coalition officially in February 1992, but most of their MPs (36 in total) did not; they formed a faction of their own, and eventually a party emerged behind this faction in spring 1994 (the constitutionality of which is very doubtful). Actually, for most of the parliamentary cycle the coalition comprised two parties, being complemented by a third, floating group of MPs who did not have party support. This coalition was dominated totally by the HDF, and this is why its voluntaristic policies damaged all three coalition parties significantly right through and to the end of the cycle (see Table 2).

In the First Parliament six (later seven) party factions were organised. The independent MPs were considered as a quasi-faction, so they formed the seventh (later eighth) group and elected their own leader. The party factions were the major actors in the parliament; their faction leaders – headed by the speaker – sat together as the House Committee, and this decided all important parliamentary organisation matters. Yet the activities of the party factions were not properly regulated in the First Parliament. This was due to the fact that a new set of coherent Standing Orders of Parliament were not passed in that particular parliamentary cycle: instead, the 'Standing Orders' were in fact little more than a series of amendments, and these created new contradictions and left a great number of legal gaps in their wake.

One of the biggest problems of the political transition so far has been the definition of the parliamentary party faction and the regulation of its activities, rights and duties. The Standing Orders of the First Parliament note only laconically in Section 16(1) and (2):

> Representatives of the parties represented in Parliament as well as representatives not belonging to parties can establish standing groups of representatives (factions) in order to co-ordinate their parliamentary activities. A standing group of representatives can be established by at least ten representatives.[10]

The actual coherence of factions was rather low in both parliamentary discussions and voting, and the faction debates before the plenary session were weak, inconclusive or missing. The faction discipline in the governing parties was bigger and this fact, coupled with the higher rate of attendance, was very important for the stability of government. The governing coalition was glued together by the common interest to stay in power. It was not by chance that they were not ready to accept a law on the political incompatibility of membership of parliament with the exercise of economic functions on the boards of enterprises.

TABLE 1

THE POLITICAL MAP OF THE HUNGARIAN PARLIAMENT (2 MAY 1990)

	votes in %	seats	seats in %
MDF	24.73	165	42.75
SZDSZ	21.39	94	24.35
FKGP	11.73	44	11.40
MSZP	10.89	33	8.55
Fidesz	8.95	22	5.70
KDNP	6.46	21	5.44
Independents	0.00	7	1.81

Votes indicate the percentages of votes cast on the party lists. The Hungarian party abbreviations in English are HDF, AFD, ISH, HSP, AYD and CDPP.

TABLE 2
THE POLITICAL MAP OF THE HUNGARIAN PARLIAMENT (7 APRIL 1994)

	seats	seats in %	changes
MDF	136	35.23	-29
SZDSZ	83	21.50	-11
FKGP-C	36	9.33	-8
MSZP	33	8.55	0
Fidesz	26	6.73	+4
KDNP	23	5.95	+2
MIÉP	12	3.11	+12
FKGP-T	9	2.33	+9
Independents	28	7.25	+21

MIÉP (Hungarian Justice and Life Party – HJLP) was the biggest successor party of the HDF, led by István Csurka. The others were not able to organise their party factions since they had less than ten MPs and therefore their members sat with the independents. This was also the case with the ISP which left the coalition (FKGP-T, indicating the name of József Torgyán, the ISP president). However, most of the ISP's MPs (36) remained with the coalition (FKGP-C) and they were able to organise a faction, but the real party, having only nine MPs, could not. This breakaway faction of 36 MPs disappeared in the second elections, in 1994, so FKGP means again the party of Torgyán.

During the First Parliament 29 MPs left (nine died and 20 resigned) and were replaced (five in by-elections in individual constituencies and 24 from the party lists). Altogether 59 people moved inside the parliament by changing factions, including 12 MPs who later formed the HJLP faction, and the nine MPs of FKGP-T who remained outside their party faction by the split in the ISP. Table 2 shows the aggregate results of both changes, that is, inside the parliament, as well as the effects of the five by-elections from 'outside'.

The Chamber

The unicameral Chamber of the Hungarian Parliament holds at least two sessions a year: from 1 February to 15 June and from 1 September to 15 December, every week on Mondays and Tuesdays (sometimes also on Wednesdays), and committee meetings on Wednesdays (sometimes also on Thursdays). Actually, the First Parliament, in addition to these regular sessions, often had long extraordinary winter and summer sessions as well and, in such a way, the plenary sessions took altogether 378 days between 2 May 1990 and 7 April 1994. The chamber has a speaker (from the biggest party), three deputy speakers (from the other parties in proportional order), and also eight recorders who are elected from among the MPs (involving first of all the parties not having the post of speaker) on the principle of juniority.

The Standing Orders of the First Parliament rule in Section 28(1) that

The President of the Republic, the Government, the Ombudsman, the parliamentary commissioner of national and ethnic minority rights, the President of the State Audit Office, the Chief Public Prosecutor, each parliamentary committee and any representative may submit proposals to Parliament. The proposals of the committees and the representatives (initiating an Act of Parliament, proposal for putting certain questions on the agenda) are independent motions.

These independent motions account for about 50 per cent of all motions, within which the committee motions comprise only about ten per cent. However, among the motions passed as Acts, or indeed any other decisions of parliament, the government's proposals represent an overwhelming majority, totalling over 90 per cent.

The proposals to be discussed have to be submitted to the speaker and directed by him to the competent committees. After the committees' discussion the bills have first the general, then the detailed debate (two separate readings) in the plenary sessions. If some bills are of lesser importance and politically non-controversial – for example, some routine issues of governance – the general and the detailed plenary debates can take place jointly. After the general debate the bills can be sent back to the committees for further discussions and specifications. MPs can submit amendments to bills in both phases, but in the detailed debate this can only be done in connection with the previously submitted draft amendments. In the case of something involving an important state interest the leading officials of the parliament, the government and all parliamentary committees may request urgent discussion of the given proposal (except for budgeting).

Parliament makes its decisions passing bills through four different kinds of majorities: namely (1) by the votes of more than half the representatives present, (2) by a simple majority of all representatives, (3) by a two-thirds majority of the representatives present, and (4) by the votes of two-thirds of the representatives of the parliament (the figure required to change the constitution). The bill will be an act if signed by the president and will become effective when it has been published in the Official Gazette (*Magyar Közlöny*).[11]

Parliamentary Committees

The system of parliamentary committees is quite extensive and sophisticated, but it is well regulated in the Standing Orders of the First Parliament in Sections 20–23. There was a six-party agreement on the committees on 28 April 1990, before the First Parliament began to work and this agreement was modified by a new six-party agreement on 28 September 1992 which changed the structure of committees and established new ones. As a result, there were Standing Committees and Special Committees, and all of their members are representatives (see Table 4). The former are engaged in preparing and dicussing the bills in their sphere of operation (that is, mostly in the legislative process), while the latter deal with particular issues of parliamentary life. The committees have a big role in parliamentary life, and they can request the presence of any officials at public hearings and testimonies, and can ask for any information and documents for their legislative work. The constitutional committee in the First Parliament served as a super-committee because all the bills had to pass through this committee for the final control. Therefore it proved to be the biggest bottleneck in legislative work. Parliament can also elect *ad hoc* and fact-finding committees for the purpose of examining certain issues or elaborating proposals. The chairperson and at least half of the members of these committees have to be parliamentary representatives.[12]

The committees are proposal-making and controlling organs of the Hungarian Parliament. The heads of authorities have to make available the data required by the committees and have to testify before them. The standing committees can turn directly with their proposals to the parliament, president, State Audit Office, Chief Public Prosecutor, and other bodies. Their major role is still in the legislative activity; they have to prepare the debate on the draft bills in their sphere of operation and to discuss matters submitted to them by the parliament or by the speaker. The standing committees of the First Parliament were rather active, they submitted 22 per cent of all proposals (34 per cent government and 44 per cent by the MPs). Among these proposals there were 12 draft bills, 40 law amendments, 127 resolutions and 16 resolution amendments.

TABLE 3
THE POLITICAL MAP OF THE HUNGARIAN PARLIAMENT (28 JUNE 1994)

	votes in %	seats	seats in %
MSZP	32.99	209	54.14
SZDSZ	19.74	71	18.39
MDF	11.74	38	9.84
FKGP	8.82	26	6.73
KDNP	7.03	22	5.69
Fidesz	7.02	20	5.18

Two MPs, counted here in the SZDSZ faction, were elected as candidates of other parties (Agrarian Alliance and Party of Entrepreneurs) which were in electoral alliance with the SZDSZ.

TABLE 4
LIST OF COMMITTEES IN THE FIRST HUNGARIAN PARLIAMENT (AFTER 28 SEPTEMBER 1992)

I. Standing committees

1. Constitutional and legal affairs (25 members)
2. Interior affairs (25)
3. Foreign affairs (23)
4. Defence (23)
5. Budgeting (25)
6. Economic affairs (25)
7. Social and health affairs (25)
8. Environmental affairs (23)
9. Cultural affairs (25)
10. Human rights (25)
11. Educational and scientific affairs (25)
12. Agriculture (19).

The memberships and chairmanships of the Standing Committees were allocated in proportion to the size of parliamentary parties. The overwhelming majority of the MPs (288 out of 386) took part in the work of these committees.

II. Special Committees

1. House Committee (the speaker and faction leaders) (11)
2. Agenda Committee (14)
3. Immunity, Incompatibility and Credentials Committee (12)
4. National Security Committee (13)
5. European Affairs Committee (16)
6. Auditing Committee (14).

Most of the 80 members of the Special Committees are also members of the Standing Committees. Thus, there were only 82 non-committee member MPs in the First Parliament.

The Members and Constituency Relations

In the process of parliamentarisation of parties the First Parliament had a decisive impact on the formation of the parties, including the recruiting and socialisation of party elites and learning the elites' roles. Given the fact that parties were only or mostly 'parliamentary' parties (that is, existing and acting in the parliament), a great cleavage emerged between the party leaderships – to an almost equal degree for each parliamentary faction – and the party memberships (the latter in any case being poorly connected due to the paucity of national party organisations). In the parliamentary factions a further cleavage rose between the 'frontbenchers' and 'backbenchers'; some leading politicians were super-active in their parliamentary roles and some others (about one-third of the MPs) were absolutely passive. This contrast was greater in larger factions, but even in the smaller factions these roles were quite clearly separated. Whereas the separation of the two roles, or the existence of a hierarchy, is normal in advanced parliaments, in

Hungary this huge gap and antagonism was produced by the difficulties experienced by transitory political elites.

The 386 members of the Hungarian Parliament can be divided into two basic groups: 176 MPs come from the individual constituencies and 210 from the party lists. The 1989 electoral law tried to preserve personal contacts between legislators and citizens by establishing an 'individual' part of the membership of parliament (45 per cent), but proportional representation has been the prevailing idea in the region and it has become the dominant part (55 per cent) in the Hungarian national assembly as well. This 'personal test' of the MPs has been working well, since actually all candidates have run in both ways (except for some top party leaders, one in 1990 and three in 1994), and the personal failure of the leading politicians in the individual constituencies has been a good indication for the whole party. One has to add that extremist politicians from all parts of the political spectrum, who themselves proclaimed (and imagined) their own large popularity and social support, failed in 1990 and failed again in the 1994 elections.

In general, we can describe four types of MPs in the First Parliament, based on the most common international typology. First, we can distinguish between 'general' and 'individual' roles – that is between those who represent a general party or political line (coming usually from the party lists), and those who represent their direct electorate in their constitutiencies. Second, we can also distinguish between interest-group-oriented MPs and professionals, or policy experts. The former try to mediate or represent the interests of certain social groups or interest organisations (trade unions or business associations); the latter, in turn, think that they are above particular interests and they perform what they perceive as the special, very sophisticated job of a professional politician; in this process their personal skills and special education matter a great deal.

In the First Parliament the first two roles were clearly formed and markedly present. The behaviour of those elected in the individual constituencies was very different from those elected on the party lists. Those playing 'individual' roles claimed to have more legitimacy, and they complained that they were busier, since they had to maintain their personal contacts with their electorate; also, they pioneered the working out of the special relations between MPs and citizens (meetings and correspondence with the electorate, in some cases even local plebiscites concerning important matters and so on). This difference was, however, still not that great, since most of those who were elected on the party lists were also constituency-based to some extent. Originally they might have run in a particular constituency, but just failed in the individual elections. This is why they subsequently tried to maintain their personal contacts with their 'would be' constituencies and to represent their interests in parliament. This led to a strange situation in the First Parliament in that there was a strange mixture of collision and collusion between the real, legal and shadow or 'self-appointed' representatives of the constituencies (or bigger regions and counties).

This shows that the Hungarian electoral law does not allow a major cleavage between 'individual' and 'general' types, since all of them have to run in the individual constituencies and those who have been defeated think, from the very beginning of their parliamentary cycle and even as 'general' types, in terms of the next elections, that is, running again (mostly) in the same constituency. Both roles comply with a third one – the territorial interest representation. The members of the First Parliament refused the idea of interest representation in general and that of functional interests in particular. The overwhelming majority of the MPs flatly denied any connections with any organised interests. Yet this was untrue to a great extent, and it was demonstrated in a parliament which refused several times to vote for a law on the incompatibility or conflict of interests of the MPs. (This denial came from the ruling idea that, whatever the situation, representatives were working in the nation's interest; such a conception was promoted by the national-conservative coalition, which tended to deny the legitimacy of particular interests in any form, but claimed the direct representation of the general or national interest for itself). The special atmosphere of the first stages of systemic change also influenced MPs in this direction. This was partly because organised interests had not yet finished their internal transformations and seemed to be very particularistic. However, the major reason was the political 'idealism' and national romanticism of the ruling coalition.

It was only a small group in the First Parliament who identified themselves as professionals, and most of these had been on the party lists. The professional level and quality of the First Parliament was rather low. This was caused not just by the lack of political expertise, but by the presence of a great number of 'by chance' politicians, who were old and frustrated. They arranged personal 'one-man shows' in the First Parliament and their performance drastically displayed the poverty of political culture in some social strata and generations, as well as a total misunderstanding of domestic developments by those coming home after some decades of emigration. The transitory political elite and its political culture requires an extensive analysis, but it can be said briefly that the low performance of most of the MPs and their inability to 'learn politics' was the decisive factor contributing to the decreasing popularity of the First Parliament. In this respect the four-year stability was counter-productive. In some ECE countries the elections were held two years after the first power transfer, and these low quality, 'by chance' politicians were, at least to some extent, selected out (70 per cent of MPs were not re-elected as an average in the ECE region). The same happened to the MPs of the First Parliament, but the country had to wait four years for this fundamental personnel change or 'natural selection'.[13]

POLICY MAKING AND LEGISLATION IN THE FIRST PARLIAMENT

I have analysed the First Parliament in its policy-making role, based on the criteria of the effectiveness, efficiency and feasibility (efficacy) of legislation. Effectiveness is used in this case as a holistic term, and refers to whether the First Parliament succeeded in promoting systemic change; efficiency relates to the internal workings and the use of time and other resources; and feasibility indicates the quality of the output. These three criteria enable us to carry out a concrete and detailed analysis of the legislative activities of parliament, including its policy-making role and attributes. The first part of this paper has focused mostly on the formal features of the First Parliament. In the second part I will concentrate on the content of its activities – that is, on its substantial side. This illustrates a much more problematic picture than the slow progress of formal institutionalisation.

As far as effectiveness is concerned, parliament as the central site of systemic change – even in its exaggerated form of overparliamentarisation – would have been expected to play a decisive role in democratic transition, and the First Parliament in many ways underlined this fair expectation, but at the same time belied it. The First Parliament did promote democratisation and Europeanisation to a great extent, but did much less in this respect than it could have done. The processes took place against a background of many setbacks and contradictions because of the authoritarian renewal embodied in the national-conservative government. These four years were a period of lost opportunities in many respects for Hungary. Hungary got off to a good start in the late 1980s and had good chances to speed up Europeanisation and democratisation in the early 1990s.

Effectiveness of the First Parliament would have meant three major changes: (1) separation of the major, constitutional changes from those of routine governance, with priority being given to the former; (2) a clear policy agenda for parliament, in which socio-political transformation and the related crisis management would play the dominant role; (3) a decisive systemic change in the parliament itself, by legitimising the roles of government and opposition, and by creating radically new Standing Orders for itself. The First Parliament failed basically in all three of the above respects.

First, the ruling coalition was unable to set priorities in basic constitutional matters with regard to everyday legislative activities. The major reason was that the constitution-making process would have presupposed a consensus with the opposition in laws requiring a two-thirds majority, and the national-conservative government was not ready to compromise. They made an effort to assume full powers, based on the simple conception of a parliamentary majority as a 'tyranny of majority'. Therefore they avoided having to deal with the most important laws that really needed to be passed. So, after four years of hectic legislative activities, even some of the most important laws were still missing (for example, the media law), or existed only in a partial and distorted form (the Act on local governments). The parliaments of transition have to perform two historical roles at the same time: they have to act as constituent assemblies and also as 'normal' parliaments, albeit with the first role being dominant. The First Parliament was unable to give dominance to its nature as a constituent assembly and performed in this role rather badly. Consequently, this role has been left, to a great extent (including the need for very radical corrections in legislation already passed), to the Second Parliament.

Second, the First Parliament did not succeed in producing a policy agenda or a meaningful policy concentration. The legislation did not follow a particular order and the legislative sequence was capricious. The real priority for the coalition government was a 'nationalist' agenda with a series of 'historical' laws, focusing on the past, not on the present. The 'historians' government' dealt all the time with the national grievances of the past – like a 'time machine' they tried to revive the political norms, discourse, habits, decorations and scenery of the interwar period (sometimes even those of the late nineteenth century) in the spirit of re-establishing an eleven-century continuity of Hungarian national history. Socio-economic legislation and the related crisis management were mostly neglected. The government returned to the relevant socio-economic laws from time to time, but left them again for the sake of past-oriented laws, including its effort to pass laws indulging in retroactive punishment for the assumed 'crimes' of the previous four decades. In these voluntaristic efforts at 'time travel', and with the aim of extending its own powers, the government regularly confronted the Constitutional Court; this was because the latter annulled many of the laws which were high on the government's agenda. There was an attempt, after a major social crisis in October 1990, to create a long-term programme for legislation; nevertheless, this failed and the government finally gave it up. It was the so-called 'Kupa Programme' in March 1991, with its dozens of proposed laws for socio-economic systemic change, coherently presented. Yet the 'nationalist' agenda won against it, and the minister of finance who elaborated it was forced out of government.

Third, parliament cannot promote systemic change in the real world by legislation, without is own internal systemic change – that is, by radically amending its own Standing Orders. The Standing Orders of the First Parliament were a peculiar mixture of different measures and regulations, a series of unusual compromises and statements that were forced upon the parliament by the ruling majority. The lack of a precise definition with regard to factions enabled the government to maintain a faction (a breakaway group from the Smallholders Party: FKGP-C) without a party for a relatively long period of time in the life of the parliament; this was in order to ensure the government's own parliamentary majority. The existence of a 'super-committee' for dealing with constitutional and legal affairs made it possible for the government to filter all the proposals from the committees and to control their activities. This was due to the fact that all legislation had to pass through this committee as a 'double check', the price being a slowing down of the whole process of legislation. As a bottom line, the government had no interest whatsoever in passing the new Standing Orders, since it was a law of the two-thirds majority type as well, and the government, again, was not ready to make a compromise with the opposition. Instead the government used the weight of its executive power in order to implement *ad hoc* voluntaristic decisions practices as far as the parliamentary procedures were concerned.[14]

The same line can be followed directly in the field of the low efficiency. The low efficiency or the limited policy-making capacity of the First Parliament can be explained in three major dimensions. First, there was the poor policy responsiveness to social demands by the national-conservative government and the parliament which it dominated. There were, in these four years, two separate worlds confronting each other: the dreams, utopias and nebulous ideology of national romanticism on one side, and the earth-bound world made up of the everyday needs of the population on the other – there was no linkage, no bridge between them. The leaders of the coalition parties were arrogant, and had a traditionalist political rhetoric which was very far from the modern European discourse and popular understanding. This led to a 'dialogue of the deaf' between governors and governed. Since the learning capacity of the traditionalists-nationalists turned out to be very low – not believing the results of by-elections and public opinion polls and indulging in such practices as intimidation of the electronic media – the only chance for the population to react came in the spring 1994 elections: they delivered their verdict by presenting the national-conservative traditionalists with a crushing defeat (reducing their total of 230 MPs in the First Parliament to 85 MPs in the Second Parliament).

Second, the preparation of bills was also very inefficient and poor, mostly because of the lack of expertise and co-ordination. The leading ideologists of the HDF tended to regard expertise as 'a bolshevik trick', so the majority of the legislative experts of ministries were fired or pushed into the background. The poorly prepared draft bills proposed by the government overburdened the committees, and the plenary sessions as well. Even so, most of the work involved with the preparation of bills was made in the plenary sessions. The lack of a real policy agenda appeared here in the form of hectic legislation; this gave the government the opportunity to over-use the 'urgency' solution in which it proposed discussions concerning many draft laws which had not originally been put on the legislative agenda. The government shifted the whole job of bill preparation and discussion from the ministries to the parliament, almost reaching the model of a 'governing parliament'. The expertise and support of organised interests was also missing, and the rancour caused by this came back with a vengeance when it came to the stage of implementing new laws.

Third, the lack of real activity on the part of the parliamentary factions of the ruling parties also caused considerable trouble. The faction discipline was rather high, but the MPs of the national-conservative coalition felt it necessary to represent their own views at least in plenary debates. A high percentage of amendments and interpellations came from the MPs of the ruling parties, a phenomenon totally unknown in west European parliaments. There were no regular days for political debates, and a special measure involving speeches before the plenary discussions was introduced (this was very counter-productive and conflict-generating in every session day, creating the atmosphere of a permanent election campaign immersed in abstract ideological struggles). The parliament was a forum for weak parties which had no real social existence, and this 'forum function' came to the forefront too often; this decreased the efficiency of legislation even further due to the wasting of time and energy on ideological confrontations instead of sober and practical-oriented legislation.

This ideologisation of legislation and the lack of proper mechanisms, procedures and skills for efficient legislation resulted in a 'cumulative effect' with regard to the implementation of laws. The whole problem of poor legislation of the First Parliament appeared in a concentrated way in the difficulties which accompanied the implementation of laws, and in the poor feasibility of most acts passed by the First Parliament. The impressive extensive legislative production (see Table 5) in fact turned out to be a very meagre intensive production, since about half of the laws passed by the First Parliament had to be amended because of their collision with other laws or with reality (that is, they could not be implemented at all, or only partly and even then they ended up creating new contradictions). There were some issues very frequently legislated by the First Parliament – for example, the regulations concerning landed property (see Table 6) – but no real legal solutions were reached for these issues. Taken as a whole, the process cannot be seen as a proper legal systemic change, but a change which was sometimes even markedly negative in its character.

The socio-political obstacle to the implementation of legislation was the constant confrontation of the government with various organised interests. The views and expertise of the latter were not channelled into the legislation in the preparation phase, and they were not called to assist in the implementation of laws touching upon their own particular concerns either. Thus, in the best cases organised interests applied a form of passive resistance, but they also put up active resistance, which was supported by a large part of the population. The historical-national romanticism and the political voluntarism led to an increasing confrontation between the national-conservative government and the different social strata or interest groups of the population. Because of the central site and high visibility of the parliament in political life this provoked an anti-parliamentary feeling. A large majority of the population did not go so far as to refuse the principles of parliamentary democracy, but their dislike of the First Parliament eventually became intense and bitter. This low popularity and the increasing unpopularity of the government came not from the necessary difficulties of democratic transition but from the degeneration of the young democracy in Hungary under the national-conservative government. The parliament's performance was outstanding with respect to the sheer volume of legislation, but it was very poor considering the setbacks experienced. These setbacks are even more serious when the favourable situation of Hungary in the late 1980s is taken into account. Therefore, as I stated at the very beginning of this analysis, the First Hungarian Parliament was with its achievements and weaknesses a classic case for the ECE region.

TABLE 5
THE HUNGARIAN LEGISLATIVE PRODUCTION IN 1990–94

	1990	1991	1992	1993	1994	1990–94
new laws	29	55	50	61	24	219
amendments	48	38	42	60	25	213
resolutions	55	73	92	103	31	354
opinions	3	3	2	2	0	10
all decisions	135	169	186	226	80	796

TABLE 6
THE MOST FREQUENTLY 'LEGISLATED' ISSUES

Issues	1990	1991	1992	1993–94	1990–94
1. social security	11	7	12	13	44
2. taxation	10	6	10	10	36
3. privatisation	6	9	11	9	35
4. state budget	2	11	8	11	32
5. courts	4	12	4	8	28
6. landed property	3	5	9	10	27
7. local governments	7	7	5	4	23
I. all frequent issues	44	57	59	65	225
II. all laws	77	93	92	121	432

THE ENTRY OF THE SECOND PARLIAMENT

The spring 1994 elections changed the political map of the Hungarian Parliament beyond recognition (see Table 3). As a result, the national-conservative coalition has been exchanged for a social-liberal one with the participation of the HSP and AFD. The new coalition and the Second Parliament has identified itself in many respects as a contrast to the approach of the old coalition and the First Parliament. First of all they have declared a policy based on the consent and acceptance of the legitimate rights of participation of the (much smaller) opposition in legislative activities as it has been reflected in the new Standing Orders passed by the Second Parliament in a six-party consent. From the outset of the formation of the new coalition it is apparent that the negative heritage and contrasting features of the earlier parliament have already determined to a great extent the entry of the Second Parliament.[15]

There has been a big change among the MPs as well. Only 13 MPs have been re-elected in the individual constituencies and 126 MPs have come back on the party lists (139 out of 386, about 36 per cent). The party lists are bearers of a strong continuity and offer 'final protection' for the party leaderships. There are 45 women in the Second Parliament (compared to the 28 in the First Parliament), and most of the new MPs (366) have an MA-level university degree. The education level of the First Parliament was more or less the same, but then there were more graduates in human sciences (literature and history) which were positions requiring them to take major decisions in parliament and within the national-conservative government itself. In the Second Parliament, alongside groups of humanities (70, which is still the largest) there are many lawyers (68), economists (51) and engineers (42); it is these latter three groups which are now dominant in decision-making.

As to a longer continuity, it is interesting to note that the Second Parliament has altogether 14 MPs who were also members of the 1985–90 Parliament. However, only six of them represent real continuity, since they were members of the First Parliament as well – the other eight MPs have returned to the parliament after four years' absence (that is, they 'missed' one parliamentary cycle).

It is still too early to discuss the characteristics of the Second Parliament, for it only began its activities in late June 1994. However, there are good reasons for supposing that, as a result of the political learning process and the personal changes, it will be markedly different from the First Parliament. The First Parliament did a good job in many ways in the legislation of systemic change and by introducing positive parliamentary practices and precedents for the democratic institutionalisation. Yet, it became unpopular to a great extent because it was unable to meet the high expectations coming from its 'central site' in the democratisation process and from the rather good starting positions based on the achievements of the transitory parliament (1985–90) which already began the democratisation process step by step. The First Parliament accumulated a lot of experiences and its positive and negative experiences alike are good points of departure for the Second Parliament.

NOTES

1. In this paper I have summarised the results of the book, A. Ágh and S. Kurtán (eds.), *Democratization and Europeanization in Hungary: The First Parliament, 1990–1994* (Budapest: Hungarian Centre for Democracy Studies (HCDS), 1995). I have described the emergence of the new Hungarian parliamentary system and its functioning in my papers, 'The Parliamentary Way to Democracy: The Case of Hungary', in G. Szoboszlai (ed.), *Flying Blind: Emerging Democracies in East-Central Europe* (Budapest: Hungarian Political Science Association, 1992), and 'Bumpy Road to Europeanisation: Policy Effectiveness and Agenda Concentration in the Hungarian Legislation', in A. Ágh (ed.), *The Emergence of East Central European Parliaments: The First Steps* (Budapest: HCDS, 1994) (hereafter I refer to it as *The First Steps*).
2. I quote here and later the official translation of the 1990 Constitution edited by the Offices of the Hungarian Parliament. Article 19(3) specifies the functions of the parliament as follows: 'Exercising this authority, the National Assembly shall a) enact the Constitution of the Republic of Hungary; b) enact laws; c) determine the socio-economic plan of Hungary; d) determine the balance of state finances, approve the state budget and its implementation; e) decide on the programme of the Government; f) enter into international agreements having outstanding importance for the foreign relations of the Republic of Hungary; g) decide on the declaration of a state of war and on the conclusion of peace; (h,i,j) k) elect the President of the Republic, the Prime Minister, the members of the Constitutional Court, the National Assembly Commissioner of Civil Rights, the National Assembly Commissioner of the National and Ethnic Minority Rights, the President and Vice-Presidents of the State Audit Office, the President of the Supreme Court and the Chief Public Prosecutor.'
3. The political negotiations in April 1990, after the founding elections between the two leading parties, led to a constitutional solution preferring a strong executive to a strong parliament, unlike the former constitution of 1989, which was produced by the national roundtable talks.

4. The Constitutional Court, in fact, has four major functions, (1) the anterior and (2) the posterior constitutional control of laws, (3) the removal of the violation of the constitution by negligence (removing legal gaps and contradictions) and (4) the explanation of the Constitution. See P. Paczolay, 'The New Hungarian Constitutional State: Challenges and Perspectives', in A.E.D. Howard (ed.), *Constitution Making in Eastern Europe* (Washington: The Woodrow Wilson Center Press (distributed by the The Johns Hopkins University Press), 1993), and also my chapter, 'The Permanent "Constitutional Crisis" in the Democratic Transition: The Case of Hungary', in J.J. Hesse and N. Johnson (eds.), *Constitutional Policy and Change in Europe* (Oxford: Oxford University Press, 1995).

5. See my paper, 'The Hungarian Party System and Party Theory in the Transition of Central Europe', *Journal of Theoretical Politics*, 6, 2 (April 1994); and I. Kukorelli, 'The Birth, Testing and Results of the 1989 Hungarian Electoral Law', *Soviet Studies*, 43, 1 (1991).

6. I have discussed all these problems in my paper, 'The Experiences of the First Democratic Parliaments in East Central Europe', *Communist and Post-Communist Studies*, 28, 2 (June 1995).

7. The necessity of the unicameral character of the Hungarian Parliament has been questioned several times since 1988, because no solution has yet been found for the representation of cultural, ethnic and religious minorities. This in turn raises the urgent need for a consensual democracy (although ethnic minorities are very small in Hungary). Consequently, the bicameral parliament as a proposal returns to the foreground from time to time, also in connection with a functional democracy and organised interests (which is discussed very briefly below).

8. See J. Hausner and A. Woytyna, 'Trends and Perspectives in the Development of a System of Interest Representation in Post-Socialist Societies', in J. Hausner, B. Jessop and K. Nielsen, *Institutional Frameworks of Market Economies* (Aldershot: Avebury, 1993), p.224.

9. I have elaborated these criteria and applied them for the analysis of the First Parliament in my paper, 'Bumpy Road', in *The First Steps*.

10. I quote here and later the official translation of the Standing Orders of Parliament edited by the Offices of the Hungarian Parliament and I try to use its wording and expressions in my paper.

11. In HCDS István Somogyvári has dealt particularly with the way of legislation and the Standing Orders: see his chapter, 'Legal Institutions in Standing Orders of the Parliaments of the Advanced Democracies', in *The First Steps*.

12. The Standing Orders of the First Parliament regulate the activities of committees as follows: 'The committees are the opinion-expressing, proposal-making and controlling organs of Parliament. Members of the standing committees can only be representatives. The heads of authorities, offices and institutes, as well as individual citizens shall make available the data required by the committees of Parliament, and/or testify before them, provide them with information and make declarations.' More specifically, 'On their own initiative, the standing committees can be engaged in all issues they consider issues of basic significance in the given field of state and social life. They can turn with their proposals directly to Parliament, the President of the Republic, the Government, the Ombudsman, the parliamentary commissioner of national and ethnic minority rights, the State Audit Office, the Chief Public Prosecutor, and in accordance with the contents of a separate law they can turn to the Constitutional Court with their motions, and the competent minister and/or head of organ with national competence with their proposals. The concerned state organs shall in merit deal with the proposals of the committees, and inform the committee about the results; the initiatives of the committees may not restrict the competence and responsibility of the state organs.'

13. For details on the parliamentary roles the paper of G. Ilonszki, 'Parliament and Parliamentarians in Hungary in a Comparative Perspective', in *The First Steps* and also G. Ilonszki and D. Judge 'Representational Roles in the Hungarian Parliament', in T. Cox and A. Furlong (eds.), *Hungary: The Politics of Transition* (London: Frank Cass, 1995). Kathleen Montgomery also made a survey on Hungarian MPs, the results have been summarised in her paper, 'Interest Group Representation in the Hungarian Parliament', *Budapest Papers on Democratic Transition*, No. 78 (1994). Seemingly the First Parliament was 'professional':

out of 386 MPs 340 had an MA diploma: 78 MPs in humanities, 75 in law, 39 in economics and medical sciences, and 38 in engineering; unfortunately, it appears that in most cases this did not lead to any political professionalism. As the other chapters of *The First Steps* show, the other ECE countries have had the same difficulties with their parliamentary elites.

14. I have discussed these issues concerning the privatisation legislation: see 'Europeanization through Privatization and Pluralization in Hungary', *Journal of Public Policy*, 13, 1 (1993).

15. The data on the political opinions (see *Political Yearbook of Hungary 1995*, p. 595) suggest that the overwhelming majority became more and more dissatisfied with the national-conservative government and the First Parliament:

Are you satisfied with the development of democracy in Hungary ?

	1991	**1992**	**1993**	**1994**
very satisfied	2.3	2.0	2.3	1.3
rather satisfied	28.2	20.0	18.0	21.9
not satisfied	39.2	44.0	44.2	41.7
very unsatisfied	21.0	28.0	30.0	23.9
dont knows	9.2	6.0	5.5	11.2

These percentages 'predicted' the results of the spring 1994 elections to a great extent, since only some 20 per cent of the population voted for the coalition parties. Public opinion polls in June 1994 indicated that the majority of the Hungarian population was optimistic about the perspectives of the democratic developments with the new social liberal coalition: namely, about 50 per cent are rather optimistic, 29 per cent cautiously optimistic and only 21 per cent rather pessimistic. This latter reflects again the election results, that is, this is the size of supporters of the previous, national-conservative government (see the survey of the Hungarian Gallup Institute in the *Magyar Hirlap*, Budapest Daily, 6 June 1994).

The Legislature in Post-Communist Bulgaria

GEORGI KARASIMEONOV

The Bulgarian legislature has emerged slowly from its legacy with the former Communist regime. Three distinct evolutionary periods are identified. November 1989 to June 1990 was characterised by a reformist Communist membership whose role was confined to the 'rubber stamping' of Communist Party measures. June 1990 to October 1991 witnessed a transitory legislative environment with an assertive opposition, a new constitution and a change in government personnel. Since October 1991 the third phase has been marked by 'polarised pluralism' in which a more active yet more divided legislature has witnessed a growing credibility gap with the electorate.

In comparison to the former socialist states in central Europe in Bulgaria Communist rule enjoyed a certain legitimacy. Even in the 1980s before the downfall of the regime the Communist Party could count on keeping its power base and political monopoly without any major opposition. This was the result of specific historical factors before and after the establishment of the Communist regime.

One major factor is the traditional pro-Russian sentiment in the population as a result of the major role played by Russia in the liberation of the country from Turkish oppression in 1878. The symbols of gratitude to Russia can be found in almost all towns and villages in Bulgaria and are sufficient to explain the special place that Russians and Russia have in the minds of the population, especially among the older generation. The lack of anti-Russian sentiment later helped to legitimise the pro-Soviet regime and Communist rule after World War Two. In that sense Bulgaria is a deviant case compared to other east European nations which, throughout their history had often been objects of Russian or Soviet oppression. The legitimisation of Communist rule was helped also by a very favourable, even privileged policy of support, especially economic, of the Soviet regime to Bulgaria's Communists who did their best to turn Bulgaria into the closest satellite of Moscow.

Another factor should not be underestimated. The Communist regime was able to achieve the modernisation of the country, which was trailing in Europe as a backward agrarian country. Industrialisation, agricultural reforms, and the introduction of mass education, although achieved in the conditions of Communist rule, brought fast economic growth, creating a

Georgi Karasimeonov is Managing Director of the Institute for Political and Legal Studies and Professor at Sofia University.

new middle class with a comparatively good living standard. Loyalty to the regime by the intelligentsia was also created, filling the vacuum left by the former 'bourgeois' intellectuals repressed or marginalised by the regime.

The political tradition of the country favoured to a great extent the influence of left political parties and values (populist-agrarian, social democratic, radical democratic, Communist). This explains the fact that the revival of party pluralism after 1989 was marked by these political currents.

The Communist Party favoured by the agreements in Yalta, which left Bulgaria in the Soviet zone of influence, was able to take power with greater ease than in the other eastern European countries. It did not even need the direct help of the Soviet army. It was able to keep that power without serious opposition until 1989.

Because of these major factors, the transition from Communist dictatorship to democracy was not preceded by year-long struggles or anti-Communist revolts against the regime. The first major opposition to the regime of Todor Jivkov, who took over the leadership in the Communist Party with Moscow's support in 1956 and kept it until November 1989, came from inside the Communist Party. The first dissidents were either former party members or reformers in the ranks of the Communist Party. The major stimulus for change came from Gorbachev's *perestroika*. That is why the change in the power structures in November 1989, which brought the reformers in the Communist Party to the forefront and ousted Jivkov and his closest associates, was achieved with the active help of Moscow.

These aspects show the differences between Bulgaria's and the central European nations' transition to democracy, especially concerning the role of the ex-Communist Party in the reform process. It is in this context that the establishment of the new democratic institutions, amongst them the new parliament, has to be analysed.

EMERGENCE AND EVOLUTION OF THE POST-COMMUNIST LEGISLATURE

Three different types of parliament and parliamentary praxis accompanied Bulgarian political life in the years following regime change. The first stage took place during the first months following the fall of the Jivkov regime in November 1989 until the first free elections in June 1990 for a constituent assembly, the so-called Grand People's Assembly. The composition of the parliament was inherited from the former regime. Its role was limited to a 'rubber stamp' whose main function was to implement the decisions taken by the reformers of the Communist Party, and consequently by the Round Table, in which the newly born opposition was represented. The parliamentary institution was included in this process as part of the 'negotiated transition' to democracy whose precedent was established in Poland where the first Round Table came to life. Through these Round Tables the transition to democracy took the form of 'negotiated' or 'tender' revolutions. If we look for historical parallels they were closer to the British conservative 'model', than the French (1789) or the Russian (1917) radical revolutionary transition characterised by violent eradication of the former ruling elite.

Practically all decisions taken by the Round Table which needed legislative approval were approved by the parliament. Most important amongst them was the removal from the old constitution of the notorious Article 1 cementing the 'leading role' of the Communist Party. No less important were the constitutional amendments implementing political freedoms, the rule of law, and party pluralism which removed the most anti-democratic components of the totalitarian system and guaranteed basic human rights and freedoms. Amongst the most important decisions of the Round Table legitimised by the old parliament were the new electoral law and the law on political parties.

A historical paradox was to take place – a parliament fully composed of Communist Party members took the major decisions ending Communist Party rule and opened the road to free elections. In other words it signed its own death sentence. Instead of sabotaging the changes, the reform wing of the *nomenclature* tried to preserve its interests in the new democratic institutions and market economy. That is why instead of resisting the reform process it tried to control it by using the financial and political resources it had at its disposal, giving it many advantages over the just established opposition.

The Communist reformers had a well prepared tactic for integration into the new system, preserving as much as possible the positions of the 'new class' born during communism, using its financial resources and influence acquired during decades of uncontrolled rule. That is why it took the road of infiltrating the new political, media and economic structures. In this process the old parliament had its own role to play as an obedient executor of the decisions of the new guard of the Communist Party.

It was the Round Table that played the role of a *de facto* parliament, becoming an extra-constitutional institution which took the place of other policy-making institutions of the old regime. Accordingly 'the round tables as such obviously have exceeded the constitutional framework of a communist state'.[1] They represented a kind of corporatist structure which not only legitimised the new political forces, but became a transitional power broker setting the rules of the democratic game.

The reigning Communists used their hegemony in the first stage of regime change to determine the pace of reforms trying to 'set a pattern of paternalistic rule, in which the reforms would be granted by them from above, and they would issue concessions on particular activities (such as free trade unions or independent newspapers) to selected oppositionist groups'.[2]

The second stage of the development of the post-Communist legislature is characterised by the election of the constituent assembly in the first free elections on 10 June 1990 (Table 1). Compared to other post-Communist transitions, Bulgaria opted for the adoption of a new constitution before undertaking major reforms on the road to democracy and a market economy. In that the country followed a historical tradition. After the liberation from the Turks following five centuries of oppression, and later after the regime change in 1944, it convoked special constituent assemblies to adopt new constitutions or major changes in them.

Some critics argue that this brought a delay of the reforms and gave advantages to the dominant Communists which in Bulgaria won the first elections. The Bulgarian experience showed that the adoption of the new constitution establishing the fundamental legal framework of a democratic state gave positive impetus to consolidating democracy. The time spent on the new constitution might have delayed some reforms, but later on it had a stabilising effect by allowing the parliament to concentrate on the adoption of new laws instead of constantly introducing changes in the old constitutional framework. The new constitution also became a barrier, restricting attempts to circumvent democratic principles. Certain deficiencies of the new constitution, sometimes a result of hasty work, cannot hide its positive role in the process of applying democracy, guaranteeing the peaceful, non-violent nature of transition.

Besides its major task, the constituent assembly had to fulfil many of the functions of regular parliaments. It adopted major changes in the legal framework inherited from the old regime. During its lifetime, a little more than a year, it voted into power two governments with radically different compositions and elected a president. It adopted measures which brought changes in the political system and the personnel in the administrative agencies.

Although the constituent assembly became the stage of a most acute confrontation between the majoritarian Socialist (ex-Communist) Party and the anti-Communist opposition, it was able in time to adopt a new constitution based on universal liberal democratic principles. Only a small radical anti-Communist minority and the parliamentary group of the Turkish minority party declined to sign the new constitution. From 400 members of the constituent assembly, 309 put their signature to it. Most of the motives of the non-signataries were political and aimed at provoking new elections. After the change of government a few months later, that same group of radical anti-Communists taking power had to accept the new constitutional framework.

The third stage of the development of the post-Communist legislature is marked by the legal framework established by the new constitution which declares the will to build a democratic and social state based on the rule of law. A new parliament was elected after the second round of free elections in October 1991. They brought a radical change in the composition of the parliament and a new majority, composed of the anti-Communist Union of Democratic Forces (UDF) and the Turkish minority Movement for Rights and Freedoms (MRF), which formed the government. With the exception of the Bulgarian Socialist Party (BSP), which became the major opposition, all other parties and coalitions were not able to overcome the four per cent threshold, although some of them were very close to it.

TABLE 1
RESULTS OF THE ELECTIONS FOR CONSTITUENT ASSEMBLY 10 JUNE 1990
(TURNOUT 91 PER CENT)

Parties	Votes	%	Seats	%
UDF	2,216,127	36.20	144	36
BSP	2,886,363	47.15	221	54
BANU	491,500	8.03	16	4
MRF	368,929	6.03	23	5
Others	-	-	6	1
Total			400	100

The activity of the newly elected legislature was marked by two different phases. The first one is characterised by initiatives and actions of the new majority attempting to introduce radical reforms in ending the Communist legacy. Most typical were the restitutional laws which restored to the old owners all real estate and land nationalised by the communists. At the same time all property amassed by the former Communist Party and its satellite organisations was put under state control. Some so-called 'de-communisation' laws and clauses were adopted, limiting access of former Communist *nomenclature* to take positions in some structures of the state apparatus. Much contested by the Socialist Party, some of them were vetoed by the president.

These attempts to radically change the economic and political power structures in the country caused a strong negative reaction in the ranks of the opposition Socialist Party. Its protest culminated in the boycott of parliamentary committees and for a short time even of plenary sessions. At a later stage the aggressive policy of the government caused a rift in the governing coalition leading to a breach between the UDF and the MRF. The UDF Government was accused of trying to establish an 'administrative dictatorship'. The growing conflicts in the ranks of the UDF and with other major political actors, especially the president, led to an early fall of the UDF Government in November 1992.

This led to a restructuring of political forces in the parliament and to the formation of a new majority by the socialists, the MRF and about 20 dissidents of the UDF, which formed their own parliamentary group. They supported a change in government which was based on an expert non-party formula. The new government, without clear party backing, was to be transitional and that is why it had great difficulties in continuing the reform process, especially in an economy where conflicting interests hampered its legislative proposals. Parliament's work was hampered by a policy of total opposition and attempts at blocking its activity on the part of the UDF opposition. The latter was able to achieve its blocking tactic mostly through the channels of power it kept in the presidency of the assembly and most parliamentary committees. For various reasons the new majority was not able to achieve consensus on the issue of electing new parliamentary committee chairs and thus it left them in the hands of the opposition, creating an unprecedented situation. A curious paradox could be observed – the major power structures in parliament were occupied by the UDF opposition enabling it to block or delay many of the legislative proposals, especially those attempting to revise formerly adopted laws. In spite of the 'procedural war' of the UDF opposition against the majority aiming to force early elections, the new so-called dynamic majority was able to keep together longer than expected. It was even able to adopt some important laws in support of the economic reform, a police law, an army law and important changes in the legal system.

CONSTITUTIONAL STRUCTURE

The new Bulgarian constitution defines the governmental system as a 'republic with a parliamentary form of government' (Article 1). The National Assembly 'shall be vested with the legislative power and shall exercise parliamentary control' (Article 62).

As was earlier mentioned two major positions opposed each other in the constitutional debates – one supported by the majority opted for the establishment of a parliamentary form of government, the minority for a semi-presidential form close to the French model. Another small minority opted for a constitutional monarchy and expressed its aim for re-establishment of the monarchy, declaring the referendum of 1946 null and void. The monarchist groups, not only in Bulgaria, were expecting that the population, disenchanted by the crisis, would easily turn to a 'saviour' coming from the former royal dynasty. Although great efforts were made to popularise the monarchist cause, and in spite of the personal popularity of the exiled king, the majority of the population is not ready to accept a change in the republican form of government, at least for the time being. This is also the case for the majority of the political parties. The polls give the monarchists about four to five per cent electoral support.

There is a certain 'allergy' in the post-Communist society towards any form of authoritarian government, which explains this general lack of approval for the return to the monarchy. The fear of a new dictatorship explains to a certain extent the choice of a parliamentary regime over a presidential. The supporters of a presidential regime argued that during the transition period there was a need for a certain degree of concentration of power in an institution which would guarantee the stability of the new democracy, especially when there is a fragmented party system and the new political elite is still adapting to the new rules of the game. At the start of the transition the Communists also supported a stronger presidency, but later when a president from the opposition came to power they opted for a parliamentary regime.

The debate over the choice of the form of government is stimulated by the weaknesses demonstrated by parliament and the executive power. They reflect also the public disenchantment after the bitter confrontation between the major protagonists in parliament – the UDF and the BSP. As mentioned earlier, this confrontation limits severely the legislative effectiveness of parliament and causes a crisis of confidence in that institution. The situation of a blocked parliament enforces the desires for a stronger president. The presidential cause is sustained by the fact that some of the post-Communist presidents retained a certain charismatic legitimacy as long-time dissidents and leaders of the anti-Communist resistance movements (Walesa, Havel, Jelev). They had a strong moral engagement for the success of democracy, but the constitutional framework limited their capacity to influence the political process. Their very high personal rating in public opinion and their personal desire to be active participants in the policy-making process brought them often into conflict with parliament and the executive. It is difficult to assess which regime, presidential or parliamentary, is more adapted to the post-Communist transition, but I am inclined to accept Kryzstov's observation that

> Parliamentary systems tend to be more inclusive: each party that won even a few seats in the parliament will have at least some influence over the decision making process, and potentially become a member of the ruling coalition. In a highly fragmented and unstable polity of countries undergoing a fundamental political, economic and social transformation, the obvious strategy for the political elites was to promote parliamentary systems in order to: 1) secure their open

participation in the political process through representative bodies; and 2) prevent development of authoritarian forms.[3]

Bulgaria's political system could be defined as parliamentary with reinforced presidential powers. They ensue from the following constitutional prerogatives. Firstly, the president is directly elected for a five-year term, with a maximum two terms. Secondly, he has at his disposition a limited veto power which allows him to send back for reconsideration any law adopted by the legislature. The latter can override the veto by a simple majority of all Members of Parliament (Article 101). Thirdly, he retains important powers as chief of the armed forces and as chairman of the Council for National Security. And, fourthly, he has a certain say in the appointment of some higher state officials. But the most important prerogatives of a strong presidency, such as the dismissal of parliament, or legislative initiative, or appointment of the prime minister, are not foreseen by the constitution. In a comparative evaluation the Bulgarian presidency finds itself between the German (mostly ceremonial) and the strong French presidency.

The question of enlarging the power of the presidency is constantly in the public debate. For one, the president himself and some of his political friends periodically bring the topic to the forefront. On the other hand, the constitution has some deficiencies and loopholes in the definition of the separation of powers and the president's prerogatives. This often causes what some political scientists call the 'war between the institutions'.

These conflicts concerning the presidential powers are nothing abnormal for the transitional post-Communist democracy. It will take time to achieve the necessary balance of powers. The Bulgarian case offers a good balance of powers as far as the popularly elected president retains enough possibilities and authority to assert a certain continuity and stability in the institutional structures, avoiding a power vacuum, especially in crises.

A constitutional change strengthening presidential powers is hardly to be expected. The fear that this could lead to an authoritarian regime is still strong enough to restrict any serious attempts for a regime change. If the transitional process is accompanied by instability and weakness of the parliamentary institution, then growing attempts at a regime change are not be excluded.

THE ELECTORAL SYSTEM AND PARLIAMENTARY ACTIVITY

By tradition, the constituent assembly comprised a greater number of members than a regular parliament, aiming to be more representative. That is why the number of MPs in the Grand People's Assembly was almost twice as much as compared to the parliament that followed – 400 versus 240. There were also major differences in the electoral system applied to both elections. For the constituent assembly a mixed electoral system was applied. Two hundred MPs were elected through the proportional system with regional lists in 31 constituencies. A four per cent threshold was introduced as well. The other half of the MPs were elected through the majority system (absolute majority for the winner in one or two ballots). The choice of the electoral system was a compromise worked out during the Round Table and was accepted as exclusive for the first elections for a constituent assembly. It was adapted to the much larger numbers of MPs which were to be elected. It was also agreed that after the adoption of the new constitution a new electoral law was to be adopted corresponding to the much smaller composition of the parliament.

Forty-two political parties and coalitions were registered for the elections held on 10 June 1990, but only four overcame the four per cent threshold. These were the UDF, the major anti-Communist coalition of more than ten parties and political organisations, amongst which the most influential were the Social Democratic Party, the Agrarian Union 'Nikola Petkov', the Democratic Party and the Radical Democratic Party. The other ones were the ex-Communist Party renamed Socialist, the Agrarian Party, the former partner of the Communists, and the Turkish minority party MRF. From the 200 MPs elected through the majority system, only six were independents or came from other parties. A majority of seats was gained by the Socialists. The second major group was formed by the UDF, while the Agrarians and the MRF had a much smaller presence (see Table 2).

It is important to note that these founding elections established a bipolar two-party configuration, with two smaller parties on the margins, which remained relatively stable in the first years of transition, reproducing itself in the following elections. Bulgaria did not reproduce the model of the founding elections in other central European countries, where the Communist parties were marginalised and the anti-Communist coalitions were able to a great extent to occupy the political space. The fragmentation of the party system, typical in Poland, was avoided.

At the same time this type of party configuration stimulated the political confrontation between both major political blocks, each of which failed to achieve dominance and depended on a third smaller party which held the balance between them. This type of party configuration influenced to a great extent the legislature and its effectiveness.

The next elections in October 1991, which could also be labelled as founding, produced almost the same parliamentary situation, the major difference being that the Socialists and the UDF exchanged places, with the UDF gaining a very small advantage. Neither of them received an absolute majority through the proportional system with regional lists in 31 constituencies and a four per cent threshold (see Table 2). The third party that entered parliament was the MRF.

The ensuing government was formed by the UDF and the MRF. The BSP remained in opposition. Less than a year later the coalition between the UDF and the MRF fell apart and a new government was formed supported by the BSP, the MRF and a group of parliamentarians that left the UDF and created its parliamentary group called New Union for Democracy. Formally, it was an expert government not tied to any political party.

TABLE 2

ELECTORAL RESULTS FROM PARLIAMENTARY ELECTIONS 13 OCTOBER 1991 (ELIGIBLE VOTES 5 540 843–84 PER CENT)

Parties (coalitions)	Votes	%	Seats	%
UDF (Union of Democratic Forces)	1,903,567	34.36	110	46
BSP* (Bulgarian Socialist Party)	1,836,050	33.14	106	44
BNRP (Bulgarian Ntl. Radical Party)	62,462	1.13	-	-
BANU (Bulgarian Agrarian Ntl. Union)	214,052	3.86	-	-
MRF (Movement for Rights and Freedom)	418,168	7.55	24	10
BANU-NP (Bulgarian Agrarian Ntl. Union – 'Nikola Petkov')	190,454	3.44	-	-
UDF-C (Union of Democratic Forces – Center)	177,295	3.20	-	-
UDF-L (Union of Democratic Forces – Liberals	155,902	2.81	-	-
BBB (Bulgarian Business Blok)	73,379	1.32	-	-
KKB (Konfederation for Kingdom Bulgaria)	100,883	1.82	-	-
Others (< 1 per cent – N = 38)	418,364	7.81	-	-

Note: * Includes nine other parties

The proportional electoral system with a four per cent threshold limited party fragmentation in parliament. This helped achieve a certain stability of the political process. Compared to Poland, where the founding elections based on proportional representation without threshold led to a strongly fragmented parliament and as a result led often to governmental crisis, in Bulgaria's parliament the situation looked much more stable. But a closer look reveals another matter of major importance which hindered this formal stability and the opportunity to become a much more positive factor in the legislative process. The deep suspicion and confrontation which existed between the major political forces – the UDF and the BSP – led to a party configuration which Sartori defined as 'polarised pluralism' or which Bulgarian political scientists labelled as 'bipolar confrontational'. When these two major players find themselves in a 'warlike' relationship, when there is a lack of real dialogue between them, and when neither of them has a clear majority or reliable partners, a blocked parliament can be the result. Such a situation can lead to similar results as in strongly fragmented parliaments.

The confrontation that ensued between the BSP and the UDF, with the small MRF in between them, created a unique situation in Bulgaria not comparable to other post-Communist countries. After the second elections, the MRF remained the decisive factor determining which of both major groups would have access to the government. This unforeseen role played by the MRF, and the tolerance shown by the other parliamentary groups, helped to a great extent to mollify the ethnic tensions in Bulgaria and the integration of the MRF in the political system.

The strongly polarised party system which dominated in parliament was one of the major factors contributing to the delay of some of the major reforms. The parliament lost a great amount of time in political strife and attempts at blocking its work instead of fulfilling its major task as legislature.

Following the founding elections and with the approach of the next ones again in the centre of public debate came the question of the electoral system. As mentioned earlier Bulgaria experienced two different electoral systems – a mixed one for the first elections and a proportional one for the second. A growing number of parties and experts tended to support a change from the proportional to a majority system. Another set of proposals opted for a mixed system or for a lowering of the threshold. Those who supported these changes were mostly aiming at overcoming the polarity in the party system and allowing a larger representation for more parties in parliament. According to them the electoral system should contribute to more responsible political behaviour by MPs.

It will take more than one electoral reform in each of the post-Communist countries until the one most geared to the needs of the transitional period can be found, if at all. The choice of the appropriate electoral system will certainly remain an open question reflecting very often preferences of different parties trying to achieve or keep their dominance in the political system, including the legislature.

THE LEGISLATURE AT WORK

The main function of a parliament is traditionally that of legislating. Two aspects are to be analysed in that connection. On the one hand, the role of the legislature in setting the policy agenda (legislative initiative) and, on the other hand, the effectiveness of the legislature in reforming the social system.

The first aspect reflects the activity of the institutions whose task is to set the policy agenda and make legislative proposals. Of major concern here is the relationship between the legislature and the executive.

The Bulgarian constitution grants the right to initiate legislative proposals to the members of parliament and to the government (Article 87). In contrast to the established democracies, where legislative proposals are mostly initiated by the executive and its various administrative agencies, post-Communist legislatures show quite another pattern. The constituent assembly as well as the regular one played a major role in initiating policy proposals. This is true for individual MPs as well as for the various parliamentary groups. Although the constituent assembly had to work mainly on the new constitution in the short period of its existence (10 July 1990 until 11 July 1991), 320 bills were introduced from which 82 reached the plenary and 63 were adopted. Most of them (47), brought a change of or supplemented old laws and only 16 were new ones. Most of the bills were introduced by MPs individually or collectively and only 23 were introduced by the government.[4]

In the legislature elected in October 1991, starting from November until November 1993, 283 bills were introduced from which 129 were initiated by the executive. In other words a change in the balance between the legislature and the executive is to be observed.

The legislative activity can formally be measured by the number of bills adopted by parliament. The case of the last legislature gives a clear indication that the quantity is significant compared to the legislatures in established democracies. Before its pre-term dissolution the 36th legislature had adopted in the period between November 1991 and July 1994 altogether 210 bills. But from the qualitative side another picture is to be observed. An analysis of the categories of law adopted reveals that from the 210 bills adopted only 25 were new laws and from them only about ten were connected substantially with the reform of the old authoritarian system. The great majority of the laws brought changes or corrections in old laws or were formal acts of approval of governments actions and decisions (ratification of treaties – see Appendix 1).

The short experience of post-Communist legislatures leads to the conclusion that for some time to come they will be much more active in setting the policy agenda and initiating new bills than legislatures in established democracies. This is because of the gigantic task of changing the old system and also the desire of parliament to keep its primordial role as the major policy maker. For a long time there will be a certain jealousy on the side of parliament towards all attempts by the executive to gain the initiative in setting the policy agenda. This is stimulated by the fear inherited from the past that too much power might again be concentrated in the executive.

A certain chaos and lack of discipline characterises policy proposals introduced by individual members on various issues. Many of the bills proposed carry the sign of incompetence and improvisation. Many of them are pure ideological documents. That adds a burden to the work of the different legislative committees and slows their effectiveness. That is why many of the bills introduced are 'dead' from the beginning and drown in the files of the various committees. The lack of experience and experts to prepare the bills, as well as the pressure of time, cause great deficiencies in this initial stage of the legislative process.

To counter these deficiencies a special Committee on Legislation was established, where all bills must be reviewed after they have been discussed in the substantive committees before they reach the plenary. The Committee on Legislation has the following major functions. First it has to review all bills introduced in parliament after they have been adopted in the substantive (standing) committees. Second, it has to prepare a proposal to the plenary with recommendation to adopt the bill, with or without changes, or to reject it. In practice, though, its major task is to review bills in legal terms, in a way helping the substantive committees. It has to look for contradictions with the constitution and other adopted bills. But as specialists observe, very often the committee exceeds its competencies and gives its view on substantive matters.

Although the work of this committee is often criticised and the committee itself labelled as the 'mini-parliament', or even censor, it plays a positive role in that it tries to bring some order and stability to the legislative process. It will take time for a tradition to be established that will normalise the legislative process as part of the consolidation of the democratic system.

The 36th legislature had 21 standing committees (Appendix 2). (The 37th legislature abolished the Committee on Legislation.) But many temporary committees were established on various issues mostly concerned with legal breaches and abuse in the work of administrative agencies, corruption and incidents with MPs.

After it has been introduced in the Bulgarian legislature, a bill passes the following stages: (1) preliminary hearings in the permanent and legislative committees; (2) report to the floor followed by first reading, debates and amendments; (3) second round of hearings in the committees; (4) second reading, final debates on the floor and final passage after two rounds of voting in separate sessions (in certain situations both votes can be in one session). After the first vote the floor can send the bill back for another hearing to the Legislative Committee which must return it to the floor not later than seven days after receiving it. After the second vote, if the bill is adopted it is signed by the President of the Assembly and sent to the state president for final signature (promulgation). As mentioned earlier, the Bulgarian Constitution invests the president with a suspensive veto when, in his judgement, the law violates constitutional provisions. In that case the bill is sent back to the Assembly, which can override the president's veto by a simple majority of all Members of Parliament. Fifteen days after its final adoption the bill becomes law.

TABLE 3
RESULTS OF THE PRESIDENTIAL ELECTIONS IN JANUARY 1992

First Round	Main Contenders	% Vote	Main Party Support
	Zhelyo Zhelev	44.66	UDF
	Velko Vulkanov	30.44	BSP
	George Ganchev	16.77	-

75.41 per cent turnout

Run-off	Main Contenders	% Vote	Main Party Support
	Zhelyu Zhelev	52.85	-
	Velko Vulkanov	47.15	-

75.92 per cent turnout

RELATIONS BETWEEN PARLIAMENTARY GROUPS

There are at least three major features to be observed in the Bulgarian post-Communist parliament characterising the relations between parliamentary groups. The first is mostly related to the practice of pluralism and the relationship between political majorities and minorities. It is one of the crucial tests for the maturity of the political elite and the consolidation of democracy in post-Communist societies. From that point of view, one of the major deficiencies in parliament's work is the 'tyranny of the majority' syndrome. It was prominent in the political practice of the UDF parliamentary group after it gained a relative majority at the October 1991 parliamentary elections. The newly established majority took an aggressive course of passing major legislative reforms, ignoring the opposition. This included the introduction of a bill imposing a ban on the ex-Communist Party. Parliamentary politics was not viewed as a balance of interests, but more or a less as an instrument for marginalising and even repressing the political opponent. This was the aim of a series of so-called 'de-communisation' laws. In the course of time this policy, labelled by some Bulgarian politicians as corresponding to 'bureaucratic' dictatorship, caused a boomerang effect and led to a growing opposition not only on the part of the socialists, but even among the UDF ally, the MRF (the Turkish minority party), which also complained of being ignored in the legislative process.

The lack of parliamentary traditions and culture, and the bitter confrontation between the major political forces, could lead to a parliament which is closer to the French revolutionary model of a 'convent' than to a pluralistically oriented assembly based on liberal democratic principles. Compromise and defeat as part of parliamentary democracy will take time to be accepted.

Another phenomenon characterising nascent post-Communist parliamentarianism is the friction between party headquarters and the parliamentary groups. For both major political blocks – the UDF and the BSP – there were moments of conflict resulting from a lack of co-ordination and different tactics employed by the party leadership and the parliamentary groups. This conflict arose from a more fundamental problem connected to the understanding and application of the free mandate fixed in the constitution (Art. 67). Bulgaria's constitution accepts the principle of the free mandate of the MPs and specifically declares unacceptable the imperative mandate typical of the former constitution of the old regime. But at the same time it creates a certain ambiguity by formulating also that the MPs represent their constituencies.

As one of the leading Bulgarian constitutionalists observes, this text of the constitution shows a 'lack of theoretical knowledge or the desire to combine two principles based on populist and political considerations'.[5] He remarks also that an inherent contradiction is to be observed in the same article that postulates that MPs are bound in their actions by the constitution and the laws in accordance with their convictions and conscience. He asks the rhetorical question – what happens when there is a contradiction between a MP's conviction and the constitution?

This ambiguity of the constitution creates tensions between MPs and their parliamentary groups when conflicts of values and interests arise. These are reinforced by the general instability of parties and parliamentary groups which often cause desertions by MPs from their parliamentary parties. This was several times the case in Bulgaria's parliament – there were individual MPs or whole groups that left their parties or were 'flicked off' (a Bulgarian terminological innovation) by the parliamentary groups themselves and remained either as independents or formed other parliamentary groups. This led to attempts to assert the parties' hold over their MPs by binding them to the decisions of party conferences and party leaderships.[6] The general political instability, partly as a result of the delayed differentiation in the party system, leads to a general instability of the parliamentary groups and their permanent fragmentation.[7] In the span of less than three years following the October 1991 elections there were several desertions which led to the augmentation of the parliamentary groups from three to five (ten MPs are needed to form a group) and to smaller groups of independents (see Table 4).

TABLE 4

CHANGES IN THE COMPOSITION OF PARLIAMENTARY GROUPS AFTER THE ELECTIONS OF OCTOBER 1991

Party Groups

Year	UDF	BSP	MRF	NUD	Ind.	New Choice	GOR	GOR+NUD (DAR)
1991	110	106	24					
1992	87	106	24	17	6			
1993	87	105	24	17	7			
1994	88	100	19	15	10+3		5	
1994a	88	87	19		11	10		14

Notes: 1994a – September.

In October 1992 17 MPs left the UDF group composed of 110 MPs and in February 1993 formed a new parliamentary group called the New Union for Democracy. In the summer of 1994 the same group split again. Five of its members joined another splinter group of the UDF and formed a new parliamentary group called New Choice.

The remnants of the New Union for Democracy joined the five independents of Civil Alliance for the Republic, a splinter from the BSP and formed the Democratic Alternative for the Republic (DAR).

In December 1993, five MPs left the MRF and joining another five MPs from the UDF, formed a parliamentary group named 'Independents'. It fell apart in the summer of 1994 after the five former UDF MPs joined the New Choice group.

In April 1993 five MPs left the BSP coalition and joined the new centre-left party the Civil Alliance for the Republic (GOR). There were also three individual MPs (each from the three major groups) that left their groups, two of them remaining independents, and one joining the UDF (from the MRF).

Another typical feature of the relationship between parliamentary groups is that they reproduce the extra-parliamentary party relationships, *ergo* their confrontation. The new political parties represented in parliament are still not able to overcome the 'election rally' syndrome which they carry with them to the parliamentary debates. The parliamentary rostrum and the parliamentary institutions are viewed by many MPs as a continuation of the electoral arena which determines in many ways their parliamentary behaviour.

The lack of parliamentary traditions and the 'revolutionary' impatience led some MPs and parliamentary groups to attempts to pressure parliament's work from the outside, through various extra-parliamentary activities. Their inability to overcome the majority's policies led to boycotts and even attempts to abandon the parliament with the aim of initiating its downfall and early elections in the expectation of favourable results. This was the case of the UDF in the summer of 1991 and later in 1993 and 1994 when it lost governmental power.[8]

In the summer of 1994 the decision by the UDF to boycott the plenary caused harsh disagreements between the leadership of the parliamentary group and the national co-ordinating committee of the UDF. The parliamentary group decided to abandon the boycott in defiance of the decisions of the UDF.

The misuse of the non-confidence vote by the UDF (six times in the span of a year) can also be seen as an example of the parliamentary intolerance existing between the major groups leading to a general ineffectiveness of parliamentary activity.

This parliamentary confrontation led to a slow down of legislative activity and the delay of debates and votes on crucial issues and bills (for example the bill on privatisation). It hampered the government's activity and stability, especially the 'expert' government of Ljuben Berov which came to power at the end of 1992. Lacking a stable parliamentary backing, it was constantly under pressure from the incoherent, so-called dynamic majority that supported him. The legislature also bore the imprint of the intolerance between the major parliamentary groups, reflecting mostly personal or party interests, and the impossibility of finding a basis for consensus even on the fundamental issues of transition.

This situation was to a great extent a result of an 'ideologically disunified elite' characterised by disagreement on the rules and codes of conduct and deep distrust of each other.[9] It led to a constant revision of adopted bills and blocked the legislative process. The overcoming of this 'blocked parliament' is bound to a change of elites and elite relationships. Piotr Sztompka introduces the concept of 'civilisational incompetence'[10] typical for the post-Communist elites. It is a result of the deep cultural legacy inherited from the distant pre-modern past of these societies and the more recent syndrome of 'fake modernity' imposed by 'real' socialism.

They lead to deficiencies in entrepreneurial culture, civic and political culture, discourse culture and in everyday culture. The agents able to undermine and slowly eliminate civilisational incompetence must be sought among the elites insulated from the impact of real socialism and at the same time exposed to the influence of modern Western culture.

Elections can help the process of rotation and stabilisation of elite structures and the creation of normal (for a liberal democracy) relations between the major elites able to balance between national and party interests. This process will depend on the consolidation of the party system which is still in a fluid state.

TABLE 5
DEMOGRAPHICS OF THE 36TH LEGISLATURE (1991–94)

	N	%
Sex		
Male	208	87
Female	32	13
Age		
25 – 35	23	11
35 – 45	97	40
45 – 55	61	25
55 – 65	39	16
Over 65	20	8
Education		
University	227	95
College	7	3
High School	6	2
Profession		
Law Related	61	25
Engineers	34	14
Economists	31	13
Medical	17	7
Teachers	9	4
Humanitarian	42	18
Journalists	10	4
Others	36	15

PROSPECTS FOR THE FUTURE

In the coming years the legislature will be under pressure from several sources. There is enormous work to be done in creating the legislative infrastructure of the new socio-economic and political system. The time pressure and the overload of various bills leads to superficiality and inconsistency in many of the bills which have to be or are adopted. The constitutional arrangement itself needs to be revised in some parts where it creates unwanted tensions between the major institutions.

The instability and weakness of the post-Communist state leads to a growing corruption and lack of resources for the enforcement of legal provisions. The rule of law is being undermined before it has even taken hold in everyday life and in the political culture of the population. If the old regime ignored the rule of law, the new regime has no authority or resources to enforce it.

The inability of the state institutions to tackle the complexity of new issues and problems, especially the growing crime rate and corruption, leads to disenchantment in the population and to a lack of credibility in the major political institution. Poll after poll show the legislature to have the lowest percentage of public approval.[11]

The confidence gap reveals not only dissatisfaction with the work of the legislature or with its members. The negative attitudes reflect a growth of disillusion with the institution itself. This creates the potential for anti-democratic tendencies and behaviour. Growing demands for a presidential system or a return to the monarchy, or desires for a 'strong hand' reveal this potential. Another symptom is the growing number of non-voters who refuse to take part in elections. This was revealed in several major local elections in June and July 1994 when more than 60 per cent of the eligible voters abstained from voting. Some politicians try to explain this phenomenon in terms of apathy, but more so this is a conscientious protest against the state of post-Communist politics as a whole and in part a disenchantment with parliamentary activity. It is a disenchantment with the bipolar confrontational party politics that has dominated political life in the years following the transition. When burning problems have to be resolved, people have difficulty accepting the parliament as a place of strife and useless debates, which often characterise plenary sessions.

This very early crisis of confidence in the post-Communist legislature, before it has stabilised, makes a political scientist very cautious in his predictions concerning its evolution and fate in post-Communist Bulgaria – more so than in other countries. Its legitimisation plays a major role in the legitimisation of the democratic system itself and vice versa. That it is why the question, will the new legislature be an agent of transformation to a modern liberal democracy or will it become prey to a growing credibility gap, remains open for the time being.

NOTES

1. K. Jasiewicz, 'Structures of Representation', in S. White, J. Batt and P.G. Lewis (eds.), *Developments in East European Politics* (London: Macmillan, 1993), p.132.
2. Jasiewicz, 'Structures of Representation', p.135.

3. Jasiewicz, 'Structures of Representation', p.137.
4. All data are from the information department of the parliament.
5. S. Stoychev, *The Constitution of 1991* (Sofia: University Press, 1994), p.19.
6. The 6th Conference of the UDF in May 1994 decided to limit the relative independence of the parliamentary groups and bound it to the decisions of the National Co-ordinating Committee of the UDF. This led to acute conflicts in the UDF, especially over the decision to boycott the plenary sessions of the parliament. A similar kind of conflict arose between the Executive Council of the BSP and parliamentary group over the no-confidence vote in May 1994 when the parliamentary group did not follow the decisions of the party executive.
7. For more information see G. Karasimeonov, 'Sea Changes in the Bulgarian Party System', in *The Journal of Communist Studies* 9 (Sept. 1993), pp.272–8.
8. The 6th Conference of the UDF in May 1994 took the decision that in case the present government remains in power the UDF should 'begin immediately actions to force early parliamentary elections, rallies, marches, demonstrations, parliamentary boycott, civil disobedience in the realm of the law'. *Democracia* 16 (May 1994), p.1.
9. J. Higley and R. Gunther, 'Elites and Stable Democracy', in J. Higley and R. Gunther (eds.), *Elites and Democratic Consolidation in Latin America and Southern Europe* (Cambridge: Cambridge University Press, 1991), p.12.
10. P. Sztompka. *Zeitschrift fuer Soziologie* (April 1993), pp.85–95.
11. A poll taken in April 1994 by the National Center for Public Opinion shows an 11 per cent approval and 79 per cent disapproval of parliament's activity. The two other major institutions – the government and the presidency receive accordingly 20 per cent and 50 per cent approval. Source: Public Opinion Poll, April 1994, Bulletin 2, p.5.

APPENDIX 1

Categories of laws passed by the 36 Legislature (November 1991–July 1994):
(a) New laws – 25 (from them only ten had a significant impact on the economic and political system like the law on privatisation, restitution of land, police, the new tax system and so on).
(b) Abolition of old laws – 8
(c) Corrections and changes in old laws – 80
(d) Formal (ratification of treaties, budget and financial matters) – 97

APPENDIX 2

Permanent parliamentary committees (21)
(1) Committee on legislation (2) on economic affairs (3) on the income, expenditures and property of political parties (4) for youth, sport and tourism (5) on administrative-territorial structures and local self-government (6) on budget and finances (7) on religious affairs (8) on foreign policy (9) on citizens' petitions and proposals (10) on health (11) on agriculture (12) on cultural affairs (13) on education and science (14) on national security (15) on ecology (16) on citizens' rights (17) for television and radio (18) on labour and social security (19) on energy resources (20) on transport (21) on military industry.

By the beginning of 1994 18 provisional committees had been established of which eight had concluded their task and presented reports to the parliament.

Institutional Development of Poland's Post-Communist Sejm: A Comparative Analysis

MAURICE D. SIMON

A comparative analysis of the Polish Sejm at three points in time (pre-1989, 1989–91, and 1991–93) reveals a developmental process that is a product of opportunity and capability. First, the institutionalisation of the Sejm is shown to be highly reflective of external political forces (political parties, elections, and unresolved constitutional issues). Second, evolving capabilities are examined in terms of the composition of the membership, the evolution of the committee system and the level of legislative activity. The study demonstrates that, despite the complexities of democratic transitional politics, the Sejm is acquiring capabilities to exercise effectively its legislative functions.

Among the East European legislatures, the Polish Parliament is of particular interest. As one of the world's oldest parliaments, it has symbolic importance for the democratic aspirations of Poles. Moreover, it stands out as one of the few examples of political assertiveness by a parliament against authoritarian patterns of governance during the period of Communist rule (Hungary is another example). At critical junctures from 1944 to 1989, the Polish Sejm operated more as a 'minimal parliament' with a limited degree of influence over policy formation and implementation than as a 'rubber stamp'.[1] Hence, it is an important test case for democratic parliamentary development in the post-Communist eastern European transitions.

The central theme of this investigation of the Polish Sejm (the key house of the bicameral parliament) is that post-Communist parliaments do indeed evolve and develop. This developmental process, identified as institutionalisation, can be viewed as a product of 'opportunity' and 'capability'.[2]

This study begins with an examination of the opportunity structure for institutionalisation provided by the changing political context of Polish politics. Forces external to the parliament – the political agenda, the emergence of political parties and their electoral performances, and unresolved constitutional issues – are the central focus.

The evolving capabilities of the parliament are then examined. Patterns of internal parliamentary development bearing on institutionalisation

Maurice Simon is Professor of Political Science, East Carolina University, USA. He gratefully acknowledges the financial support of the Research and Creative Activities Committee and the Vice-Chancellor for Research of East Carolina University which helped fund this study.

include the composition of the membership, the evolution of the committee system and the level of legislative activity. The capabilities of the parliament are considered through comparison of the Polish Sejm at three points in time. The base point is the Communist period of rule (1952–89) when, with the exception of the Solidarity period of 1980–81, the Sejm operated as a typical minimal parliament. The second is the tenth term of the Sejm of the Polish People's Republic (1989–91) – the 'contractual parliament' of the initial transformation to democracy and the market economy. The third is the first term of the Sejm of the Republic of Poland (1991–93) – a highly fragmented multi-party parliament.[3]

OPPORTUNITY: THE CHANGING POLITICAL CONTEXT

Three Contexts of the Sejm

For most of the pre-1989 period, the Sejm of the Polish People's Republic functioned as a mature Communist 'minimal parliament'. As elaborated in previous studies, the Sejm was in a subordinate position to the hegemonic Communist party-state authorities, but was not simply a 'rubber stamp' fulfilling primarily symbolic functions.[4] In the wake of organised civil opposition in the 1980s, the ruling Communist authorities permitted the Sejm to adopt a more active role in governance, particularly in expressing plural demands for policy change and exercising expanded administrative and supervisory control functions. The representative and oversight functions of the Sejm were enhanced, resulting in an intensification of parliamentary activity and the expression of a broader range of political positions – always limited by both externally and self-imposed restrictions.

The Polish Round Table talks of 1988–89 which followed the political confrontations, stagnation and impasses of the post-1981 martial law regime of Wojciech Jaruzelski were meant to open up a fruitful dialogue and limited co-operation between the Communists and the recalcitrant opposition. The atmosphere of economic and political crisis yielded the agreement to hold 'compartmentalised' (manipulated) legislative elections in the summer of 1989 which produced a more representative, but still heavily Communist-dominated parliament. However, a fascinating set of developments resulted in the toppling of the Communist party-state and the seating of the 'contractual parliament' – the tenth term of the Parliament of the Polish People's Republic which lasted from 1989 to 1991.[5]

The tenth term of the Sejm was a strange moment in Polish history. This 'transition' period was marked by shifting political allegiances, intense policy demands and expectations, heated elite competition, successful and unsuccessful institutional innovations, and a very fluid political environment. Despite the immaturity of the political system and the odd configuration in the Sejm (37.6 per cent of the deputies were Communists; 22.4 per cent *former* Communist allies, and 35 per cent 'oppositionists'), the parliament began to function in a rather 'normal' fashion.

By 1990, Lech Walesa had unleashed his 'war at the top', thus contributing further to the fragmentation of the Solidarity forces. His successful campaign for the presidency set the stage for the 17 October 1991 parliamentary elections. With 69 political parties participating, the electoral outcome placed 29 parties in the Sejm. As a result, it took nine months to form a stable governing coalition. Thus, the first term of the Sejm of the Polish Republic (1991–93) took place in a political context of a highly fragmented and competitive political party system with strongly divergent policy orientations on the part of elites and public opinion.

The Sejm in the Post-Communist Political Arena

The complicated political and constitutional evolution of post-Communist Poland has critically affected the Sejm's actual performance. It embodies the confusion and contentiousness of contemporary political currents. This can be illustrated by a· fuller review of political and constitutional developments in the 1989–93 period.

The political context (4 July 1989 to 31 October 1991) in which the 'contractual parliament' operated was marked by constitutional ambiguity, political divisiveness and a lack of clear directions. Although the constitution of 1952 was still in operation, it lacked legitimacy and credibility. In accordance with the Round Table agreements, a number of critical constitutional revisions were established on 7 April 1989 which created uncertainties with respect to parliament's role in the new political system.

Two of the most important revisions[6] can be identified as: (1) The introduction of 'competitive, but not confrontational' ('compartmentalised') elections to the Sejm and fully contested elections to a newly established Senate.[7] The Polish United Workers' Party (PUWP) lost its monopoly role as a party and its dominance over the electoral process. (2) The elimination of the collegial head of state – the Council of State – and the creation of the position of the President of the Republic.

The outcome of the 1989 elections ultimately yielded a large Solidarity presence (161 seats) in the Sejm and nearly total Solidarity domination of the new Senate (99 of the 100 seats) where it could exercise veto power over bills passed by the other chamber. Following the June elections, Jaruzelski was barely able to muster enough votes in the Polish National Assembly (270 positive votes, 233 negatives, 34 abstentions, and seven invalid ballots) to assume the presidency. The subsequent approval of his nominee,

General Czeslaw Kiszczak, as prime minister (237 to 173 with ten abstentions) only bought a short reprieve for the Communists. A week later, on 9 August, the United Peasant Party (UPP) and the Democratic Party (DP) joined the Solidarity coalition. By 18 August Kiszczak had resigned as prime minister and on 24 August Solidarity's Tadeusz Mazowiecki was confirmed by the Sejm as the new prime minister.[8]

This created a very delicate constitutional and political situation. The 7 April 1989 amendments gave the President of the Republic considerable powers analogous to the model of the Fifth French Republic. The president, elected by the National Assembly (the combined membership of the Sejm and the Senate) by a majority of votes was deemed the supreme representative of the Polish state for both internal and external affairs. Serving a five-year term, he could veto parliamentary laws (which could be overturned by a two-thirds majority vote of at least half of the members of the Sejm) or send them to the constitutional tribunal which would rule on their validity. The president was also given important powers to select his candidates as prime minister and president of the national bank – both of whom would have to be formally approved by the Sejm. Moreover, he was given considerable leverage with the government through his ability to convene and preside over sessions of the Council of Ministers. In the realm of national defence, he was designated Commander in Chief of the Armed Forces and was to chair the Committee for National Defence. He also had the power to declare a state of emergency or institute martial law.[9]

A critical aspect of the April 1989 amendments was the president's ability to dissolve parliament in three very carefully specified circumstances: (1) if the Sejm, over a period of three months, was unable to approve a prime minister and his cabinet; (2) if the Sejm was unable to approve the budget in the three months after its submission; and (3) if the Sejm had adopted laws or resolutions preventing him from exercising his responsibilities as guarantor of the state's international obligations. These provisions were clearly intended to enhance presidential power in cases of legislative inertia. However, the two chambers combining in the National Assembly could curb presidential excesses through impeachment proceedings – ultimately to be decided by the Tribunal of the State.[10]

The political context in which Jaruzelski found himself dictated cautiousness and temperance. Realising the parliamentary mathematics and the mood of the public, he tried to recede into the background. For Walesa, however, the difficult economic and social conditions which were spurring the fragmentation and break-up of the Solidarity coalition, dictated a 1990 run at the presidency. Throughout 1990, he railed at the various forces that he felt were holding back Polish momentum, levelling blistering criticisms of the 'contract Round Table Sejm' which he identified as incapable of effective representation (knowing, of course, the deep suspicions of many citizens about the participation of the former Communists). Jaruzelski felt the pressure and resigned from the presidency; in September the Sejm set a November election date.[11]

The tone of the campaign suggested that if Walesa won the election he might seek to assert the powers of the presidency at the expense of the Sejm. Under the constitutional revisions of 27 September 1990, the President of the Republic would be elected by direct popular vote. This enhanced the prestige of the office and indicated the possibility of a movement away from a parliamentary form of government and a tendency to move toward presidentialism. Questions were raised about the balance of power between the president and parliament.[12] Walesa's weak showing in the first round of the elections, followed by his landslide victory in December, generated confusion about the direction of Polish politics. Fears of an 'imperial presidency' circulated among Walesa's opponents as he entered office and complicated the formation of a new government to succeed Mazowiecki's. Walesa first designated Jan Olszewski as his prime ministerial candidate, but the two disagreed on ministerial appointments and at the end of two weeks Olszewski withdrew as a candidate. Jan Bielecki was Walesa's second choice, but it took lengthy negotiations to form and gain approval of his cabinet. Walesa aroused additional concerns by suggesting that he would form his own political council which some of the Sejm leadership saw as diluting the power of the prime minister.[13]

It became evident in 1991 that the best way to resolve the political and constitutional issues of presidential, prime ministerial and parliamentary relations would be to move beyond the transitional 'contractual parliament' and to hold new parliamentary elections. However, deep divisions existed with respect to the electoral law. From the autumn of 1990 and throughout 1991 there was an intense fragmentation of parliamentary clubs and political parties/groupings. This was facilitated by the 28 July 1990 Law on Political Parties – a liberal law which permitted organised groups of 15 or more members to be registered and acknowledged as political parties, resulting in their proliferation. Most of the parties/organisations preferred a highly proportional system of voting that would guarantee them seats in the parliament, while Walesa and his supporters argued for more restrictive majority or threshold formulae tilted toward the large parties and coalitions. The struggle over the voting system became heated and was interpreted as a struggle between presidentialism and parliamentarism. Moreover, Walesa aggravated the parliament by pushing for special powers and decrying what he interpreted as its irresponsible behaviour. Ultimately, on 1 July 1991, Walesa signed the bill.[14]

How might the tenth Sejm be evaluated? While the Mazowiecki period witnessed considerable support for the government programme, during 1990 the consensus began to break down. With the election of Walesa and the appointment of the Bielecki Government, a continuous process of fragmentation and intensified conflict emerged. The government struggled, often unsuccessfully, to pass its key legislation. During the electoral campaign, the Sejm was especially antagonistic toward the government, opposing its proposals for special economic powers, turning down the constitutional amendments designed to strengthen executive power, rejecting a nominee for president of the National Bank of Poland, and fighting legislative proposals to counteract economic corruption. On the one hand, the tenth Sejm ended 'in an atmosphere of chaos and complete disintegration'. On the other hand, it was highly active and produced a large number of important laws concerning state administrative reforms, economic reforms, co-operatives, local self-government, privatisation, political parties, budgetary matters, and corruption.[15] The results of the 27 October 1991 elections evidenced the confusion, fragmentation, and contentiousness of Polish society. The presence of 29 different parties within the Sejm greatly complicated the task of forming an effective governing coalition. As a consequence, the institutional 'war at the top' between Walesa, the Sejm, and the prime minister worsened. By May 1992, Walesa was describing the institutional competition as a 'Bermuda Triangle'.[16]

Following the October elections, Walesa nominated Bronislaw Geremek of the Democratic Union to form a government, but he was unable to win support from either the right-wing Christian Democratic parties or the Centre Alliance. The Alliance lobbied for its candidate – Jan Olszewski – but Walesa balked. Bielecki's resignation on 25 November prompted Walesa to nominate Olszewski on 5 December 1991. Yet this came only after his repeated calls for constitutional reform and bolstering of the executive, as well as his negative comments on Olszewski's sharp disagreements with the Balcerowicz economic austerity programme. Although the Sejm confirmed the government on 6 December, internal wrangling and Walesa's dim view of Olszewski's cabinet led to the prime minister's resignation on 17 December and his subsequent formation of a cabinet and programme with Sejm approval on 21 December. Nearly two months had elapsed since the election.[17]

The next six months (until Olszewski's dismissal on 5 June 1992) found Walesa, Olszewski, and the Sejm in full internecine conflict. The prime minister, a strong critic of the shock therapy reforms, promised to stabilise the economy. In February 1992, he asked (unsuccessfully) for special powers to govern by decree to facilitate a programme that entailed a variety of seemingly inflationary measures in contradiction to the existing austerity programmes. The plea for more governmental power was a challenge to both Walesa and the Sejm. Throughout his stay in office, Olszewski waged a 'decommunisation' campaign designed to root out former Communists in government and politics. The charges and counter-charges touched many raw nerves. Moreover, the 'Parys Affair' generated fundamental questions about presidential versus prime ministerial authority over the military and raised Sejm concerns over political manipulation of the military.[18]

By May, Walesa again was pressing hard for enhancement of presidential powers. Olszewski was on the defensive, especially following the resignation of his defence minister after a special parliamentary commission deemed the minister's charges of an army conspiracy to be unsubstantiated and therefore recommended his removal. Moreover, Olszewski's methods and record brought about erosion of support from the leadership of his coalition partners. Following Walesa's formal call on 26 May for the Sejm to oust Olszewski, the interior minister released supposedly incriminating police files suggestive of ill-doings by Walesa and other leading politicians. This was the final straw. On 5 June, 1992, Olszewski and his government were removed from office.[19]

Waldemar Pawlak of the Polish Peasant Party (PSL), the president's immediate nominee for the post of prime minister, was accepted by the Sejm, but also had great difficulty forming a working coalition government. Despite the fact that Pawlak assured the potential coalition partners that he would seek presidential and governmental harmony, a month of haggling prevented Pawlak from forming a government and he tendered his resignation. With Walesa bearing down on the parliament, Hanna Suchocka (Democratic Union) proved acceptable as the prime ministerial choice. A seven-party coalition was put together, composed of the liberal 'little coalition' (UD, KLD, PPG) and four other parties, including the conservative Christian National Union.[20] Suchocka, facing considerable adversity, proved to be surprisingly capable in reducing the political tensions that preceded her by maintaining the coalition and restoring confidence in the economy while holding to the Balcerowicz reforms and negotiating the institutional 'Bermuda Triangle'.[21]

The hard political experiences of 1989 through to July 1992 provided compelling arguments for seeking harmonisation of the presidency, government and parliament. This took the constitutional form of 'the Little Constitution' or the Constitutional Act of 1992. A variety of parliamentary and extra-parliamentary groups had been working on such a document since 1990, but sharp differences prevented agreement until the summer and autumn of 1992.[22] The Little Constitution, while replacing the 1952 Constitution, is seen as an interim document, rationalising inter-institutional relations. It is unclear how 'interim' it is.

The Little Constitution moves Poland further in the direction of a hybrid presidential-parliamentary form of government. It clarifies and delimits the powers of the president, specifies procedures for the dissolution of parliament, and delineates how governments may be formed and dismissed.

Most of the president's powers are retained from 1989. One important modification is the emphasis placed upon the president's superior role in matters of internal and external security of the state. He is advised by the Council of National Security, is supreme Chief of the Armed Forces, and appoints (in consultation with the defence minister) the Chief of the General Staff and various military commanders including the heads of the specific services. When state security is imperilled, martial law may be invoked by the president, but only for a period of three months; during that period, there is a prohibition against dissolution of parliament or amendment of the constitution. In normal times, the president may only dissolve parliament if it fails to approve the budget within three months of its introduction; if the Sejm has removed a government by a vote of no confidence, but is unable to select a new prime minister by absolute majority; and when the Sejm cannot produce a majority vote for their nominee to the Council of Ministers. There are several other circumstances under which the president can dissolve parliament. Finally, the president cannot request the government's dismissal, but is able to replace individual cabinet ministers under the prime minister's request.[23]

The most important parliamentary changes clarify inter-institutional relations in the formation of new governments. A complex five-stage process has been delineated: (1) the president designates the prime minister and appoints a cabinet (upon the motion of the prime minister). This government is empowered, but must win a vote of confidence by absolute majority within 14 days. (2) If, however, the vote of confidence fails, the Sejm may elect its own prime minister by absolute majority; (3) If this, too, fails, the president can request another vote on his candidate, this time by simple majority; (4) If this fails, the Sejm may now select its nominee by simple majority; (5) If all of these procedures fail, the president can either dissolve parliament or appoint a government for a six-month term; the president must gain a Sejm majority for this government within the six months or, alternatively, the Sejm must choose its own by majority. If this final step does not result in a government, the parliament is dissolved and new elections are organised.[24] Several other changes are responsive to the turmoil of 1989 to July 1992. The Sejm can put certain bills on an accelerated track to improve the flow of important legislation. Moreover, the Sejm agreed to sanction the issuance of governmental decrees holding legal status, with the exception of certain areas: budget, constitutional reforms, presidential and parliamentary election laws, regional government laws, ratification of international treaties, and civil rights legislation.[25]

There was also clarification of the Senate's role. All Sejm-approved bills are to be sent to the Senate which has 30 days to either amend or reject them. Such amendments or motions to reject may be overturned (by an absolute majority) of the Sejm. In the absence of the absolute majority vote, the Senate's actions are accepted.[26] Another provision of the Little Constitution stipulates that all legislative amendments of the Senate must specify the methods by which they can be financed without expanding the budget.[27]

Under the Little Constitution, the status of the government has been strengthened. Votes of no confidence on the Council of Ministers or individual ministers require that a minimum of 46 Sejm deputies sponsor the motion and act upon it within seven days; the vote must carry by an absolute majority and, in the case of failure, no subsequent vote is possible for three months – and only then if the motion is sponsored by 115 deputies. In the area of ministerial selections, the prime minister is no longer reliant on Sejm nominations in reorganising the composition of the government. The Council of Ministers, under the new provisions, can also give priority to its bills and require the parliament to deal with them according to the stipulated urgencies. Finally, the Council of Ministers is able to request extraordinary decree powers.[28]

While the reforms of the Little Constitution did not bring an end to the political wrestling during the remainder of the first term of the post-Communist Sejm, they did represent a serious effort at rationalising or institutionalising the external and internal interactions of key constitutional organs. By the time of the surprising successful vote of no confidence on the Suchocka Government on 28 May 1993, Polish legislative politics had gained a more positive stature. With the regularisation (or rationalisation) of the legislative process, the sorry record of the Olszewski period of the first term was seemingly reversed. The Suchocka coalition had managed to hold together and press forward with a legislative agenda that included an emphasis on conservative fiscal policy, privatisation, softening some of the social costs of the economic reforms, and withstanding the political restlessness of industrial workers and public sector employees. Only the quirky miscalculations of the parliamentary parties and Walesa's desire to apply his own 'political shock therapy' accounted for the vote of no confidence and dissolution of the parliament.[29] This suggests that there is some room for optimism that the post-Suchocka parliaments can approximate democratic 'normalcy'.

CAPABILITY: THE INTERNAL DEVELOPMENT OF THE SEJM

This section focuses comparatively on the internal development of the Sejm. First, it examines the composition of the Sejm – party representation and some important characteristics of the deputies. Second, it analyses the committee system and committee activities. The third subject is the overall legislative activity profile of the Sejm. This analysis affords insights into the evolving capacities of the Sejm to deal with the political agenda.

COMPOSITION

Parties and Interests

During the Communist period of rule, deputies to the Sejm were, in essence, selected rather than elected. 'Consent elections', controlled by the hegemonic Polish United Workers' Party, placed either Communists, reliable members of two allied 'co-operating' political parties (the United Peasant Party and the Democratic Party) or members of three Catholic political associations (Znak, Pax and the Christian Social Association) into the parliament. The nominations and candidates' lists were determined through the co-ordinating mechanisms of the Front of National Unity dominated by the PUWP. As a result, there was considerable stability in representation and full assurance of Communist dominance.

From 1952 to 1980, party/association representation in the Sejm remained within clearly established limits. The dominant PUWP, avowedly representing the working class and collective national interests, held from 62.4 per cent to 52.1 per cent of the deputies' seats. The United Peasant Party, composed primarily of citizens from farming communities and intelligentsia of rural background, ranged from 25.7 per cent to 21.2 per cent of the total deputy seats. The Democratic Party, whose members came mainly from the intelligentsia, small business and segments of the services sector, held between 8.5 per cent and 5.9 per cent of the seats. Non-party deputies, many of whom were members of the three Catholic associations, ranged from 13.7 per cent to 8.7 per cent of the deputies.[30]

The 'compartmentalised election' of 31 July 1989 was meant to yield a new configuration for the tenth term of the Sejm through inclusion of the Solidarity forces – the citizens' committees. The electoral outcome did yield a Communist bloc victory (276 seats) with significant representation of the Solidarity forces (161 seats) and the non-Communist-affiliated candidates (23 seats). However, the defection of UPP and DP deputies to the Solidarity coalition on 17 August 1989 ended the Communist bloc's control of the Sejm. The Solidarity group (the Citizens' Parliamentary Club), was now joined by the UPP with 76 seats and the DP with 27 seats, producing a 264 seat majority over the combined PUWP (161 seats) and the non-Communist-affiliated deputies (23 seats).[31]

From July 1989 to October 1991, there was a constant shifting in the number and composition of the parliamentary clubs. At the end of July 1989 there were seven parliamentary clubs; by the end of 1990 there were 11; and by the end of October 1991 there were 15. Such fragmentation complicated the functioning of the Sejm.[32]

The electoral results on 27 October 1991 produced a new parliamentary landscape with a proliferation of parties represented in the tenth term of the Sejm. Table 1 presents the nine top parties, their seats, and the percentages of votes won in the elections.

TABLE 1
MAJOR PARTY REPRESENTATION IN THE 10TH TERM OF THE SEJM

Party	Seats	% Votes
Democratic Union	62	13.5
Democratic Left Alliance	60	13.0
Catholic Election Alliance	49	10.7
Polish Peasants' Party-Program Alliance	48	10.4
Confederation for an Independent Poland	46	10.0
Centrum Civic Alliance	44	9.6
Liberal Democratic Congress	37	8.0
Peasant Alliance	28	6.1
Independent Self-Governing Labor Union, Solidarity	27	5.9
Total	401	87.2

Note: The remaining 59 seats and 13.8 per cent of the vote were distributed among small parties.
Source: Rocznik Statystyczny, 1992 (Warsaw, Glowny Urzad, 1993), Table 3 (103), p.66.

The first term of the post-Communist Sejm was marked by considerable changes in the number and composition of the parliamentary clubs. At the beginning of the term, 17 clubs ranging in size from three to 62 deputies were in existence; by 31 May 1993, there were 11 clubs ranging in size from 16 to 59 members and six clubs of three to seven members. Throughout the term, a variety of parliamentary clubs and circles were established and either persisted, changed their names, or ceased to exist, thus reflecting the continuous turmoil in the political arena.[33]

The party system and parliamentary club situation in Poland demonstrates the important institutional evolution from Communist monocentrism and Sejm dominance to a transitional pluralism with the Communists in the Sejm minority, to what can be termed 'hyperpluralism' and fluid coalitional Sejm politics.

Incumbency

Despite the rather stable representation of parties and associations in the Sejm during the Communist period, there was a considerable amount of deputy turnover. For example, perhaps as a result of the 1970 political crisis, at the beginning of the sixth term of the Sejm in 1972, only 37 per cent of PUWP deputies, 39 per cent of UPP deputies, and 38 per cent of DP deputies were incumbents. Fewer than half of the deputies from the sixth term were selected for the seventh term (1976–80), with incumbents constituting 44 per cent of PUWP deputies, 45 per cent of UPP deputies, and 38 per cent of DP deputies. Successive incumbency from the fifth through the sixth and on to the seventh term of the Sejm included less than 20 per cent of all deputies.[34] Apparently the Communist authorities did not place a high premium on experience in the functioning of the Sejm.

The volatile political conditions of 1989 resulted in nearly a clean sweep as far as experience is concerned in the composition of the tenth Sejm. 422 (91.7 per cent) of the deputies were serving for the first time, while 32 (6.9 per cent) had served for the first time in the ninth term.[35]

There was greater carry-over from the tenth term of the Sejm to the first term of the post-Communist Sejm. However, the volatility of the political system is evidenced by the fact that less than one-quarter of the members of the 'contractual parliament' were re-elected to office; 335 deputies (72.8 per cent) were serving as deputies for the first time, while only 113 (24.6 per cent) continued on as incumbents from the tenth term. Eight deputies (1.7 per cent) hailed back to the ninth term.[36]

Demographic Composition

From 1952 to 1991, the Polish Sejm was populated primarily by middle-aged deputies. In any given term, more than half and up to 70 per cent of the deputies were in the 40–59 age bracket.[37] In the first term of the non-Communist Sejm, there was a notable jump in the proportion of younger deputies – 35 (7.4 per cent) in the 20–29-year bracket and 135 (29.3 per cent) in the 30–39 bracket.[38] This large representation of members under 40 made the first Sejm of 1991–93 the youngest in age composition since 1952. The advent of democracy was accompanied by the infusion of new, younger aspirants into the political arena.

There was also a trend in the direction of educational upgrading of the Sejm membership. From 1952 to 1980, the percentage of deputies with higher education ranged from 32 per cent to 55 per cent.[39] The tenth Sejm and the first post-Communist Sejm had 392 (85.8 per cent) and 357 (77.6 per cent) members, respectively, having higher educational status.[40] In the more democratic context of post-1989 politics, educational credentials seem much more essential for service as a deputy.[41]

An occupational profile of the membership of the tenth Sejm indicates that specialists and administrators dominated: non-technical professional specialists occupied 105 seats (22.9 per cent); top directors in workplaces 69 seats (15.0 per cent); scientific employees in all areas 42 seats (9.2 per cent); middle and lower level directors in workplaces 38 seats (8.3 per cent); state administrative officials at all levels 31 seats (6.8 per cent), and activists of political, social, and union organisations 25 seats (5.4 per cent). Farmers, holding 59 seats (12.9 per cent) were the only significant non-managerial/non specialist group.[42]

Data regarding the professional backgrounds of deputies to the first term of the post-Communist Sejm utilised a somewhat different classification, but show similar patterns. The leading groups were: farmers, 52 seats (11.3 per cent); administrators 47 seats (10.2 per cent); politicians 41 seats (8.9 per cent); academicians 38 seats (8.3 per cent); doctors 20 seats (4.3 per cent); and elementary/secondary school teachers 19 seats (4.1 per cent).[43]

One final demographic aspect of the Sejm must be noted – the representation of females among deputies. From the first Sejm of 1952–56 to the ninth Sejm of 1985–89, the trend seemed to be in the direction of increasing representation of women. From a low of 19 women deputies in the second Sejm, the number rose to 106 in the eighth Sejm of 1980–85 (23.4 per cent). In the tenth Sejm, however, women deputies dropped to 62, and in the first term of the post-Communist Sejm to 44 (9.5 per cent).[44]

What emerges from this examination of demographic trends is a portrait of a Sejm which is becoming younger, more educated, and increasingly professionalised in background. At the same time, the tenth and the first Sejms included a large number of legislative novices and were unrepresentative of female citizens. While under Communism an informal quota system was used to assure presumed proper representation of various groups, the post-1989 competitive environment produced representation based more on educational and professional credentials, as well as political expertise.

DEVELOPMENT OF THE COMMITTEE SYSTEM

Polish parliamentary analysts have emphasised the central role of the standing committees of the Sejm in handling the details of legislation too complex for the parliament as a whole. The committees are designed to provide specialised expertise, increased opportunities for discussions, and the best setting for thorough deliberation.[45] Given the ambitious agenda of the post-Communist transformations, the committees have become even more prominent legislative actors.

Number and Size of Committees

Earlier research for the Communist period depicted a rather well-developed committee system. During the eighth term of the Sejm, there were 22 permanent committees covering a wide range of functional areas. The committees varied in size from 19 to 53 members. Committee assignments numbered 697, meaning that over half of the deputies served on more than one committee.[46]

The tenth term of the Sejm operated with 23 permanent committees, varying in size from 13 (the Committee on Constitutional Responsibilities) to 62 members (the Committee on Agriculture and Food Economy). There was a total of 445 committee assignments, with 240 deputies belonging to one committee, 184 to two committees, 31 to three or more committees, and 12 to no committees. In keeping with the unusual political environment of the 'contractual parliament', there were 14 extraordinary committees that operated for limited periods of time during the tenth term.[47]

The first term of the post-Communist Sejm expanded the number of permanent committees by one (a new committee dealing with European System Affairs) to 24. At the beginning of the term, a total of 452 members were serving on committees, 261 on one committee, 184 on two, seven on three or more, and eight on no committees. By the end of the term, there was a reduction in committee participation – with 427 members serving, 244 on one committee, 183 on two, nil on three or more, and 33 on none. Seven special committees also operated to examine specific policy issues.[48]

Committee Activity

Studies during the Communist era show a trend toward expansion of committees and sub-committees. During the first term of the Sejm (1952–56), committees met a total of 247 times – an average of 61.7 times per year. By the sixth term (1972–1976), the committees met 1,057 times – an average of 264.3 meetings per year.[49]

Available data on the committees' operations since 1989 also show a high degree of overall activity. During the tenth term, the 23 full permanent committees held a total of 2,188 sessions. Their presidia met 769 times and their sub-committees 1,052 times. Certain committees are prominent for their large number of full member sessions – the Legislative Committee with 518; the Economic Policy, Budget and Finance Committee with 187; the Social Policy Committee with 182; and the Agricultural and Food Economy Committee with 130. Given the pressing political, social and political agenda of the 'contractual Sejm', these were logical committees for high activity profiles. The permanent committees were also active in adopting decisions in the form of *disiderata* (requests to agencies that they undertake specific actions), issuing opinions (interpretations of rules/activities) and field trips (generally on-site inspections). These activities function to hold administrative agencies responsible to the Sejm. During the tenth Sejm, 167 *disiderata* and 229 opinions were adopted by the permanent committees. Moreover, 93 field trips were undertaken. The permanent committees most active in issuing *disiderata* were the Committee on Health (30) and the Committee on Agriculture and the Food Economy (24). The most active committees issuing opinions were the Committee on Foreign Affairs (58) and Deputy Rules and Affairs (47). Field trips were most numerous by the Committee on Relations with Poles Abroad (24) and the Committee on the Economic System and Industrial Policy (15).[50]

A similar profile of activity is presented by the first Sejm of the post-Communist period. The 24 permanent committees met 2,132 times with 678 presidia meetings, and 122 sub-committee meetings. The Legislative Committee was the most active in holding full sessions (456), followed by the Committee on Economic Policy, Budget, and Finance (195). There were 82 *disiderata* and 304 opinions issued, as well as 74 field trips. The committees most active in issuing *disiderata* were the Committee on Health (18) and the Committee on Agriculture and the Food Economy (16). The most prominent committees in adopting opinions were the Committee on Deputy Rules and Affairs (84), the Committee on Foreign Affairs (29), and the Legislative Committee (22). Field trips were most numerous by the Committee for National Defence (19) and the Committee on Education, Science, and Technical Progress (18).[51]

The pattern of development of the committee system in the Sejm suggests that as a functioning body it has the structural capacity to deal with the complex array of problems associated with the post-Communist transformation. The committee system involves the majority of deputies in specialised roles and affords them the opportunity to develop expertise. The levels of activity of the committees seem appropriate to the agenda. While specific decisions that have been taken may not have resolved existing problems, the Sejm committees appear to be working seriously and strenuously.

Legislative Activity

Earlier studies of the Communist Sejm concluded that in terms of numerical indicators of activity it would have to considered a 'minimal' parliament. From 1952 to 1980, the number of Sejm meetings was rather low. Excluding the summer recess, the Sejm met about once a month, with most meetings taking one day each. Over this period, the number of meetings per term varied from a high of 59 to a low of 18, while the actual days of meetings ranged from 71 to 22. During the seventh term (1976–80), there were only

28 meetings.[52] The tenth 'contractual parliament' showed a much higher level of activity. In its term from 4 July 1989 until 31 October 1991, it held 79 meetings, with the days of meetings totalling 177. The meetings varied from one to four days in length. In 1989, it met 17 times over 33 days; in 1990, it met 30 times over 67 days; and in 1991, it met 32 times over 77 days. Indeed, in keeping with the heavy agenda of the transition, the Sejm met continuously during this term except for an August 1990 recess.[53]

The first post-Communist Sejm (24 November 1991 to 31 May 1993) held 45 meetings, with the days of meetings amounting to 135. It held four meetings over eight days in 1991, 29 meetings over 86 days in 1992 (recessing in August), and 12 meetings over 42 days in 1993.[54] This can also be considered a very full schedule congruent with the significant policy agenda of this period.

Comparison of the legislative productivity of the Sejm indicates a great difference in the activity levels from the Communist to post-Communist periods. From 1952 to 1980, the largest number of laws passed was 174 (second term, 1957–61); the range for the remaining terms was from a low of 36 (the fifth term which was of three years' duration) to a high of 103 in the sixth term (1972–76). The number of bills introduced, but not passed, throughout this period was very low, ranging from two to four.[55] In stark contrast, 248 laws were passed during the tenth 'contractual parliament' term – 33 in 1989, 107 in 1990, and 108 in 1991. The majority of these laws (156) came at the initiative of the government, with 105 introduced by deputies, 15 by senators, and four by the president. Of the 248 laws adopted, nearly half (120) were considered in their first reading at a committee meeting; 22 were considered in first and second readings at full meetings of the Sejm without referral to committees. Also in contrast to the Communist Sejms, in the new democratic context a notable number of bills (78) were withdrawn, formally rejected (36), or otherwise delayed or rejected (of the 16 in this category, four were rejected by the Senate). During the course of consideration, 41 of the adopted laws were amended, 169 underwent editing (changes creating a uniform text), and only 38 emerged without amendments.[56] This heavily loaded agenda primarily concerned reforms associated with the market and democratisation emphases of the transition.

The first post-Communist Sejm also assumed a heavy legislative burden: 335 bills were introduced, 94 which were passed, 43 which were withdrawn or rejected, and 133 which did not complete the legislative process. The government (Council of Ministers) continued to play a prominent role in legislation, introducing 91 bills, 47 of which were adopted – giving it a much higher success ratio than the deputies' bills. Only eight of the government bills were withdrawn or rejected, while 36 did not complete the legislative process. Twenty-six bills were introduced by Sejm committees, of which 14 were adopted, one was withdrawn or rejected, and 11 did not complete the legislative process. The legislative role of the president seemed slightly increased, as he introduced ten bills: of which four were adopted, one was withdrawn or rejected, and five did not complete the legislative process. The Senate had the least visible role, introducing only nine bills: four were adopted and five did not complete the legislative process.[57]

The first post-Communist Sejm processed the adopted bills with considerable thoroughness: 53 received their first reading at a full meeting of the Sejm as compared to 41 in Sejm committees; 44 of the bills received two readings, while 50 received three readings. The great majority of the bills (82) were considered by both the Legislative Committee and specialised committees, while only three were considered by specialised committees without the participation of the Legislative Committee, and another three without the participation of any committee. Five were considered only by specialised committees.[58]

Beyond formal laws, the tenth and first Sejms have been engaged in making 'decisions' (or 'resolutions' – *uchwaly*) of importance for the functioning of the state. The 'contractual' Sejm made 162 such decisions during its term, 34 concerning the internal operations of the body itself (rules changes, selection of organs and changes in their composition, taking away seats, confirming elections); 39 concerning the appointment of members of the main state organs; 29 dealing with the state budget and financial plans; 63 concerned with gaining information relevant to law. Eleven such decisions were rejected, four were retracted, and one was superceded by another decision. Eight proposed decisions were left pending at the end of the term.[59]

Even more such decisions were taken up by the first post-Communist Sejm: 232 decisions were introduced, 135 were adopted, 40 were either withdrawn or rejected, and 57 were not completely processed as the term ended. These decisions (also referred to as resolutions, declarations and appeals) were categorised as follows: 55 concerning the internal operations of the Sejm, 32 concerning appointments or removals from state organs, nine concerning the state budget and financial plans, 30 concerned with gaining information related to laws, and nine connected with other matters. Of the 57 decisions that were not adopted, 37 remained under consideration in committees, 15 were discharged to committees for initial review, and five were directed for their first reading at a full meeting of the Sejm.[60]

Another set of evidence reflecting the high activity level of the tenth and first Sejms concerns the systematic questioning of government officials by deputies – 'interpellations' requiring formal responses and more information-oriented 'questions'. During the tenth Sejm, 609 interpellations were undertaken, 508 by individuals, 101 collectively (100 in the name of deputy groups, one in the name of a Sejm committee). These interpellations elicited 470 written responses and 139 oral responses. Moreover, 150 questions were offered in Sejm meetings with officials.[61]

Such questioning, seeking to promote governmental accountability, continued in the first term of the post-Communist Sejm: 773 interpellations were registered, 693 individual and 80 collectively; these received 715 written responses and 55 oral responses; (three interpellations were withdrawn). 508 deputy questions received 295 oral and 213 written responses. The largest numbers of interpellations were directed to the following officials: the Prime Minister 248; the Minister of the Spatial Economy and Construction 74; the Minister of Health and Social Welfare 57; the Minister of Finance 56; and the Minister of Labour and Social Policy 53. The emphasis in questions followed a similar pattern.[62]

Constituency Service

Constituency service is one more dimension of the Sejm's activity which deserves mention. Data for the tenth or 'contractual Sejm' indicate that the Sejm and its organs receive a large number of written inquiries and comments that take a variety of forms. During this term, deputies had to sort out and respond to 60,969 constituent inquiries: 28,363 of these were addressed to the Marshal of the Sejm; 58,124 items were acted upon ('facilitated', in Polish parlance) by deputies and staff by the end of the session. Of these items, 10,097 involved requests, 3,058 sought replies from specific agencies, 1,807 were petitions, 875 wanted notes of introduction, 807 registered complaints, 507 were protests, and 40,923 letters focused on a variety of matters. At the end of the term 2,845 of the items were still under consideration.[63] While data are not available for the more recent terms, it is probable that constituency demands will multiply as democratic politics develop.

This consideration of Sejm activities, while not emphasising actual policy debates and internal processes, does suggest that the legislature is responding to the opportunities afforded by the new democratic environment. The legislative load and associated responsibilities are expanding – perhaps faster than is manageable for the many relatively new representatives and the often divided political parties. Adopting a long-term perspective, it is possible to say that the Sejm as an institution is developing positive capabilities to meet the new challenges.

CONCLUSION

Any serious evaluation of the institutional development of the Polish Sejm since 1989 must rise above the fascinating, chaotic politics of the transition and transformation periods. It makes better sense to adopt a long-range comparative perspective to determine whether there is some progressive evolution of the parliamentary bodies. The interplay between the opportunity structure presented by the political environment and the capacity of political elites/institutions to respond should be the key analytic focus.

This comparison does present a rather positive set of institutional responses to the political environment. When the Round Table agreements afforded the Communist opposition a meaningful opportunity for electoral and parliamentary participation, they responded in innovative and ultimately successful ways. The unanticipated (by all sides) and embarrassing 1989 compartmentalised election results did not have to spell the end of Communist rule in Poland. It was the application of external societal pressure and internal parliamentary maneouvring that reversed the equation of power in the Sejm. Moreover, the 'contractual parliament', while unrepresentative of the political division of social forces, adapted and functioned rather successfully despite the inclusion of so many strange political bedfellows. The Mazowiecki and Bielecki governments, in tandem with the Sejm, pressed forward with necessary but often unpopular sets of legislative programmes. In the transitional period, it was to be expected that parliamentary fragmentation would occur (the fading and resurrections of the Communists and the break-up of the Citizens' Parliamentary Club, for example). What was probably not to be expected was the ability of so many deputies to overcome their political distaste for many of their parliamentary colleagues and to learn the very difficult rules of the democratic game and to cope with their responsibilities. Perhaps this was somewhat facilitated by the fact that the Communist Sejm was more than a 'rubber stamp'. Its 'minimal parliament' character provided an institutional basis for effective change during the transition.

In a similar vein, it is possible to look positively at the institutional development of the first term of the post-Communist Sejm. In the wake of the first full and free democratic parliamentary elections of the post-Communist period – with a proportional representation election law that nearly guaranteed fragmentation – it was to be expected that the Sejm would be a difficult zone of operations for so many young, highly educated, and eager novice politicians. Moreover, the unleashing of the 'war at the top' and the difficult institutional inter-relationships ('the Bermuda Triangle') could only make matters worse. There was a more conducive opportunity structure for political conflict in the first post-Communist Sejm. Hence, the record of the Olszewski Government was quite dismal. Yet, at the same time, lessons were being learned in 'the school of hard knocks'. The necessary work of a parliament was being carried out in the permanent and special committees. The necessity for some constitutional reforms – ultimately in the form of the Little Constitution – impressed itself upon the consciousness of parliamentary and governmental elites, as well as upon Walesa. The political parties and clubs continued to refine their programmes and methods of operations, not only to attract electoral support, but to gain legislative credibility. Thus, there emerged among analysts a much more favourable image of the Sejm during the period of the Suchocka Government. It operated much like minority governing coalitions in other multi-party parliamentary systems. Obviously the ambitions and self-centred policies of a number of the political parties and leading political elites brought about the dissolution of the first Sejm, but is this really so abnormal or a sign of ineffectiveness in a political environment of transformation? Again, a review of the structural characteristics, the 'demographics', the activity levels, and constitutional innovations associated with the first-term Sejm suggest that capabilities to function more democratically and more effectively are being developed.

Before concluding, some attention must be paid to the more mundane world of democratic politics. Given the artificial stability and harmony of Communist politics and the 'subject' orientation of the previous political cultures, the unpredictability and messiness of the new democratic political game has been disorienting and aggravating for many (perhaps the majority of) Polish citizens. The steady decline of confidence in institutions, including the Sejm, is a manifestation of this orientation. Moreover, high expectations about the benefits of the new system, combined with the many sacrifices connected to adopting a market economy, have stimulated public displeasure directed toward the parliament and the representatives. Such public attitudes, while troublesome, cannot be said to be indicators of the failure of parliamentary development. In the long run, the commitment of the representatives to the institution, their ability to function in their roles, and their ability to find new structural, constitutional, and legislative solutions for Poland's problems will determine how we evaluate the evolution and performance of the Sejm.

NOTES

1. D.M. Olson and M.D. Simon, 'The Institutional Development of a Minimal Parliament: The Case of the Polish Sejm', in S. White and D. Nelson (eds.), *Communist Politics: A Reader* (London, Macmillan Education, 1986), pp.73–97.
2. D.M. Olson and P. Norton, 'The New Legislatures of Central Europe: The Paradox of Opportunity and Capability', unpublished manuscript, 1994.
3. D.M. Olson, 'Compartmentalized Competition: The Managed Transitional Election System of Politics', *Journal of Politics* (May 1993), pp.414–41; J. Wasilewski and W. Wesolowski (eds.), *Poczatki Parlamentarnej Elity: Poslowie Kontrakowego Sejmu* (Warsaw, IFIS, Polish Academy of Sciences, 1992).

4. Olson and Simon, 'The Institutional Development of a Minimal Parliament', pp.93–7.
5. Olson, 'Compartmentalized Competition', pp.414–41.
6. Two additional important revisions were the establishment of the Senate as the second chamber of the parliament and measures taken to assure a fair and independent judiciary. See S. Gebethner, 'The Dynamics of Institutional Change in the Polish Political and Constitutional System', unpublished manuscript, 1993.
7. R.C. Taras, 'Voters, Parties, and Leaders', in R.F. Staar (ed.), *Transition to Democracy in Poland* (New York, St. Martin's Press, 1993), p.23; Olson, 'Compartmentalized Competition', pp.414–41.
8. G. Stokes, *The Walls Came Tumbling Down: The Collapse of Communism in Eastern Europe* (New York, Oxford, 1993), pp.127–30; J.F. Brown, *Surge to Freedom: The End of Communist Rule in Eastern Europe* (Durham, Duke University Press, 1991); pp.93, 286–7.
9. Gebethner, 'The Dynamics of Institutional Change', pp.5–6.
10. Gebethner, 'The Dynamics of Institutional Change', p.6.
11. Stokes, *The Walls Came Tumbling Down*, pp.212–13.
12. Gebethner, 'The Dynamics of Institutional Change', p.11.
13. A.A. Michta, 'The Presidential-Parliamentary System', in Staar (ed.), *Transition to Democracy in Poland*, p.59.
14. S.P. Ramet, 'The New Poland: Democratic and Authoritarian Tendencies', *Global Affairs*, VII (Spring 1992), pp.146–8; G. Stokes, *The Walls Came Tumbling Down*, p.213; S. Gebethner, 'Polish Political Parties After the Parliamentary Elections of 1991', unpublished manuscript, 1992, p.10.
15. A. Goszczynski, 'Outgoing Sejm: End of an Era', *Warsaw Voice* (3 Nov. 1991), p.5.
16. Taras, 'Voters, Parties, and Leaders', pp.43–4; Michta, 'The Presidential-Parliamentary System', p.62.
17. Ramet, 'The New Poland: Democratic and Authoritarian Tendencies', pp.49–50; Michta, 'The Presidential-Parliamentary System', pp.63–4.
18. J.F. Brown, *Hopes and Shadows: Eastern Europe After Communism* (Durham, Duke University Press, 1994), pp.76–7; Taras, 'Voters, Parties, and Leaders', pp.35–6; Michta, 'The Presidential-Parliamentary System', pp.62–7.
19. Michta, 'The Presidential-Parliamentary System', p.67; Brown, *Hopes and Shadows*, pp.76–7.
20. Brown, *Hopes and Shadows*, pp.76–7.
21. Brown, *Hopes and Shadows*, p.77.
22. A. Rapaczynski, 'Constitutional Politics in Poland', in A.E.D. Howard, *Constitution Making in Eastern Europe* (Washington DC, The Woodrow Wilson Center Press, 1993), pp.118–26; J. Elster, 'Constitution-Making in Eastern Europe: Rebuilding the Boat in the Open Sea', in J.J. Hesse (ed.), *Administrative Transformation in Central and Eastern Europe* (Oxford, Blackwell Publishers, 1993), pp.208–14; A.E.D. Howard, 'Constitutional Reform', in Staar (ed.), *Transition to Democracy in Poland*, pp.100–103; Gebethner, 'The Dynamics of Institutional Change', pp.19–27.
23. Gebethner, 'The Dynamics of Institutional Change', pp.20, 24–5; A. E. D. Howard, 'Constitutional Reform', p.102; Michta, 'The Presidential-Parliamentary System', pp.71–2.
24. Howard, 'Constitutional Reform', pp.101–2.
25. Michta, 'The Presidential-Parliamentary System', p.71.
26. Gebethner, 'The Dynamics of Institutional Change', p.22.
27. Michta, 'The Presidential-Parliamentary System', p.71.
28. Gebethner, 'The Dynamics of Institutional Change', p.22.
29. L. Vinton, 'Walesa Applies Political Shock Therapy', *Radio Free Europe/Radio Liberty Report on Eastern Europe*, 2:24 (11 June 1993), pp.1–11; A. Sabbat-Swidlicka, 'Poland: The End of the Solidarity Era', *Radio Free Europe/Radio Liberty Report on Eastern Europe*, 3:1 (7 Jan. 1994), pp.81–6.
30. Olson and Simon, 'The Institutional Development of a Minimal Parliament', p.79.
31. E. Najlewajko, 'Poslowie Sejmu X Kadencja: Charakterystyka Ogolna', in J. Wasilewski and W. Wesolowski (eds.), *Poczatki Parlamentarnej Elity: Poslowie Kontraktowego Sejmu*, p.75.
32. Kancaleria Sejmu, X Kadencja, *Niektore Dane Statystyczne o Pracy Sejmu i Jego Organow*

(Warsaw, Wydawnictwo Sejmowe, 1991), pp.7–9.
33. Kancaleria Sejmu, *Sejm Rzezypospolitej Polskiej I Kadencja Informacja o Dzialalnosci Sejmu* (Warsaw: Wydawnictwo Sejmowe, 1993), pp.13–15.
34. M.D. Simon and D.M. Olson, 'Evolution of a Minimal Parliament: Membership and Committee Changes in the Polish Sejm', *Legislative Studies Quarterly*, V (May 1980), p.214.
35. Kancaleria Sejmu, X Kadencja, *Niektore Dane Statystyczne*, p.7.
36. Kancaleria Sejmu, *Sejm Rzeczypospolitej Polskiej*, p.10.
37. *Rocznik Statystyczny 1992* (Warsaw, Glowny Urzad Statystyczny, 1993), Table 5 (105), p.67.
38. Kancaleria Sejmu, *Sejm Rzeczypospolitej Polskiej*, p.10.
39. Simon and Olson, 'Evolution of a Minimal Parliament', p.215.
40. Kancaleria Sejmu, X Kadencja, *Niektore Dane Statystyczne*, p.7; Kancaleria Sejmu, *Sejm Rzeczypospolitej Polskiej*, p.10.
41. Najlewajko, in her analysis of the tenth term emphasises that 73 per cent of the deputies had attained doctoral degrees or the rank of professor. She notes the high social ranks of professionalism defined by titles and scientific degrees. Najlewajko, 'Poslowie Sejmu X Kadencja', p.79.
42. Najlewajko, 'Poslowie Sejmu X Kadencja', p.79.
43. Kancaleria Sejmu, *Sejm Rzeczypospolitej Polskie*, p.11.
44. *Rocznik Statystyczny 1992*, Table 5 (105), p.67.
45. Simon and Olson, 'Evolution of a Minimal Parliament', p.219.
46. Simon and Olson, 'Evolution of a Minimal Parliament', p.221.
47. Kancaleria Sejmu X Kadencja, *Niektore Dane Statystyczne*, p.41.
48. Kancaleria Sejmu, *Sejm Rzeczypospolitej Polskie*, pp.52–3.
49. Simon and Olson, 'Evolution of a Minimal Parliament', p.221.
50. Kancaleria Sejmu X Kadencja, *Niektore Dane Statystyczne*, pp.45–8.
51. Kancaleria Sejmu, *Sejm Rzeczypospolitej Polskie I Kadencja Informacja o Dzialalnosci Sejmu*, pp.52–3.
52. Olson and Simon, 'The Institutional Development of a Minimal Parliament', pp.75–7.
53. Kancaleria Sejmu X Kadencja, *Niektore Dane Statystyczne*, pp.16–20.
54. Kancaleria Sejmu, *Sejm Rzeczypospolitej Polskie*, pp.23–4.
55. Olson and Simon, 'The Institutional Development of a Minimal Parliament', p.76.
56. Kancaleria Sejmu X Kadencja, *Niektore Dane Statystyczne o Pracy Sejmu i Jego Organow*, pp.20–21, 81–110.
57. Kancaleria Sejmu, *Sejm Rzeczypospolitej Polskie*, pp.30–31.
58. Kancaleria Sejmu, *Sejm Rzeczypospolitej Polskie*, p.27.
59. Kancaleria Sejmu X Kadencja, *Niektore Dane Statystyczne*, pp.22, 135–7.
60. Kancaleria Sejmu, *Sejm Rzeczypospolitej Polskie*, pp.31–2.
61. Kancaleria Sejmu X Kadencja, *Niektore Dane Statystyczne*, p.23.
62. Kancaleria Sejmu, *Sejm Rzeczypospolitej Polskie*, pp.36–9.
63. Kancaleria Sejmu X Kadencja, *Niektore Dane Statystyczne*, p.79.

The Legislature of the Czech Republic

JANA RESCHOVÁ and JINRIŠKA SYLLOVÁ

The Czech Parliament has come through two big changes: the period of transition and the emergence of a new statehood. The parliament has experienced a new party system and coalition–opposition partnership. The changes have required a new constitutional and legal framework. The Czech Parliament has established itself in the political system, and has been empowered to exercise unique roles and competences. The internal structure of the parliamentary institutions developed during the transition process.

EXTERNAL FACTORS

The Parliament of the Czech Republic was constituted as a legislature of a sovereign state on 1 January 1993 as a consequence of the split of the Czechoslovak federation. Constitutional and general perception of the new sovereignty was marked by the emphasis on the continuity and traditional values of parliamentarism, the original roots of which were to be found in the pre-war Czechoslovak Republic.

The Czech legislature existed before 1993 as a legislature of the state member of the federation. Originally, it was established in 1968 under the name of the Czech National Council. Under the federal constitution – neither the Czech nor the Slovak constitution was written – the Czech Parliament consisted of one chamber and had 200 members elected directly in one-mandate constituencies for a four-year term. As a parliament of the Czech Republic it was given some important powers: power over the legality of the administration acts, the right to give consent to international treaties that have direct impact on the law of the republic, and the right to abolish administrative regulations that did not comply with the constitution or any legal provision. Its presidium appointed the Czech Prime Minister and members of the cabinet and it had power to dismiss them. The presidium also appointed other higher state officials, the general prosecutor for instance, and fulfilled on the regional level other functions that on the national level usually are reserved for the president. Also, the National Council played a legislative role. Basically, it deliberated and passed laws that were 'left and not provided' by the federal legislation and a few laws that were explicitly listed in the constitution. The latter included, electoral

Jana Reschová is a lecturer in the Department of Political Science at the University of Economics, the Czech Republic, and Jindriška Sillová is a member of the Parliamentary Institute, Parliament of the Czech Republic.

laws, laws by which new ministries or other administrative authorities were established, and laws on economic planning. The National Council also had the right to initiate a bill in the federal legislature.

This constitutional framework lasted till the adoption of a new constitution at the end of 1992. The power given to the parliament was very well accommodated to the one-party system that guaranteed the use of power both inside and outside the parliament. A chaotic situation emerged when the new political elite came to power and the new system did not exactly fit the old constitutional pattern. Nevertheless, the parliament, once it was given the power, proved rather unwilling to give it up.

Passing the new constitution, the National Council renamed itself in the Chamber of Deputies and its members remained in office as members of one of the chamber of the new bicameral parliament.

The Czech Parliament under the Current Constitution

The Constitution of the Czech Republic was adopted in December 1992. According to its wording the Czech Parliament consists of two chambers: the Chamber of Deputies and the Senate. The Chamber of Deputies has 200 members, elected every four years under a system of proportional representation with a five per cent (or seven, nine, or 11 per cent – depending on the number of coalition partners) threshold. The Senate has 81 senators, who are elected under a majority system and hold office for six years. The elections to the Senate are held every second year when one-third of its membership comes up for re-election. The electoral systems are not the only difference. Candidates to the chamber are to be 21 years and over while candidates to the Senate are to be 40 years and over.

Another difference between both chambers lies in the stability of the mandate. The Chamber of Deputies, unlike the Senate, can be dissolved. The president dissolves the chamber only in cases specified by the constitution: when the chamber is inactive and does not consider the bill when asked by the cabinet, or is not capable of reaching the attendance majority, or when the adjournment of the session is longer than 120 days per year, or when the chamber rejects the appointment of the prime minister who was nominated by its chairman. Also, only the Chamber of Deputies can vote on a motion of non-confidence in the cabinet and only the deputies (not senators) interpellate the cabinet and its members. This stems from cabinet accountability to the chamber. The Senate, on the other hand, has power to give assent to the president's appointees of the Constitutional Court and to set up legal procedure for impeachment.

The Czech Parliament under the Interim Constitution

The constitution itself includes interim provisions which have been implemented since it came into effect. The current Czech Parliament in fact consists of only one chamber, the Chamber of Deputies. The Chamber of Deputies fulfils the power of the Senate but, until the Senate is constituted, the chamber cannot be dissolved.

The main reasons for introducing the bicameral legislature were contradictory and often weak in argument. Some differing arguments suggest that the bicameral system provides a better opportunity to improve the law-making process. In other words, the first chamber, being under the close eyes of the second, would be cautious when attempting to pass a bill with evident loopholes. The second chamber is supposed to play the role of a watchdog and guarantor of perfect legislation. However, the role of the Senate in the legislative process is by no means clear: is it really supposed to guarantee a better deliberation of bills? If yes, the constitution does not provide that the Senate is bound to make the final decision. A looser interpretation of the Senate's function in the legislative process would suggest that the Senate, having no obligation to take part in the ordinary process concerning a resolution on a bill, does not enter into it if it does not want to. Then would its main function only be when the Chamber of Deputies is dissolved? Supporters of the Senate have pointed out that since the Senate cannot be dissolved it can play the role of a stable institution. Arguments that the Senate should adopt only bills on private law and the Chamber of Deputies the bills on public law were also put forward. The opponents of the bicameralism, on the other hand, have argued that the Senate is not an institution which the current political system makes necessary.

In order to make clearer the debate about the second chamber it is useful to remember a crucial fact with regard to the break-up of the Czechoslovak federation. The question at stake was whether the federal parliamentarians elected at the same time with the parliamentarians to the Czech legislature would execute their mandate even after the split of the federation or not. One of the solutions that was considered was that of the interim Senate which would be constituted not as a result of the general elections but by transferring the former federal MPs, who in 1992 were elected in the Czech Republic, to the Czech Senate. This solution appeared as a kind concession. The only inconvenience was the number of the MPs involved. They totalled 174. Their number as well as their composition would necessitate substantial changes of the draft of the constitution that few MPs would be willing to undergo. Additionally, federal representatives would form a noticeable opposition to the Czech cabinet leaders, and the Senate would be a body with a very narrow cabinet majority to deal with.

The coalition is no less divided about the future practical functioning of the Senate as far as the new electoral law and the term of the elections are concerned. The latest prognosis is that the elections to the Senate will be held, along with elections to the Chamber of Deputies, in 1996.

Parliament–Government Relations

The development of relations between the government and the Chamber of Deputies in the Czech Republic is at an early stage. Its only solid foundation is the constitution. According to the constitution, the government is accountable only to the Chamber of Deputies. Its instruments are the vote of confidence in the government (on the request of at least 50 deputies), and interpellation of the government and its individual members. Moreover, a member of the government is bound to appear before the Chamber of Deputies and its organs whenever requested to do so.

The mechanism permitting the parliament the acquisition of impartial information on the activities and particularly the economic management of the government is represented by the independent Supreme Control Office. It is an authority the functionaries of which are appointed by the president on the proposal of the Chamber of Deputies. The Office elaborates its standpoints for the Chamber of Deputies and the official conclusions are public.

The Chamber of Deputies establishes also other organs and nominates the functionaries of the organs of control, both of an administrative or public character. It has acquired these powers on the basis of the acts adopted before the adoption of the constitution. It can be expected that some of them will gradually be transferred to the government. So far, however, the parliament has opposed such transfer. It endeavours to preserve the widest possible control power over the government and other state authorities. It also has some powers over the self-governing municipal authorities.

The uncertain interpretation of the provisions of the constitution concerning relations between the executive and legislative powers results in a tug-of-war between the Chamber of Deputies and the government. This has become manifest particularly in the drafting of the bill on the Rules on Procedure of the Chamber of Deputies in 1994 in which the deputies proposed, for example, the incorporation of the duty of heads of all administrative authorities to appear before the parliamentary committees and give their explanations to the matters under review. The government refused this and a number of other provisions[1] extending, in its opinion impermissibly and unconstitutionally, the powers of the Chamber of Deputies into the executive field and declared them unconstitutional.

Legislation and the President

Under the constitution the president can interfere with legislation only in the phase when the act has been adopted by both chambers of the parliament. In the course of the legislative process it is not the duty of the parliament to inform him about the reviewed and adopted acts, although it is done currently and regularly. Adopted acts are sent to the president for signature.

Within 15 days from the dispatch of the act the president is entitled to return the adopted act to the parliament (that is, veto it), with the exception of a constitutional act. The reason for the return of the act must be given, but the president has no power to propose its amendment or modification. In practice the president uses his right of veto minimally. In 1993 only one act was returned. The Chamber of Deputies votes again on the returned act, but its confirmation requires a qualified quorum and majority (absolute majority of all deputies). If the act has not been confirmed, it is deemed not to have been adopted. The only act returned in 1993 by the president was not confirmed by a qualified majority. Such a case, however, can occur only if the attitude of all deputies of the government coalition is not uniform. Should the act be supported by coalition deputies, the president's veto would have been outvoted by a qualified majority. Consequently, the president plays only a supplementary role in legislation, consisting of the correction of those acts which had obtained only a problematic and mostly only a narrow majority. His right of veto has rather a preventative effect, because it represents a threat that an act which has not reached a state guaranteeing the support of at least a good number of coalition deputies will be returned.

Apart from the right of veto the president has the right to dissolve the Chamber of Deputies, but only in the exceptional cases of its inaction or the inability of political parties that form a government that can achieve a vote of confidence in the Chamber of Deputies. At present this provision of the constitution cannot be applied, because the Chamber of Deputies cannot be dissolved until the Senate has been established.

Legislation and the Constitutional Court

The constitutionality of laws and their accordance with international human rights regulations are controlled by the Constitutional Court established in 1993. The control of the court is subsequent to the passage of a measure. The proposal to institute proceedings before the Constitutional Court may be submitted by the President of the Republic, a group of at least 41 deputies and a group of at least 17 senators. After one and a half years of decision-making of the court it seems that the deputies will frequently use their right to initiate proceedings. It is quite natural in case of the deputies of the opposition who endeavour to achieve a legal solution which has been rejected in the parliament. However, it is used also by groups of deputies of the government coalition in cases in which they would probably be unsuccessful in attaining a change of an act in the Chamber of Deputies. An example of such submission is the proposal to abolish the provisions of the Act on Extra-Judicial Rehabilitation restricting the restitution claims to persons with a permanent address in the Czech Republic. The proposal calling for the abolition of this provision was submitted by 53 coalition deputies after it had become obvious that a similar amendment (adopted initially by the Federal Assembly) would not acquire a sufficient majority in the Chamber of Deputies.

At present the rulings of the court seem to suggest that it is becoming an effective organ whose possible participation in legislation must be taken into account by the parliament at the very time of adoption of laws.

System of Political Parties

In the first and particularly the second year after the revolution of 1989, a considerable number of political parties and movements were created, most of which were without mass membership and organisation. Even at present the Act on Association in Political Parties is very liberal, a fact contributing to a relatively high number of existing political parties. The Ministry of Interior registers every political party which complies with legal requirements – in the first place the submission of at least 1,000 signatures of persons in support of its foundation (who need not be its future members) and of the statutes which do not contradict the law. At present some 75 political parties and movements are registered, about the same number as two years ago. The crystallisation of political parties began in 1991 with the split of the strongest government political movement, the Civic Forum, successively into three political parties. The spectrum of strong political parties included at that time the Czechoslovak People's Party as the strongest Christian party which had existed also in the socialist era, the Czechoslovak Socialist Party as the renewed centrist party, and the Communist Party. Also the Social Democratic Party began acquiring support and was joined successively by the deputies of the former Civic Forum of left-wing orientation, including a number of important personalities.

The new Republican Party of Miroslav Sládek began representing the right-wing radicals, and the Movement for Self-Government Democracy the nationalist Moravian tendencies. The election year of 1992 encouraged the proliferation of political parties. The system based on the co-operation of anti-Communist forces began to turn into a standard pluralist system. This process was reflected also in the results of the 1992 elections to the Czech National Council, which has since become the Chamber of Deputies of the Parliament of the Czech Republic. The Government of the Czech Republic was formed by the right-wing parties grouped around the strongest Civic Democratic Party. It has the support of 105 out of the 200 members of the Chamber of Deputies.

Since the origin of the Czech Republic on 1 January 1993, or actually since the 1992 elections, the Czech Republic has had a pluralist system of political parties, the principal polarity of which consists of right- and left-wing parties. All important democratic right-wing parties are represented in the government. Several explanations can be forwarded for the instability and inability of the left and centre to find a platform for co-operation.

TABLE 1
CECH PARLIAMENTARY PARTIES AND THE ORIENTATION OF THEIR SUPPORTERS IN 1993

Political party	Left-oriented supporters, %	Centre-oriented supporters, %	Right-oriented supporters, %
Right-wing parties			
Civ Dem	1.5	27.1	71.4
Civ Dem Alli	5.6	36.4	58.0
Chr Dem	2.5	43.2	54.3
Rep Assn	21.2	32.7	46.2
Political centre			
Lib Union	22.4	69.7	7.9
Mor/Siles Mov	13.9	63.9	22.2
Left-wing parties			
Cz Soc Dem	39.5	56.7	3.7
Left Bloc	87.8	12.2	

Source: STEM/Stredisko empirichých výzkumu – Centre for Empirical Research, Lidové
noviny, 1993, July 25
Notes: Abbreviations of the names of political parties

Civ Forum	Civic Forum
Civ Dem	Civic Democratic Party
Civ Dem Alli	Civic Democratic Alliance
Chr Dem	Christian Democratic Party, coalition partner of ODS
Chr Union	Christian Democratic Union – Czech People's Party
Rep Assn	Association for Republic Republican Party of Czechoslovakia
Lib Union	Liberal Social Union, political movement consisted in 1992 of Chechoslovak Socialist Party renamed to Liberal National Social Party (**Lib Nat**), Agricultural Party and Party of Greens
Mor/Siles Mov	Movement for Self-Government Democracy – Association for Moravia and Silesia renamed in 1993 as Czecho-Moravian Center Party (**Cz Mor**)
Cz Soc Dem	Czech Social Democratic Party
Left Bloc	Left Bloc, the coalition of Communist Party (**Com**) of the Bohemia and Moravia and the Left Alternative, in 1993 created as a separate party
Dem Left	Party of Democratic Left, created after the split of Communist Party in October 1993
Club Non	Club of Engaged Non-party Members
Free Dem	Free Democrats/Civic Movement
Soc Party	Czechoslovak Socialist Party
Lib Dem	Liberal Democratic Party
Rom Init	Romani Civic Initiative
Democratic Left	Democratic Left

First, one of the strongest parties is still the Communist Party and other left-wing parties, particularly the Czech Social Democratic Party, are afraid of co-operating with it. Second, there exists a deeply rooted prejudice of the citizens against any left-wing ideas and statements, based on the long-term experience of the socialist state. Third, there is a general instability of opposition political parties and their clubs in the Chamber of Deputies. In particular, the political parties that oscillate about the political centre show extreme instability. Fourth, there is an unwillingness that still prevails – both among citizens and the intellectual elite – in becoming involved with any political party. Finally, the opposition is weakened by the success of government policy and the consequent entrenched position of the government. The party membership and electoral support is given in Tables 1 and 2.

TABLE 2
NUMBER OF REGISTERED MEMBERS OF THE MAIN POLITICAL PARTIES

Political party	**Number of Registered Members**
Parliamentary parties	
Right-wing parties	
Civ Dem	**22 000**
Civ Dem Alli	**2 500**
Chr Union	**80 000**
Rep Assn	40 000
Political centre	
Lib Union	*
Lib Nat Soc	**17 000**
Czecho-Mor Center	*
Left-wing parties	
Cz Soc Dem	10 000
Left Bloc	200 000
Non-parliamentary parties	
Club non	7 000
Free Dem	

Notes:

abbreviations	see Table 1
bold figures	a qualified estimate, supported by the figures given in the questionnaire by the respective party
ordinary fig.	estimate
*	figures are not known

Source: Newspaper estimates, author's questionnaire

At present it seems that the first four factors could be overcome by the 1996 elections, facilitated by the codification of the financing of political parties, which will improve significantly their economic situation but will also prevent illegal revenues reaching them. It is expected that in the next parliamentary elections the citizens of the Czech Republic will choose from the plurality of political parties, with one or two extraordinarily strong parties dominating on the right wing and one or two dominating on the left.

Proposing Candidates for Deputies

The elections to the Chamber of Deputies are based on a proportional electoral system. The lists of candidates are drawn up by political parties. The voter can award up to four preferential votes in one list of candidates. The selection of candidates is not formulated by any legal rules and is governed by the organisational norms of the political party concerned. The electoral system is based on large electoral districts, with every electoral district represented by more than 20 deputies. This system in itself determines the tactics of election campaigns the principal burden of which lies on the shoulders of the leading representatives of the parties. In practice, the voter votes for the political party and its policy, and only secondarily selects certain individuals in the given electoral district. This determines also the selection of personalities for the top positions on the parties' lists of candidates, which is not governed by the candidate's domicile but usually by the tactics of the party.

In the Chamber of Deputies this proportional electoral system results in the suppression of the electoral district for which the deputy has been elected. Nevertheless, a certain link with the district remains, as it is assumed that the deputy will be on the list for the same district in the next election again. This relationship is maintained particularly through the party work in the district and in the case of parliamentary functionaries and members of the government by meetings with voters and visits to districts. The limited links of the deputy with the electoral district are replaced by negotiations within the political party mechanism. Party members in the regions transmit their views to the central level by way of decisions of executive councils and congresses, especially in the government coalition parties. The opposition parties apply both this approach and the direct contact of the deputy with the electoral district.

Interest Groups

The role of interest groups is by no means easy to describe. One of the reasons for the lack of precise identification lays in the transformation of the roles of social actors as well as in the change of the object of interest. Political as well as economic reform has been carried out mainly by the government without any visible support for an alternative policy; therefore the initial and relevant channel for putting forward interests has been the state administration (ministries), which traditionally have had a big influence in drafting bills and proposals. Another reason relates to the fact that all former interest organisations witnessed a flux in membership, and structure, and funding. The new interest groups began to constitute their organisations, collect membership and establish relations with the state administration and the legislators. At the initial stage of their activity the groups appeared to be more efficient in acting as 'civic committees' at ministries and in promoting changes in the minister's decisions rather than going to the parliament and seeking a long legislative procedure. In other cases, when a change of legislation was required interest groups directly involved MPs in their activities. They asked parliamentarians to be members or leaders of their associations or they collected MPs signatures to demand the Constitutional Court to quash a piece of legislation (as in the case of the restitution law). Some interest groups act independently from the parliament and seek to present their drafts of legislation to the ministries.

Interest groups that support candidates in the electoral campaign cannot be identified. Candidates affiliate themselves on party lists and depend mainly on party financing. Political parties in parliament get support from the state budget and from other sources that are not usually disclosed. The amount of the state financial grant depends on the number of votes cast for the party at the last election. Thus even the 'independent' candidates who ran in the elections on the list of a party do not represent particular interest groups nor do they declare financial resources for their campaign.

Some interest groups were inherited from the past but were substantially reorganised (trade unions, Union of Women, for instance), some were established soon after the political changes (Chamber of Commercial Lawyers) and, others started to operate only after the economic reform freed their status of autonomous economic subjects (Chamber of Physicians, Chamber of Farmers, for example). Up to now, however, it has not been clear how different interest groups influence the parliament.

Trade unions' strategy for co-operation with the parliament has not been specified in terms of financial support for candidates (and, officially, no MP represents trade unions in the Czech legislature). Moreover, trade unions did not wish to link their programme with any political party. Trade unions rely more on their influence in a tripartite partnership (the regular meetings of three partners: the cabinet, trade unions, and the Association of Employers) rather than on any non-institutionalised action. Until now that is, with one rare exception: early in 1994 the trade unions called a demonstration as a response to Labour legislation which had been unsuccessfully modified in committee. Despite the fact that the demonstration was big in terms of the number of participants, its results as far as the subject of dispute were minimal. The bill was passed and the Constitutional Court rejected the legal challenge of unconstitutionality.

Another possible influence of interest groups can be detected from the

Register of Interests. According to the Law on the Protection of Public Interest which was adopted by the precedent parliament, all members of the cabinet as well as MPs should register whether they are employed, run businesses, or are involved in companies and hold positions on boards or administration. After the law entered in effect for the parliamentarians elected in June 1992, 127 MPs out of 200 registered their outside parliamentary activity. Table 3 indicates that there is no substantial difference in outside activity of MPs along the coalition–opposition line. We can even see that some of the opposition MPs are more active in business affairs than are the coalition MPs. According to the data from the registrar 90 MPs are in some form associated with a company.

TABLE 3
OUTSIDE ACTIVITY OF MPS

Faction	MPs/N	MPs/%
Civ Dem	40	61.5
Chr Dem	5	50.0
Civ Dem Alli	7	50.0
Chr Union	8	53.0
Left Bloc	24	68.5
Cz Soc Dem	10	62.5
Lib Union	12	75.0
Mor/Siles Mov	9	64.2
Rep Assn	1	7.0

Note: Factions are presented here as they were in time of registration, that is, autumn 1992. In the meantime some of the MPs stopped their outside activity.
Abbreviations see Table 1.

The law also provides that MPs should register any income, gifts and benefits whose amount is higher than the monthly salary of the parliamentarian. The salary itself has always been a subject of public discussion because it is an easy target for the evaluation of parliamentarians' work. The total of salary, extra premium and benefits which an 'ordinary' parliamentarian acquires is about four times higher than an average employee salary.

In case of a breach of law, which also provides that MPs should not abuse information and knowledge on their behalf or on behalf of third persons, a procedure before the Chairman of the House on the request of any MP is available. If the outcome of the procedure proves that the 'action' was justified, the Chairman of the House makes the revelation public. There is no 'punishment' other than the publicity of the committed abuse. The factions may impose sanctions on their own members and get rid of bad examples but until now there has been no unanimity, either in the house or in factions on how to treat 'busy' MPs and how to deal with possible negative consequences.

The conflict of interest includes situations in which an MP assumes public duties on behalf of private interests. The problem arises as to when one should explain what exactly encompasses the scope of the privacy and to what extent it concerns relatives. Does it include, for instance, wives and/or children? The fact that there were doubts about the fairness of the privatisation process led one of the coalition partners (Civic Democratic Alliance) to voice the view that parliamentarians' close relatives should not be allowed to be members of boards of the privatised enterprises. Another proposal is to impose the obligation on state officials (MPs, members of the cabinet, president of the Court of Accounts, principals and mayors of cities) to declare all new assets. This idea crossed the coalition–opposition borders and met a common feeling that there was something wrong in conferring too much power and trust on those who were given a unique opportunity to acquire assets illegally in this age of transformation. It also opened opportunities to start businesses without any specific qualifications. One of them was a 'consultancy entrepreneurship'. Generally, a market for all sorts of consultants was open. This kind of entrepreneurial background of consultancy had a special attraction for several MPs.

INTERNAL FACTORS

The Position of Members

In early 1990 the Czech National Council faced the problem of restructuring its membership. The decision to reduce the majority of Communist deputies who were elected in 1986 resulted from the Round Table negotiations at the national level, and all legislatures, both federal and republic, as well as local boards, experienced the same decision. Under a law passed by the Federal Assembly, political parties were given the limited power to recall some of their members who were parliamentarians. The process was co-ordinated both by new political movements and by old parties. As a result 18 Czech deputies were recalled (14 of them were Communists, four of them were from the Socialist Party). Another 46 deputies resigned, the majority of them were Communists. The result of the switch in political representation was the following: 82 seats for Communists, 17 seats for Socialists, 17 seats for the People's Party, 51 seats for delegates of Civic Forum and 33 seats for unaffiliated deputies.

The change in membership not only meant a break with the one-party system in the parliament but also with the social and professional composition of the National Council. As a consequence the until then 'guaranteed' representation of women, qualified and elite workers or agro-co-op leaders was lost. However it would be misleading to put a lot of emphasis on the 'calculated by numbers' representation of social and professional groups. This change required representation by people who were not professionally and directly involved with the power structure of the Communist Party. Consequently, artists, advocates, physicians and technology scientists, who were – as occupational groups – less tied up with the previous structure of imposed political power, entered the parliament as rather visible and numerous groups. Since the elections in 1990 there are no data available on the professional or occupational background of MPs. Female representation at that time was considered compromised with the Communist Party and new women groups were not as strong in their membership and organisational structure.

The Czech legislature during the period of 1990–94 had a very low incumbency rate. The first challenge in membership resulted from the reconstruction of political representation. The second came from the general election in June 1990 and the third from the elections held two years later. In 1992, although 41.5 per cent of elected members were incumbents they became members only shortly before the first elections in 1990. The same phenomenon applies to the members of the presidium and to the chairmanship. Only four members of the presidium and one vice-chairman and two committee chairs from 1990 remained in office after the elections in 1992. The year of 1993 did not mean changes in the stability of positions in the parliament. The members of the presidium remained in office as well as the committee chairs.

The newly assumed legislative functions in 1990 required fully involved parliamentarians rather than part-time visitors. The idea of parliamentarians who are on duty on a professional basis materialised slowly. However, until 1992 the 'professionalisation' did not prohibit occupations or other professional positions that would be incompatible with the mandate of a parliamentarian.

In late 1992 MPs faced a new and different situation due to the fact of becoming members of the legislature of a sovereign state. There were new issues to overcome: to make and adopt a new constitution, to establish relations with other parliaments, to deal with the new scope of legislation and to transform its image of a regional parliament to one of a fully sovereign body; and, as a consequence, to elect the president, to nominate judges to the Constitutional Court and members of the Court of Accounts, and to act as the second chamber for the time being when the Senate is not established.

There were new external and internal party relationships to establish.

Overnight the faction leaders became, if not competitive leaders of the respective parties, at least the important mediators and interpreters of party strategies. There were different executive–parliament relations to establish according to the new constitution and the need for new Rules of Procedure. The chamber is no longer prior to the cabinet in establishment and the latter no longer depends on the legislature's appointment nor does it seek its confidence, since the constitution gives it the mandate to act without any parliamentarians' formal approval. A different majority–opposition relationship also emerged which, unlike at the former national level, gave to the government coalition more power and opportunities to act in concert and to save the dominance of the cabinet in the chamber.

All this represents new challenges to parliamentarians, who were given the opportunity to assume new tasks six months after they had been elected. Although MPs perform their functions on a professional basis, they are not forbidden to have outside incomes. It seems symptomatic that parliamentarians, even when their little part-time jobs offer small incomes, prefer to keep them as a way back after the term is over. It is also interesting to know that some MPs keep their 'license of entrepreneurs' without practising it during the term.

The outside activity of MPs may prove that MPs are not certain about their position, which can be threatened by dissolution, re-selection, by-elections or by the next election. This can also reflect dissatisfaction with MPs' salaries. However, the MPs are pretty safe in their position as representatives. The chamber cannot be dissolved for the time being while it substitutes for the Senate. This fact of a relative temporary stability probably influences the feeling of autonomy of MPs from their coalition, parties and voters. Also, the salary, higher fees and better facilities provided to MPs are still under consideration.

Legislative Activity of Members

The constitution grants legislative initiative to deputies and their groups. However, as in many other countries, most bills are drafted by the government.

The initiation of legislation by government is possible in two ways. In the first case the Chamber of Deputies may adopt a resolution requesting the government to draft a bill on a certain subject. The character of such a resolution, which is used very rarely, is not clear so far, as it is not certain how far it is binding on the government. In 1994 the opinion prevailed in writings and in the government that a resolution of the parliament requesting the government to take up legislative initiative is not binding for the government; however, it can be assumed that under certain circumstances its unsubstantiated disregard could result in a vote of no confidence in the government. In 1993 a resolution was used only once when the government was requested by the Chamber of Deputies to elaborate a schedule of reform of administrative units. The resolution, initiated by the opposition, was seconded by most coalition deputies with the exception of the strongest coalition party, the Civic Democratic Party, although even some of its deputies voted for its adoption.

In the second case the legislative initiative rests with the government and was prompted by the fact that the deputies had proposed a new act or an amendment as an initiative of the deputies and their proposal was rejected by the chamber, which stimulated the government to draft a bill concerning the matter in question.

The general picture of legislative initiative in 1993 is given in Table 4. The government initiated a great majority of bills and all of them, submitted to the plenary meeting of the Chamber of Deputies by the end of the year, were adopted.

TABLE 4
PROPORTION OF GOVERNMENT AND MPS' BILLS CONSIDERED AT PLENARY
MEETINGS IN 1993

	Considered	Adopted	
Number of Bills	87	79	91%
Number of Government Bills	63	63	100%
Number of Members' Bills	24	16	67%

The initiative of the deputies in a plenary meeting was represented in 1993 by 24 bills, which is a considerable percentage. Eight of them were rejected. In most cases the bills were presented by groups of deputies, some of which comprised both coalition and opposition deputies. As can be seen in the table, these bills have been most likely to succeed. Less successful were the bills presented by the opposition only or those presented by the beputies of a single club. bills submitted by individual beputies were less successful too.

Although legislative initiatives were rare in 1993, a number of deputies' bills were concerned with the fields generally reserved for government initiative (building saving, school laws, ecological law, insurance companies). Apart from that the deputies were concerned with the drafts of purely political laws. Their number includes the act on the non-legality of the communist regime and opposition to it. Several bills submitted mostly by opposition deputies concerned social security legislation.

According to the constitution and other legal provisions, the deputies' power to initiate a bill is rather large. A deputy's bill is reviewed by the same procedure as any other bill, including the government bills. The government has the right to express its opinion on every deputy's bill and its standpoint is read during the review of the bill in the parliament. A negative standpoint, naturally, reduces the probability of the adoption of the act. Nevertheless, most bills submitted by the deputies of the coalition parties are submitted because the government either does not want to codify the given problem at all or does not intend to codify it at the time, or the government solution is the opposite from the opinion of the deputies. From the number of legislative initiatives of the groups of deputies, reviewed in 1993, for instance, the bill on savings banks on housing, initiated by a group of deputies and modified in accordance with the government comments, codified the matter much earlier than it would have been by the government. The adopted amendment of the Act on Social Need was drafted by the deputies earlier than it would have been by the government. The most important act adopted on the basis of the deputies' initiative in 1993 was the Act on the Supreme Control Office. The group of deputies submitted the bill, although a government bill was expected. The comments could not prevent the adoption of these legal norms in the Chamber of Deputies, because their adoption was envisaged.

Neither the present Act on Rules of Procedure of the Chamber of Deputies nor the constitution specify a term within which the parliamentary committees or the plenary meeting of the Chamber of Deputies can be ordered to review a bill. For this reason some bills can be postponed by the Organisational Committee which is responsible for the agenda of the Chamber of Deputies. Nevertheless, such practice has not developed and every bill is allocated to one of the committees generally by the first session of the Organisational Committee following its presentation. The reason for postponing the bill can be – and is – only the wish of the initiator of the bill.

The government as a whole has no right to interfere with the bills presented by the deputies except for the expression of its standpoint which may comprise also individual comments. (Table 5 summarises governmental opinions on MPs' bills in 1993). Consequently, the government has no right to propose amendments. Nevertheless, it is obvious that amendments and supplements may be submitted by individual ministers who are deputies.

The government has no right to propose amendments to its own bills. The practice is that the proponent of the bill has the right to express his positive or negative attitude to the proposed amendments or supplements in the plenary meeting of the Chamber of Deputies together with the reporter. This statement frequently represents a guideline for the voting of the

Chamber of Deputies or at least for the voting of the deputies of the government coalition.

In 1993 several acts were adopted by a majority consisting of the deputies of some opposition and some coalition parties. These cases concerned either autonomous decisions of the members of the parliament (as in the case of the adoption of the amendment of the Act on Social Need which was drafted practically in co-operation by deputies of the coalition and of the opposition) or disagreement within the coalition parties, some of which decided to support a solution assented to also by the opposition (as in the case of the Act of Consumer Protection). These cases did not concern very important acts, but their existence has proved that the parliament still occupies a strong position within the political system and that it is able to extricate itself from the grip of the decision-making of the executive power and of political parties.

TABLE 5
GOVERNMENTAL OPINION TO THE MEMBERS' BILLS IN 1993

	All	Positive		Negative		Neutral	
	no.	no.	%	no.	%	no.	%
MPs' Bills Considered	24	13	54	9	37	2	8
Coalition MPs' Bills	14	11	78	2	15	1	7
Opposition MPs' Bills	7	2	28	5	71	0	0
Joint Bills	3	1	33	1	33	1	33
Group Bills	19	9	47	8	42	2	10
Single MP's Bills	5	4	80	1	20	0	0

Notes:
Positive opinion of government means that government agrees in its decision with a bill without any comments, or agrees with some amending proposals.
Negative opinion means that government does not agree with the bill or does not recommend to adopt a bill.
Neutral opinion means that government went through the bill and has some amending proposals.

Position of the Chambers in the Legislative Process

The constitution does not give the chambers equal power to legislate. The Chamber of Deputies is the first to deal with a bill. It is also the only one to adopt the Budget Bill and the Final Accounting Bill. After a bill is passed in the chamber it is referred to the Senate, which either adopts the bill, rejects it, returns it to the chamber or does not consider it at all. In case the bill is amended by the Senate, the chamber has to pass the amended version of the bill. In case the changes do not pass, the original bill is to be adopted by an absolute majority vote. The same majority applies if the Senate rejects the bill. The new vote on the bill does not take place in cases where the Senate by resolution does not consider the bill at all.

Some of the pieces of legislation and some of the resolutions, however, have to be passed by both of the chambers. It is so for the Rules of Procedure, electoral law, constitutional laws, declaration of war, resolutions accepting foreign army services, and consent to international treaties and conventions on human rights. The predominance of the Chamber of Deputies overshadows the role of the Senate in the ordinary legislative process. The Senate, however, has the power to legislate when the Chamber of Deputies is in a state of dissolution. Then, it passes so-called 'legislative provisions' which are submitted by the cabinet only.

Organisation of the Chamber of Deputies

The organisation of the work of the chamber was until the end of 1992 concentrated in the hands of the presidium. It was elected by the full chamber usually at the beginning of the new term. It was a body large in number and one that originally reflected the party composition of the chamber. In early 1990 it was composed of 25 members with the chairman of the chamber and four vice-chairmen. Since the general elections in June 1990 the presidium no longer mirrored the party representation and its members were coalition party members. After the constitutional change at the end of 1992 the presidium as such was abolished. Instead, the Chamber of Deputies elects its chairman and vice-chairmen. The current chamber has four vice-chairmen who represent cabinet coalition parties.

In December 1992 the Organisation Committee was set up. It has 30 members and its composition reflects proportionally the party composition of the floor. The chairman and vice-chairmen are members *ex offici* and other members are delegates from party caucuses. They are not elected by the floor. Currently, 16 members are from the coalition parties. The committee's task is to deliberate the agenda for the floor. However, the agenda is submitted at the beginning of the session to the voting of the floor. The floor also votes on the shortening of the time for deliberation that is set by the Rules of Procedure at 60 days. Usually, the government asks for the shortened procedure caused by the urgency of the subject. However, urgency has become a rule.

The chamber works on a regular basis. The committee meetings and meetings of commissions are scheduled for three weeks and the full chamber for one week. The following week is reserved for the MPs' constituencies.

Parliamentary Parties

Political parties in the Czech legislature have experienced both cohesion and fragmentation. On the one hand there is little left from the party caucuses in 1990, on the other the present coalition has kept its party structure firm.

In early 1990 four caucuses were formed in the Czech legislature. Before parliamentary elections in 1992 there were 11. In 1994, although the same in number, the caucuses changed in their composition as well as in their names. Cohesion is a phenomenon of the coalition parties and the hard-liners' Communist faction. The non-coalition parties suffer permanent split and flux. The left bloc split in two factions (left bloc and Communist Party), Moravians formed two factions as well, and a new faction was set up by some MPs from the Liberal Social Union and Republicans. Some of the MPs chose to stay formally out of any of the factions as independents.

The factionalism has not been fragmented as dramatically as used to be the case in the former federal legislature. Nevertheless, even the present Czech legislature experienced a phenomenon that was labelled in political jargon as 'political tourism': one of the MPs changed his party affiliation three times within one year.

The coalition majority having the support of 105 votes out of 200 seems to be safe by a tiny majority but in fact it has not been jeopardised by the rest of the 95 MPs nor by its individual unloyal members. The cabinet in parliament is strong in its capacity to overcome the internal coalition variances as well as by its ability to handle successfully any possible discrepancy between the cabinet and the majority leaders on the one hand and 'back-benchers' in the parliament on the other hand.

The 'mystery' of the stability of the coalition government probably lies also in the fact that the so-called opposition might be considered rather as a 'co-operative' institution. This would explain that some of the non-coalition factions take more or less co-operative attitudes towards the cabinet. Therefore the majority of the 'opposition' factions deserve to be called rather non-cabinet parties. The willingness to co-operate with the cabinet rather than to criticise it at any price, as one may expect from an opposition, has taken different shapes: Social Democrats offered the cabinet a 100-day moratorium free of any criticism, Liberal Nationalist leaders came to a gentleman's agreement with the Civic Democratic Party on mutual support, and even Communists voted for proposals which were considered as issues deserving more unanimity.

The Parliament and the System of Political Parties

All important political problems are discussed first within the individual parties, then by the inter-party groups and only subsequently by the state authorities. One of the significant supreme unofficial bodies specialising in the discussion of legislation before the plenary meetings of the Chamber of Deputies is the so-called Coalition Thirteen consisting of the leaders of the government coalition parties (who are members of the government), the chairman of the Chamber of Deputies, vice-chairmen of the Chamber of Deputies (who are the representatives of the coalition parties) and the chairmen of the government coalition deputies' clubs. However, the mechanism is still in the process of development and in 1993 there were some serious political decisions adopted by the parliament without recourse to these procedures and even against the decisions of these groups. This concerned particularly the act on the non-legality of the Communist regime and resistance to it which had been drafted practically without the participation of the government and the chairmen of coalition parties. The government expressed its general consent to the draft, with several principal comments which were submitted as amendments and adopted by the Chamber of Deputies.

The government coalition parties form a stable majority in the Chamber of Deputies which – if a coalition agreement has been reached and party discipline is observed – is capable of adopting any resolution or act. The opposition must be approached only in case of constitutional acts, the adoption of which requires the consent of a 3/5 majority of deputies present. Such agreement, however, has not been achieved since the beginning of the existence of the state and no constitutional act has been adopted.

Organisation of Parliamentary Committees

The Rules on Procedure as well as the contemporary practice have stabilised the situation in which permanent committees represent the principal legislative bodies. They are elected in the Chamber of Deputies so that every deputy is a member of one committee, except for the Mandate and Immunity Committee, membership of which is not counted for this purpose. No functionary of the Chamber of Deputies or member of the government may be elected to any legislative committee.

All other committees are permanent groups of deputies performing their respective tasks in the legislative process as well as conceptual and political tasks. In 1994 the Chamber of Deputies had (and still has) ten legislative committees. Their specialisation does not correspond accurately with the division of the ministries in the government; most committees deal with the subjects of two ministries or with some general problem concerning a major number of ministries. The Constitutional and Legal Committee has a special position as it is responsible for the review of the legislation and policy of the Ministry of Justice on the one hand, and is considered a guarantor of legal compatibility of most bills on the other hand. The Legal Protection and

Security Committee is concerned with the problems of the Ministries of Interior and Defence. Partly special also is the position of the Petition, Human Rights and Nationalities Committee which deals with the legislation in the field of human rights and reviews petitions delivered to the Chamber of Deputies.

Character of Parliamentary Committees

The members of the committees are elected by the Chamber of Deputies without the application of the principle of proportional representation. This principle of committee composition, however, is expected to come from the adoption of the new Procedural Rules of the Chamber of Deputies. It has emerged recently because the coalition parties, due to the incompatibility of functions, have fewer members in the committees than corresponds with their proportionate representation in the Chamber of Deputies, which is a paradoxical situation. In one of the committees – the Petition, Human Rights and Nationalities Committee – the opposition even prevails over the coalition. Also the chairmen of the committees are elected by the Chamber of Deputies. At present they are all members of the government coalition parties in approximate ratio to the number of their deputies (6–2–2).

The bills for review are allocated to the legislative committees by the Organisational Committee with the understanding that most bills are reviewed at least by two legislative committees. The committees prepare a joint report for the floor of the chamber which contains the bill in the wording on which the committees have agreed. The report is supplemented with amendments adopted in one cmmittee and rejected by the other committee. The initial wording of the bill is discussed if the Chamber of Deputies requests it.

The committees are specialised bodies dealing with the bills and other matters in a general and detailed discussion. The bill is presented by its proponent – on behalf of the government by the appropriate minister or vice-minister. If the committee requests personal attendance of the minister, the latter must comply. The proponent and the reporter, who is the most important person for the review of the bill, invite experts, as a rule – the proponent the persons who have directly participated in the drafting of the bill, the reporter and the committee the persons of their own choice. In the course of the discussion, objections are submitted to the legislative project as a whole as are amendments on which the proponent takes a position. The result is usually a compromise, expressed in the report submitted by the committee to the Chamber of Deputies. As a number of deputies (including those of the coalition parties) have opinions of their own on a bill's provisions, it is usual that a government bill is modified to a certain extent in committee. The number of amendments adopted in the committees and presented to the chamber in the joint report varies and depends on the scope of the bill and the controversial nature of the matter.

As the description of their work has revealed, the committees are expert bodies. At the same time, however, they cannot renounce their political character which is manifested in the voting on the bill as a whole, and on its individual parts. If it is a government bill which the government coalition has decided to adopt, the system of club discipline manifests itself in these early phases. Similar is the case of opposition bills which are often rejected in the committees.

The professional support of the committees has been very weak so far. Every committee has its own secretariat which, however, comprises only two people – the secretary and the administrative worker. The committees have no permanent professional background facilities, and invite experts only on an *ad hoc* basis to assess individual bills. All committees are served by the Parliamentary Information and Research Centre, which elaborates expert studies, and by the Legislative Department which affords legislative technical and legal advisory assistance, every bill being allocated to one legal expert.

Composition of Parliamentary Committees

The composition of the committees depends on several factors. One of them is the necessity of allocation of all deputies (with the exception of the functionaries of the chamber and the members of the government) which means that the average number of members of one committee is 19 deputies. Another criterion is the intention to provide a majority of government deputies in all committees, if possible. The result is that most committees have one or two more coalition deputies than opposition deputies. The next criterion is the distribution of committee membership among the individual coalition parties (every party wants to have a proportional representation in all committees, minor parties want at least one member) and of the opposition.

It is only in the framework of the above-mentioned requirements that the members of the committees are selected in the party factions on the basis of further criteria, such as professional education and experience, political experience, negotiating ability, authority, position in the political party, special professional or other interests, and work in the Chamber of Deputies in the preceding period. Generally speaking the members of the more important committees, comprising – apart from the Constitutional and Legal Committee – the Budget Committee, the Foreign Relations Committee and the Economic Committee, are selected by the individual clubs from the number of deputies enjoying political support within their party, experienced and knowledgeable in the problems to be dealt with by the committee. The same criteria are applied also to the proposed committee chairmen. Other criteria are often impossible to satisfy, especially by minor parties.

Each deputy may be the member of one committee only. Some deputies must start as beginners in a given field and gradually get acquainted with its problems. It can be expected that the faction will support their allocation to the same committee in case of their re-election, as it had been the case of some deputies re-elected in 1992. From 60 re-elected deputies 41 were elected to the same committee (or the committee dealing partly with the same problems, since the division of the ministries had been partly changed). Some of them became chairmen of the committees of which they had been members in the preceding period.

Constituency Relations

Direct Contact between Individual Citizens and Legislature

The public polls indicate, that the knowledge of citizens about their representatives is very poor. If the elector is willing to contact the parliament, he or she may select from several possibilities.

1. Contacting an individual MP. Voters usually write letters to MPs or visit an MP in the parliament building. They may also make contact in the constituency during the MP's hours in the constituency or during party meetings with MPs. The voters may choose any MP they prefer, though it is common to select from MPs representing their electoral district, or from MPs representing their favourite party. The choice depends on various factors, for instance, where the profession or specialisation of an MP is connected with the problem concerned (for example, an MP was a doctor and worked in the hospital which the voter complained about), the constituency or residence of an MP is connected with the problem concerned (typically problems concerning local authorities), the political party represented by an MP is interested in the problem concerned (some parties are interested in self-government issues, others in agriculture), or the voter knows the respective MP's activities connected with his problem (for example, one MP is known for his private bills concerning disabled people).

2. Contacting president and committees. Voters frequently address letters containing questions, complaints and proposals to the president of the Chamber of Deputies. His office is one of the authorities (besides the office of president and the office of prime minister) substituting for the ombudsman office missing in the Czech Republic. The committees and their chairmen are addressed by individual citizens mostly in case of complaints concerning government officials or offices subordinated to government departments operating in the field of the committee's responsibility.

3. Petitions. Any citizen has the right to deliver a petition. The chamber has a Committee on Petitions, Human Rights and National Minorities, which is responsible for considering and answering the petitions addressed to the parliament. The initiators of the petition are allowed to come to the chamber building and to explain the opinion of petitioners.

Direct links created by the contacts between voters and MPs result in various activities of the chamber. The most important are the interpellations of the opposition MPs. The primary source of information for the great percentage of all the interpellations on ministers and government is a letter from a voter. Coalition MPs do not often interpellate but they use so-called internal interpellation. They use the internal way through the government structure to obtain useful information or to provide the necessary impact on governmental structures. Other results of the contacts are legislative initiatives and amendments to government bills. Less effective but more frequent are visits of groups or committees at various places, or MPs' questions addressed to the state authorities.

Indirect Contact between Citizen and Legislature

Continental understanding of representation leads more into indirect relations between legislature and voters. The intermediary bodies of the contact appears to be political parties and interest groups. An important influence on members is provided also by the mass media. The diversity of the media, including the regional and private ones, established especially in the year 1993–94, formed the basis of the plural society, which has a decisive impact on the behaviour of the politicians including the legislators.

POLICY ATTRIBUTES

The type of issue certainly influences the way in which the executive and the legislature work. The year of 1993 was exceptional in that it offered the opportunity for the MPs to deal with big issues of the constitution, constitutionalism, new or renewed institutions, and the way of establishing the role of the parliament itself. The process has happened in two ways. On the one hand the parliament has lost some of the constitutional powers that it had been granted under the federation. On the other it has been given a larger scope of issues to deliberate and decide on. For instance, while the current Czech Cabinet was appointed, according to the Federal Constitution, in 1992 by the Czech Parliament (precisely by its presidium), the Constitution of 1993 confers the power of appointment on the President of the Republic. The parliament itself had to decide on the constitutional limitations of its inherited supremacy. The possibility of the current parliament influencing the appointment of the cabinet is not lost, however. The chairman of the Chamber of Deputies nominates the prime minister provided that the president's two previous appointees failed in a vote of confidence.

Another example of an issue which is inherited from the pre-constitutional period is the power to nominate boards of different agencies that supervise the work of public corporations (radio broadcasting and television). This power unlike the above-mentioned, did not result from the old Communist constitution but from demands to transform the media and to free their status from the state during 1990–92. The parliament, it was thought, would better guarantee both the openness and the scope of the process. Although in both cases bargaining, negotiations and compromises among political leaders in and even outside parliament seemed to be the dominant factor on the final decision, both examples prove that the parliament, once granted the power, shows little willingness to give it up.

If we were to test the hypothesis that the policy activity of parliaments would be greater on issues which are new rather than old, and salient rather than quiet, we would have concluded that since every issue in the transitional period is new and attracts the public eye the Czech Parliament is very active. None the less, the Czech legislature is specific on some points. The 1993 Parliament dealt with transitional issues which had already been on the agenda in the previous federal state or the Czech Republic, therefore the new element was to reshape or to modify solutions adopted by preceding legislators. Additionally, new issues needed to be dealt with because a new independent state was founded. Moreover, new issues came to light when it was thought that new values should be manifest and established together with the new state. And lastly, the novelty of issues arose from the very substance of any policy implementation. In all these categories of new issues the activity of the parliament differed. While the activity seemed to be great for the constitution and for the 'Law of the Legitimacy of the Communist State', it was less salient for economic reform issues. The activity of the parliament appears to be more dependent on whether or not the cabinet covers the issue rather than on the novelty of issues.

The great activity does not necessarily mean that the parliament improves its image of an institution that is the core of the decision-making process. This activity produces counter-productive and inefficient effects which do not offer quick solutions. Thus the executive, which is more unified, enters as an arbiter who knows and implements quick and efficient solutions. And since the cabinet shows its predominance over the legislature in handling economic issues, the parliament itself pays more attention to framing the cabinet and ministries' action into legal limits. These attempts focus on the transparency of the privatisation process, on the legal protection of citizens and on the accountability of state functionaries.

It is also worth mentioning the stages at which the parliament gets the most involved. The Czech legislature is allowed to interfere in different stages of the law-making process. From drafting, deciding on the agenda, modifying specific articles of the bill on the floor, to rejecting the government's bill. Despite this, the parliament's involvement is not threatening in principle to the cabinet. It forces the cabinet and its members to present the bill only after bargaining among leaders of the coalition and being sure of a positive result.

The findings do not offer solid arguments, apart from general perception, that the activity of the legislature is greater when interest groups disagree among themselves. For the moment it seems that the activity of the parliament depends on how the coalition leaders are able to prevent cleavages before taking the floor rather than to seek support among individual MPs across party affiliation. Presently, the practice suggests that interest groups act through parties rather than independently.

In the period under consideration the Parliament of the Czech Republic did not have to solve any government crisis, pass a vote of no confidence, review principal transformation measures or pass through any critical reversals. That is the reason why it has proceeded further than the former Federal Assembly of the CSFR while the stabilising its relations with the government and other bodies established on the basis of the Constitution of the Czech Republic. The resulting state can be described as a state of equilibrium between a stable parliament and a stable government, not lacking dynamic and disputable moments both in legislative activities and in the practical development of further powers of both bodies.

NOTES

1. For example, providing that the Chamber of Deputies reviews and approves the budget and final account of the Children and Youth Fund, decides about the Statutes of the Economic Chamber and the Agrarian Chamber, elects the Chairman of the Czech Bureau of Statistics, and elects the members of the agencies active in the field of culture.

The National Council of the Slovak Republic: Between Democratic Transition and National State-Building

DARINA MALOVA and DANICA SIVAKOVA

The third post-Communist parliament in Slovakia faced two new important tasks in June 1992: on the one hand the Slovak National Council[1] had to continue a democratic transition, and on the other hand it had to build a new national state. This paper[2] focuses on the development of the Slovak Parliament since the election of 1992. First, it studies the impact of building a national state on the development of parliamentarism. Second, consideration is given to the formation of the party system inside the parliament. Third, it examines the stability of government in new democratic conditions.

EXTERNAL FACTORS

Constitutional Structure

The Slovak Parliament has considerable powers stipulated by the Constitution passed on 1 September 1992. The constitution established the government, according to the common tradition of the former Czecho-Slovakia, as *a parliamentary democracy based on proportional representation and a multi-party system*. The Slovak Parliament is uni-cameral and its name is the National Council of the Slovak Republic. The single chamber consists of 150 members, elected by universal suffrage (21 years old and over) through proportional representation, for a four-year term. According to Article 73, clause 2, of the Slovak Constitution the members 'shall be the representative of the citizens, and shall be elected to exercise their mandates individually and according to their best conscience and conviction. They are bound by no directives'. A representative who becomes a minister or the president must give up his/her seat though still retaining the right to participate in parliamentary proceedings.

Important powers of the National Council which require the consent of three-fifths of the members (90) are those of electing and recalling the president; adopting constitutional statutes; amending the constitution; and

Darina Malova is Assistant Professor of Political Science, Department of Political Science, Comenius University, Slovakia; Danica Sivakova is a Policy Analyst, Department of Information and Analysis, National Council of the Slovak Republic.

declaring war (Article 86). Other powers listed in Article 86 include proposing referendums; establishing government departments and other government bodies; debating 'basic issues'; approving the budget; and giving consent to contingents of troops to be sent outside Slovakia. The general impression must be of a legislature of more than average political weight.

At the time of writing the new constitution, there was some speculation, probably fostered by Prime Minister Meciar's forceful style, that the executive branch would prove to be powerful and would dominate the parliament. Some constitutional powers given to the prime minister, such as the right to recall a member of the cabinet, the right to return laws to the parliament, the right to join voting on a bill with a vote of confidence of the cabinet, and the establishment of a position of state secretary nominated and recalled only by the cabinet were interpreted as authoritarian provisions aimed at strengthening the prime minister's power and supremacy of the executive branch of government.[3]

In fact, both the government and the prime minister are in weak positions. The one-chamber Slovak Parliament has so many constitutional powers of control over the government that even in a two-party system it would be difficult to discipline individual members. Slovakia has been developing a multi-party system without strong party discipline. The government is responsible to a legislature which has a good deal of autonomy and in which party discipline is weakened by the stress put on an individual representative's independence. The prime minister does not have sole control over his ministers because any of them can be brought down, against his wishes, by a vote of the National Council. Moreover, in the spring of 1993 the Constitutional Court decided that the president can make a free decision if the prime minister requests him to remove a minister. The Slovak Prime Minister, therefore, does not have the freedom to 'hire and fire' his ministers. The prime minister's only constitutional freedom in this area is that of not appointing anyone he does not want and he may be under political pressure even to do this from a coalition partner if his own party does not have an absolute majority in the parliament. In fact, there has been constant trouble over the position of ministers, irrespective of whether they belonged to the prime minister's party or not. Since the 1992 election till March 1994 seven ministers either resigned or were replaced by the prime minister, and one minister was brought down by a vote of no-confidence; it means half of the positions were changed out of 16 ministerial posts. The executive's instability was ended by a vote of no-confidence in the whole government in March 1994.

The political institution that has developed in two years of independence has been the presidency. Although originally the proposed powers of the president involved a right to propose legislation directly in parliament, in the final version it was deleted. But gradually the president has gained more political weight, first with respect to the nomination of ministers and, second, he has established informal councils for national minorities and regular meetings with political parties. Moreover, he pushed hesitating representatives of the opposition to take a decision about the unstable minority government. In mid-March 1994 President Kovac gave a report on the state of the republic to the National Council. He emphasised the necessity of a broad coalition government. After his speech a vote of no-confidence in the government was initiated. It was passed by 78 out of the 82 deputies present, the Movement for Democratic Slovakia (HZDS) and the Slovak National Party (SNS) having withdrawn.

Considerable powers of the Slovak Parliament can be explained by the political culture common to the Czechs and the Slovaks in the first Czechoslovak Republic, where the parliament was the dominant political institution. The National Council, according to the Slovak Constitution, is relatively independent of the government with respect to setting its own agenda, legislative powers and control of the government.

Administrative Structure

The parliament possesses important rights related to the functioning of the administrative structure. The parliament can establish government departments and other governmental bodies, albeit decided in accordance with governmental proposals. Furthermore, any member of the parliament may submit an oral or written request to a member of the government and any head of state administration office (including senior civil servants) asking for an explanation of any administrative decision. It could be argued that political traditions of the former Czechoslovakia and the Communist legacy have influenced this configuration of the relations between parliament and the administrative structure. A common view of the Communist state administration originated from assumptions of high centralisation and secrecy. It seems, on the contrary, that the Communist Party, by introducing party control over administration (through establishing the same departments at Central Committee level, controlling government departments through party basic organisations and introducing advisory committees) undermined the centralisation of state administration. Although, after the collapse of the Communist regime, party institutions disappeared, the system of advisory committees has been maintained. Moreover, recently a new political practice has developed – so-called MPs' inquiries. The minister can ask any member to investigate some issue, for example, privatisation projects, and provide a report for the ministry. The Members of Parliament can initiate an inquiry based on the request of voters, organisations or according to their own decision. The National Council has discussed cases of such inquiries, especially with respect to privatisation.

Another indirect indicator of informal linkage between the administration and individual members is provided by the fact that several MPs were promoted to administrative posts as 'experts', during both Meciar's and Moravcik's governments. This model of carrier often begins in a political party which chooses candidates according to their specialisation to be later nominated to respective parliamentary committee. Then, the Member of Parliament, having access to detailed information in committee, can challenge the minister, and, consequently he or she can be nominated by his or her party to be a minister in a new government or for another top administrative post.

Legislation

Bills may be proposed by the deputies, the committees and the cabinet. The legislative process continues in the office of the President of the National Council who distributes bills to committees. In his choice of committees he is restricted only by a provision according to which every bill has to be considered by the Constitutional and Legislative Committee. However, any committee has a right to ask for a consideration of any bill. Most bills are proposed by the government, moreover, the government has a right to review and to recommend or not to recommend a bill proposed by members to the parliament. After debate in committees, a bill is submitted to the floor session. The first speech is by the sponsor of a bill, followed by a rapporteur or several rapporteurs, if members of different committees did not appoint a common one. After a bill has been passed by the parliament, the Slovak President, the prime minister and President of the National Council have to sign the act. The president or the prime minister can refuse to sign the bill, and they have a right to return it to the parliament. Only in the event of members voting to pass the bill again do they have to sign it.

In the 10th election period of the Slovak Parliament 232 laws were passed, and the ratio of governmental to private members' bills suggests a quite active legislature (see Table 1).

TABLE 1
RATIO OF GOVERNMENTAL TO PRIVATE MEMBERS' BILLS

	N	%
GOVERNMENTAL BILLS	174	75.0
PRIVATE MEMBERS BILLS	58	25.0

Notwithstanding considerable powers, the parliament is only relatively independent and autonomous of government, as bills proposed by the members and the parliamentary committees are reviewed by the government, who may not recommend these private bills to the parliament. In a well-developed party system it would mean that a chance of such a bill being passed would be very low. However, in an unstable party system with low party discipline, opposition bills have a chance of being passed. Even some members of governing parties have voted for them.

Electoral System

Both post-Communist elections in the former Czecho-Slovakia became a central part of the democratisation process. In effect, they *produced new parliaments and governments, they legitimised the break-up of the Communist regime, and they legitimised political elites* which were recruited on the basis of nomination by negotiating forces during the 'Velvet Revolution'.

The first post-Communist election law introduced a proportional representation system that existed in the first Czechoslovak Republic between the two wars, thus abolishing the majority system of the Communist regime. The law has attempted to limit political fragmentation and extreme pluralism of parliaments typical of the pre-war Czechoslovakia. First, the new election law put forward a provision establishing a threshold for a party's entrance into parliament. A party had to receive at least five per cent of the vote in order to gain seats in the federal parliament. Moreover, according to the law on political parties, only parties which had reached at least two per cent of the vote could receive federal financial support after the elections. These amendments were strongly supported at that time by the most recognised political leader, Vaclav Havel, who stressed the negative consequences of the unlimited proportional representation election law for the First Czechoslovak Republic, which subsequently experienced a fragmented party democracy. The following fragmentation in all three parliaments in former Czecho-Slovakia was not foreseen, and also not prevented by party discipline.

The threshold for the Slovak National Council in 1990 was only three per cent and consequently seven political parties out of 36 gained seats in the parliament. In the Slovak Republic, before the election of 1992, the threshold for a single party was increased to five per cent, and a new provision on election coalitions of parties was passed in an effort to prevent fragmentation: a threshold of seven per cent for a coalition of two–three parties or movements, and a ten per cent limit for a coalition of more than four parties or movements was established. Under these conditions only five out of 23 political parties that submitted party lists for the election to the

Slovak National Council succeeded in entering the parliament. There are four election districts – Bratislava (registered voters as of 1992 = 342,703, with 12 seats); Western Slovakia (registered voters 1992 = 1,238,529, with 50 seats); Central Slovakia (registered voters 1992 = 1,146,399 with 47 seats); Eastern Slovakia (registered voters 1992 = 1,042,442 with 41 seats).

For the 1994 election the five, seven and ten per cent thresholds were maintained. These influenced the formation of election coalitions. There are unlikely be substantial amendments to the election law as the coalition formed in March 1994 was diversified and moreover, deputies themselves were satisfied with the electoral system (see Table 2.).

TABLE 2
DEPUTIES' SATISFACTION WITH ELECTORAL SYSTEM

	N	%
YES	66	68.0
NO	27	27.8
NO OPINION	2	2.1
NO ANSWER	2	2.0

Source: See note 2.

The 1990 and 1992 elections in former Czecho-Slovakia were characterised by high voter turn-out as compared to other central and eastern European countries; in Slovakia 95.4 per cent of the electorate participated in 1990, and in the second elections 84.2 per cent of eligible voters cast their votes. In the third elections of 1994 voters' participation dropped to 75.7 per cent.[4]

Voters' preferences in Slovakia have indicated two general trends: on the one hand, a substantial level of electoral volatility, mainly if there are some broad political movements or coalition of political parties, which split after the election; and on the other hand an increase in electoral stability based on traditional collective identities (ethnic and religious, and/or links with the previous regime). Both these trends can be linked to rising voter apathy and electoral absenteeism. Such tendencies of party formation and voters' behaviour in post-Communist countries can be explained by the absence of stable social and economic interests, and, consequently, also by the absence of stable party loyalties.

The PR system in Slovakia has led to a multi-party fragmented parliament, where it appears difficult to obtain the three-fifths of votes necessary to reform the political system. After April 1993, when a group of eight MPs left the HZDS, Prime Minister Meciar attempted to re-construct the cabinet and obtain a majority by changing the political rules. There were several proposals, firstly, HZDS was asked to sign 'a pact of acceptance of the state's interests' by parliamentary political parties. Secondly, the prime minister advocated a chancellor's system of government or the implementation of a presidential system instead of parliamentary. The opposition did not respond positively to these proposals. Moreover, the Slovak Parliament in June 1993 did not pass another governmental bill on the State Defence Council, which would have allowed Prime Minister Meciar to declare a state of emergency, and to act without parliamentary approval and control. Furthermore, HZDS sought to change the law on the Slovak Parliament, which would have allowed the replacement of dissenting MPs. All these proposals were defeated. It could be argued that the PR system has prevented substantial changes to the political system. Moreover, it seems that the PR system, even with a threshold requirement, which favours big parties, has produced a multi-party system and coalition government. The specific characteristic of the system is the formation of political parties along ethnic, religious and ideological lines.

Party System

Immediately after the break-up of the Communist regime politics was dominated by broad citizens' movements which lacked organisation, consistent political programmes and discipline. After experiencing political fragmentation in the parliament, some political parties concentrated on building external party organisation. This helped to stabilise some parties. In May 1992, 91 political parties were registered in Slovakia and 23 of them submitted lists of candidates for the elections, while in August 1994, 64 political parties were registered and 20 of them submitted lists of candidates (only 18 met the condition required by the election law, that is, 10,000 signatures of citizens supporting the party).

The party system in Slovakia has gradually been structured along two main cleavage lines. The first is national and ethnic identity. The Slovak National Party and Hungarian minority's parties emerged a few months before the first post-Communist election of 1990 at a time of broad citizens' movements. The other salient identity line expresses different attitudes to religion and/or to the Communist past. The Christian Democratic Movement appeared also before the first election and its leader, J. Carnogursky, was originally a founding member of Public Against Violence. The post-Communist Party of the Democratic Left has a relatively stable electorate supporting values of social security and, thus, it divides society according to attitudes towards the former regime. The 1992 election brought again a broad movement into parliament, as the winning political force was the Movement for Democratic Slovakia. The split of the ruling movement is similar to that of Public Against Violence, the main source of division can be identified as personal tensions among political leaders and not the programme's or value differentiation. During 1993–94 two factions left HZDS and established a new party, the Democratic Union. The rest of HZDS remained unified around its leader, Vladimir Meciar, and again won the 1994 early election.

Another specific aspect of the party system in Slovakia is the extreme fragmentation of right-wing political forces, caused by non-cooperative elite behaviour before the election of 1992. Leaders of the Civic Democratic Union (ODU, a part of the former VPN), KDH, the Democratic Party and the Hungarian Civic Party were not able to form an election coalition. In September 1993, the first step to integrate the right-wing political forces was made and four political parties (the Conservative Democratic Party, the Christian Democratic Party, the Democratic Party, and the Hungarian Civic Party) founded the Club of the Right in Slovakia. In summer 1994, the opening of the election campaign interrupted this development.

It could be argued that broad political movements without strong organisation and new political parties with weak party discipline cannot dominate parliament as an external factor. Such a composition was characteristic of the Slovak Parliament until a new coalition government under Jozef Moravcik was formed in March 1994. The leaders of the five parliamentary clubs set up a Coalition Council to deal with any problems of co-operation and to set up a preliminary agenda for government meetings. Later, the Coalition Council used to meet also before parliamentary sessions to facilitate voting on governmental bills. The coalition partners informed each other about the voting of their representatives in the parliament. (Those practices are vaguely reminiscent of those of the 'Great Five', the group of coalition parties in the First Czechoslovak Republic.) The Hungarian minority parties, which had endorsed the new cabinet under certain conditions (that were later included in the government programme), were allowed to send representatives to meetings dealing with minority issues.

While in the previous two elections most of the parties preferred to register alone this changed in 1994. Political parties attempted to increase their chances of overcoming the threshold by forming new political groupings, that is a coalition of parties or an agreement among two or more parties on a common list of candidates. Following are the main groups which had been formed (see Table 3).

There can be identified internal and international factors influencing the emergence of the party structure in Slovakia. Among the internal factors are, firstly, the existence of ethnic and religious cleavages; secondly, the dependence of parties on state financial support; thirdly, the need to build territorial structure to gain support in local elections; and, fourthly, the necessity to build links with interest organisations. The international factors involve the efforts of Slovak political parties to belong to international political organisations to legitimise their own existence and to find political counterparts in European political structures. This can determine also the emergence of a division of parties along the left–right dimension, which is now lacking in the whole of central eastern Europe.

TABLE 3

NEW POLITICAL GROUPS

Political Group	Subjects Included in the Political Group
Common Choice (Left Bloc)	Party of the Democratic Left (SDL) Social Democratic Party of Slovakia (SDSS) Green Party (SZ) Agricultural Movement (HP)
Christian Democratic Movement	Christian Democratic Movement (KDH) Permanent Conference of the Civic Institute Liberal Party (announced support for the KDH)
Democratic Union	Democratic Union (DU) National Democratic Alternative (New Alternative)
Democratic Party	Democratic Party (PS) Party of Entrepreneurs and Craftsmen (SPZ)
Movement for Democratic Slovakia	Movement for Democratic Slovakia (HZDS) Farmer's Party (RS)
Hungarian Coalition	Coexistence Hungarian Christian Democratic Movement Hungarian Civic Party

Political parties are the main actors in candidate nomination and election campaigns. Candidates are selected by the parties, which prepare lists of candidates for submission to an election commission in each election district. Candidates do not necessarily have to be members of the party, but compared to the 1990 election there has been a substantial decline in picking up so-called independent candidates, that is, non-members of the party. Parties place candidates on their lists in order of preference. Voters must select a party list and either accept the top names on the list or specifically select four other names that may appear. Thus the advantage lies with the top names. However if a lower listed candidate receives at least ten per cent of the total votes cast for that party, he/she will be elected regardless of their position on the list (this raises the prospect of a lower listed candidate, once on the ballot, waging his/her own campaign). These lists also provide alternate members if members should have to give up their seats.

The crucial role of the political parties in candidate nomination has been confirmed also by the deputies (see Table 4.)

TABLE 4
ROLE OF POLITICAL PARTIES IN CANDIDATE NOMINATION

Ways of Nomination to Parliament	N	%
I PUT MYSELF FORWARD	8	8.2
I WAS IN MY PARTY	70	72.2
PARTY ASKED ME	11	11.3
SOC. GROUP ASKED ME	5	5.2
OTHER	3	3.1

Source: see note 2.

Interest Groups

The legalisation of the citizens' rights of association, assembly and petition has encouraged a rapid growth in the number of civil associations. While before 17 November 1989 there were 306 officially permitted associations and organisations in the whole of Czechoslovakia, there were 9,845 organisations registered in Slovakia alone in December 1994. Different organisations have formed different modes of links between interest groups, parliament and/or government and political parties.

The first way is reminiscent of pluralist civil society, as most citizen's associations and interest groups function independently of political parties, government and the parliament. Since some organisations are affiliated with political parties, the second type of relations between interest groups promotes the elitist model of parliamentarism with a top-down relationship. Those political parties which are more stable (KDH, SDL) give the same or similar rights and status to professional clubs and other organisations as they attribute to their district organisations, including the right to propose candidates for elections, to participate at the highest level in national or executive bodies, and to receive financial contributions from the party budget. The third mode of interest representation has been institutionalised by the second post-Communist government that set up the tripartite system and passed the Act on Collective Bargaining at the end of 1990. The government is represented in the Council for Economic and Social Agreement (RHSD) by seven ministers (vice-minister, finance, economy, labour and social affairs, health, agriculture, transport); employees have six representatives of the Confederation of Labour Unions and one of the Confederation of Arts and Culture, and employers have seven representatives selected by the Association of Employers' Unions and

Associations. The composition of the RHSD is set up by the Statute of the Council and its agenda reflects current bills in the legislature. This corporatist arrangement can impose restriction on the powers of the legislature, but when the government was losing support in the parliament, it did not work. Instead, leaders of labour unions and business before the passage of important bills organised meetings with parliamentary parties and committees. This behaviour of labour unions and business associations reveals that interest groups would rather accomplish their objectives with the government and/or its agencies, but if they fail then they turn to the legislature. The fourth trend in interest group formation is related to the emergence of central co-ordinating bodies of different organisations, and it is vaguely consistent with a societal corporatism. Top bodies of interest groups promote co-operation and representation of interests from 'below' in order to improve their influence *vis-à-vis* the government and parliament in decision making. This is related mainly to business and professional associations. It seems that these interest groups are able to lobby committees, party clubs and individual MPs, because bills concerned with the establishment of specific trade or professional chambers which imposed compulsory membership and stipulated a monopoly of such organisations in some profession or trade (for example, Chamber of Medical Doctors, Slovak Chamber of Industry and Trade) were initiated by cross-party groups of members.

The main conflicts between the government, the parliament and interest groups were related to privatisation and social policy. While representatives of investment funds and private enterprises asked to continue privatisation using the voucher method, the representatives of state companies demanded direct sales to a management, transformed into limited liability companies or so called employees' privatisation, in other words, the sale of enterprises to employees. Furthermore, representatives of the small and medium size of businesses protested against the new tax system and the act on National Security Fund, which were introduced in January 1993, claiming that they disadvantaged them in comparison to state-owned companies. After several mass protests and lobby activities the parliament amended the law. Labour unions during 1993 protested against governmental social policy. The government's proposal to cut welfare programmes – pension security system and family support schemes raised criticism also in the parliament. Oppositional parties in June 1993 substantially amended the bill on child allowances and family support that was passed, but Meciar refused to sign, arguing that it would create a deficit in the budget. Meciar's government proposed new bills that were negotiated in the tripartite and parliamentary parties and finally passed.

With respect to interest groups one can conclude that they have undergone serious changes in their organisation and mode of representation. They are fairly well organised, centralised and represented by one administrative or co-ordinating body. This provides better conditions for the government to deal with them. The legislation stipulating powers of selected interest groups is a stabilising factor. Different models of interest representation link the government, the parliament, political parties and interest groups. They do not exclude each other during the transition of post-Communist societies, when all political, economic and social institutions and actors are in flux.

The study of the Slovak Constitution, electoral system, and formation of party system suggests that these institutions do have important political consequences for the new democratic legislature. Although some institutions have the same impact as in well-established democracies, other adopted institutions can raise new elements, such as the formation of political parties and the division of the electorate along identity lines. Further it could be argued that some new institutions and organisations – presidency, political parties and their bodies (Coalition Council), interest groups (mainly if they have institutionalised access to the government in a specific way, like tripartite system) have gradually limited the dominating position of the legislature. Another factor contributing to the restriction of parliamentary sovereignty has emerged from informal linkages between administrative agencies and deputies and it is based on the possibility of deputies' investigations.

INTERNAL FACTORS

The Members

According to the constitution the individual representative appears to have considerable power. This is indicated by the right to 'interpellate', that is, raise some query that has to be answered. It may be followed by a vote of confidence. Thus any individual representative can attack the government, especially as only 30 members are needed to move a no-confidence vote.

After the collapse of the Communist regime the social and professional backgrounds of deputies have gradually changed. The first change is related to the substantial increase in the number of MPs with a university education. Before November 1989 only ten per cent of deputies had a university degree; after the 1990 election this ratio increased to 50 per cent, and after 1992 it was 67 per cent. The opposite tendency developed with respect to manual workers. Gender composition of the National Council has been ranging from 29 per cent of women before November 1989 to 12 per cent in June 1990. Further changes have taken place in the age composition of the National Council, the most evident is the decline of the proportion of deputies over 60 years (20 per cent since November 1989).

After the 1992 election the proportion of newly elected deputies reached almost 50 per cent. The most new members were nominated by HZDS. Almost the same proportion of new members have entered the National Council after the early 1994 elections; again HZDS and a new party – the Association of Workers in Slovakia – had most new members. However, due to the formation of election coalitions (the Common Choice and the Hungarian Coalition) also other, more established parties have brought more new deputies into the parliament.

The above-mentioned proportion of private and governmental bills suggests that deputies have had a notable interest in law-making. This behaviour has been encouraged by the possibility of individual MPs proposing a bill. Passing a bill depends on several factors. First is the importance of the bill: it is likely that less important bills will be approved even if only submitted by one member. The second determining factor is the slowly developing party discipline which sometimes determines voting and which forms a division between the ruling parties' and the opposition's voting behaviour. The third aspect influencing the likelihood of passing the bill is timing; often before the end of session or the end of year more bills are accepted. Another indicator of interest in the legislature is whether members quit their job or they continue. Though there are always complaints about the 'working' discipline of MPs who very often do not show up in the parliament, according to our findings 73 out of 97 members stated that they do not have any other occupation beside membership of parliament.

Parliamentary Parties

According to the constitution, it appears that the National Council is relatively powerful and independent from external factors. The main actors slowly limiting its independence are political parties, but their power is much more visible within the parliament than outside.

The selective emphasis on democratic tradition of the first Czechoslovak Republic in adopting political institutions led to the establishment of the PR system and a threshold, but also to the rejection of party discipline and its instruments. The latter was determined also by the negative experience of the First Republic,[5] but to a greater extent the Communist regime. Consequently, loose party discipline stimulated gradual fragmentation of the parliament. Before the 1992 elections no substantial changes had been made to limit possible fragmentation, however, some parties asked their candidates to sign an informal version of a 'commitment'; however this could not be used like an official document.

Moreover, a new political institution within the parliament was established, the so-called *Politicke Gremium* (Political Consultative Body), composed of the leaders of parliamentary parties. Its purpose is 'to discuss political issues', essentially to set up an agenda for parliamentary sessions. Vice-Chairmen of the National Council can also participate in its meetings. Decisions of the *Gremium* are not binding on deputies.

The 1992 election brought six political parties into the Slovak Parliament with the percentage of the vote and number of the seats according to a PR system as shown in Table 5.[6]

TABLE 5
PERCENTAGE OF VOTE AND NUMBER OF SEATS ACCORDING TO PR SYSTEM

Political Subject	% of the Vote	Number of Seats
Movement for Democratic Slovakia/HDZS	37.0	74
Party of the Democratic Left/ SDL	14.7	29
Christian Democratic Movement/KDH	8.9	18
Slovak National Party/ SNS	8.0	15
Co-existence-Hungarian Christian Democratic Movement/Spoluzitie-MKDH	7.9	14 (9 + 5)

The ruling parties in Slovakia, the HZDS and the SNS, which entered into an informal coalition after the 1992 election had gradually fragmented, so before the 1994 election there were nine parliamentary clubs. The broad governing coalition had four parliamentary clubs; the SDL, the Democratic Union (associated in the club of non-affiliated members formed of the former HZDS members), the KDH, and the National Democratic Party – New Alternative (organised in the other club of non-affiliated MPs). There were the two clubs of Hungarian parties (the Coexistence and the Hungarian Christian Democratic Movement) and two opposition parties (the HZDS and the SNS).

The early election in 1994 brought seven political groups to the National Council. The composition of parliamentary clubs is even more fragmented, as the Hungarian Coalition formed again two separate clubs and members representing other political parties and nominated on KDH and HZDS party's lists and on the coalition list of the Common Choice did not join respective parliamentary clubs.

TABLE 6

COMPOSITION OF PARLIAMENTARY CLUBS

Political Subject	% of the Votes	Number of Seats
Movement for Democratic Slovakia	35	61
Common Choice	10.4	18
Christian Democratic Movement	10.1	17
Hungarian Coalition	10.2	17
Democratic Union	8.6	15
Association of Workers in Slovakia	7.3	13
Slovak National Party	5.4	9

Source: see note 7.

Thus, the formation of parliamentary parties in the National Council has been determined firstly by weak party discipline, secondly by the fragmentation of ruling political parties, thirdly by an easy possibility to form a new parliamentary club and, consequently, establish a new political party; and, finally, the establishment of a new broad coalition government that created a new political institution – the Coalition Council, considerably limiting powers of the legislature. The Coalition Council mediates different opinions of coalition parties on legislative proposals and facilitates support for governmental proposals in the parliament. With respect to MPs' opinions on the current party discipline it is interesting to find out that a lot of them demand more discipline (see Table 7).

TABLE 7

DEPUTIES' OPINIONS ABOUT THE DEMANDS OF PARTY DISCIPLINE

Should be:	N	%
Much Stronger	13	13.4
Somewhat Stronger	33	34.0
As it Should Be	43	44.3
Somewhat Less	2	2.1
Much Less	1	1.0
No Answer	5	5.1

Source: see note 2.

Responses of deputies on the relationship between parliamentary groups and their party's national executive also suggested that gradually the parliament can be dominated by political parties (Table 8).

TABLE 8
WHO HAS THE MOST SAY IN PARTY POLICY

Deputies' Responses:	N	%
Parliamentary Club	9	9.3
National Executive	74	76.3
No Opinion	2	2.1
No Answer	12	12.4

Source: see note 2.

Committees

It is often said that the strength of a legislature is indicated by the power of its committee system. By this criterion the National Council has considerable power, it can establish committees (whose chairmen are elected by secret ballot) in order to introduce legislation and 'for purposes of supervision' (Article 92). This last phrase probably refers to Article 85 which states that when the National Council requests a member of the government, senior civil servants or representative of other administrative and political body to participate in one of its sessions or committee meetings, they are obliged to do so. The power to summon any minister or senior civil servant very much strengthens the monitoring role of the committees. They have to share their role of initiating laws with the government and with individual members.

The National Council has a system of permanent committees to consider legislation. According to the Act on the Legislature's Procedures only one committee has to be established, the Mandate and Immunity Committee. Other committees should be formed according to different fields of administrative, economic and social policies. After the 1992 election ten permanent committees were established. Later, on 26 October 1993, the parliament voted to establish the Committee for Privatisation. Two committees exceed other committees by their size, the Committee on Economics and Budget and the Committee on Constitutional Law and Legislation; they each have 20 members. The Committee for Environment and Ecology has only nine members (see Table 9).

A look at the internal division of functions among committees shows that the Committee on Constitutional Law and Legislation is supreme compared to other committees, as it is the only committee reviewing all bills. Parliamentary parties try to nominate to this committee their best lawyers, as some very important, though detailed amendments can be made before a bill is submitted to the floor session. Chairmen of the committees are elected by secret ballot, and their main function is to call meetings and to distribute bills. Their role in policy formulation is weak and often they follow the instructions of party leaders.

TABLE 9
LIST OF COMMITTEES IN THE NATIONAL COUNCIL OF THE SLOVAK REPUBLIC (1994)

Committee of NC SR/ Number of Mandates	HZDS	SDL	SNS	KDH	ESWS	MKDH	IND1	IND2	NON AFF.	TOTAL
1. Mandate and Immunity Committee	4	3	-	2	-	1	4	1	-	15
2. Constitutional Committee	9	4	1	2	1	-	2	-	1	20
3. Economic and Budgeting Committee	8	3	-	3	1	1	3	1	-	20
4. Committee for Agriculture, Forest and Water Economy	2	2	1	2	-	1	2	-	-	10
5. Committee for Civil Service Regional Management and Nationalities	6	3	1	1	2	-	1	-	1	15
6. Committee for Health and Social Affairs	7	3	1	1	1	-	2	1	-	16
7. Committee for Petitions, Law Protection and Security	6	3	2	2	-	1	1	-	-	15
8. Foreign Affairs Committee	5	1	-	2	-	1	1	2	-	12
9. Committee for Education, Science and Culture	3	4	1	2	1	1	3	1	1	17
10. Committee for Environment and Protection of Nature	2	1	-	1	2	-	2	1	-	9
11. Committee for Privatisation	3	3	2	2	1	-	1	-	-	12

Source: Political Structure VI. 1994.

Members used to be placed on committees according to party ratio, their education and occupation. In interviews most members declared that the selection of individual deputies for different committees was decided at meetings of party clubs. Proposals of parliamentary clubs used to be accepted by the floor usually without changes.

After the 1994 election a new parliamentary majority composed of the HZDS, the SNS and the ZRS (the Association of Workers in Slovakia) used two possibilities provided by the current Act on Legislature Procedures to change the composition of committees. First, the above act does not exactly stipulate the way committees are to be composed; second, although parliamentary clubs nominate their members to sit in committees, the floor has to approve the nominations. Due to the common vote of the HZDS, the SNS and the ZRS in the plenary session, the original proposals of parliamentary clubs have been changed and the new coalition has a majority in ten out of 11 parliamentary committees (the committee's structure has been maintained in the 1994 Parliament). Compared to the composition of committees in the former parliament, the number of members of the Committee for Environment and Ecology increased from nine to 19, as most of the opposition deputies were shifted to this committee without considering their professional background and interest. Numbers of deputies in other, more important committees were reduced.

Paragraph 38 of the Act on the Legislature's Procedures defines the committees as 'initiating and controlling bodies of the National Council', mainly during the time when the parliament is not in session. Among their powers the following are crucial: consideration of bills, international agreements, submission of own drafts of bills, consideration of administrative policies, including reports of ministers, and complaints of citizens, organisations and state administration. It seems that deputies agree with such powers of the committees, but they wish to exercise more power over the cabinet (see Table 10).

TABLE 10
THE MOST IMPORTANT FUNCTION OF PARLIAMENTARY COMMITTEES

	...IS		...SHOULD BE	
	N	%	N	%
Check on Government	9	9.3	27	27.8
Preparing Legislation	74	76.3	57	58.8
Demands of Groups	10	10.3	11	11.3
Other	3	3.1	2	2.1
No Opinion	1	1.0	-	-

Source: see note 2.

According to paragraph 50 of the act the committees should co-operate with administrative agencies in the legislative process; they can ask any administrative agency to provide information and the administration is obliged to do so. Also the committees can ask for expert reports, and they can institute inquiries into administrative agencies, state-owned enterprises, or other organisations.

The committees can establish permanent or temporary commissions composed of deputies, experts, or representatives of different economic and political organisations. This provision was written in the old Communist procedures and did not stipulate the powers of such commissions. Consequently, with the developing parliamentary procedures a new paragraph was added introducing investigatory commissions. Such commissions can be formed to investigate matters that appear to violate the public interest. After accomplishing the investigation (here, administrative bodies are obliged to provide required information) the commission submits its findings to the National Council with its recommendations. So far, only a few investigatory commissions have been established dealing with violations in foreign trade and privatisation. However, the results have not usually brought any clear position, and there has only been one recommendation for a matter to go to the cabinet.

Procedures in the committees are further regulated by the above-mentioned act, though quite often they are more informal compared to the chamber. Ministers or their delegates present and explain cabinet bills, as do the sponsors of other bills. The committee selects one rapporteur preparing the committee report that is submitted to the plenary session. Voting on controversial or complicated bills proceeds by section and paragraph, with members proposing amendments. The final voting on proposed amendments is collective, and the majority decision is valid. It means that the majority in the committee can stop some amendments proposed for the floor session. However, any individual amendments can be proposed directly on the floor.

Setting the agenda for committee meetings follows from the current legislative work of the parliament. The President of the National Council has the power to distribute bills to committees, however, any committee has a right to ask to consider any bill. Members of the committees can decide the order of bills. It seems that their standpoints on bills are partly influenced by party decisions, their personal preferences and/or lobbying by some interest groups.

The Chamber

The unicameral chamber, as stipulated by the constitution, has considerable powers over the cabinet; including a vote of no-confidence, electing the president and members of the Constitutional Court. Moreover, ministers, the chairman of the Constitutional Court and the General Prosecutor are obliged to participate in the session if the National Council requires it by passing a resolution.

Article 82 of the constitution says it is 'continually in session' which means that it can only be adjourned by its own decision, and it cannot adjourn for more than four months. After the opening session, sessions are convened by the President of the National Council who can call an emergency session on the request of 30 members. The President of the National Council is elected by an absolute majority (76) of members. He convenes it and chairs its proceedings with the help of vice-presidents who are similarly elected. Together with the President of the Republic and the prime minister, the President of the National Council signs all laws it has passed.

Consistent with the power of individual representatives is the fact that the National Council is in charge of its own agenda. The agenda is set at the beginning of the session. Any deputy can propose a change or amendment. The agenda should be passed by a majority of the present members.

The first speech on a bill is that of the sponsor, then a rapporteur or several rapporteurs, if members of different committees did not appoint a common one. To shorten debate, a ten-minute limit on individual statements can be approved by members.

Bills may be proposed by the deputies, the committees, and the Government of the Slovak Republic. However, in the preparatory draft of the new Slovak Constitution the same power was given also to the president, but in the final version it was rejected on the grounds that such power complicated the legislation in the Czecho-Slovak Federal Assembly. Most of the bills are proposed by the cabinet, and most of them are passed, though sometimes with substantial amendments. However, the members lack the bill-drafting staff and administrative and legal support available to the cabinet. With respect to the voting of deputies, according to our interviews parliamentary clubs decide in most cases about member's position (see Table 11).

TABLE 11
DECISION ABOUT MPS POSITION ON DRAFT OF LEGISLATION

	N	%
Parliamentary Club	50	51.5
Party Group	2	2.1
MP Himself	26	26.8
Somebody Else	17	17.5
No Opinion1	2	2.0

Source: see note 2.

The National Council provides some additional financial resources for the clubs of parliamentary parties or of non-affiliated members, including offices and a financial contribution from the budget of the parliament according to the proportion of the members in the individual clubs.

The committees do not have their own funds. Their expenses, related, for example, to the need for independent analysis, are reimbursed by the Office of the National Council. The members have the right to approve the amount of their own salaries and fund additional expenses. This is a very sensitive issue in societies that have undergone a difficult economic and social transformation bringing a considerable decline in living standards. In spring 1993, an increase in deputies' salaries produced public discontent, as the salary, including all connected spendings, was five times that of the average salary in Slovakia. A bill on conflict of interest has not been passed, and there is no clear information about the extra-parliamentary incomes of the members.

Attributes of Policy

With the Slovak economy performing poorly in 1993 – unemployment increased from 11.5 per cent to 13.8 per cent, the budget deficit reached five per cent, inflation exceeded 30 per cent, and the Slovak crown was devaluated in July by ten per cent – it was the main issue on the political agenda. Debates in parliament and the mass media focused on privatisation, as it rapidly slowed down in Slovakia: Meciar's government preferred standard methods and put voucher privatisation only in second place. The opposition disagreed with direct sales to foreign companies or to state managers, arguing that the cabinet concentrated too much economic power, controlling the Ministry of Privatisation and the Fund of National Property and that Meciar's cabinet diverted money to the state budget, which was illegal. In April the cabinet approved the amendments to the 'law on bankruptcies' which the parliament passed in May (the Party of Democratic Left from the opposition voted for it). The amended bill delayed the breakdown of indebted state-owned companies. The opposition voted against the amendment saying that this bill 'would prolong the agony of the post-socialist centrally planned economy' and it would stop economic reform.

In September the cabinet discussed the 1994 budget. The debate began in a tense atmosphere due to the worsening economic situation, the minority position of the cabinet, and vacant ministerial seats. Although the opposition parties emphasised that the budget proposal was unrealistic, the budget was passed with some changes related to the assumed growth of unemployment and with zero growth of the GDP.

After the establishment of a new broad coalition government in March 1994, the main interest was to amend the budget and to begin voucher privatisation. While the amendment of the budget, aiming at an increase of funds for education and health care by increasing consumer taxes on selected products, did not cause tension in the coalition, proposals for voucher privatisation have raised conflicts between the Minister for Privatisation (NDS-NA) and the Minister of Economy (SDL). The main line of this conflict is in the resistance of the current management of state enterprises (more or less connected with the post-Communist Party) to provide information on the real value of enterprises and thus avoid privatisation by the voucher system. SDL and its supporters prefer privatisation by establishing employees' share-holding companies that allows management to own a bigger part of the shares; this conception is closer to HZDS' programme. In September 1994 the broad coalition government started the second wave of voucher privatisation, which has been delayed by the new government formed after the 1994 election that brought HZDS again into power. Further conflicts about privatisation can be expected.

During 1993 the living standard in Slovakia dropped dramatically and in the middle of the year almost one-fifth of families were living below the poverty line. Although the reporting of regular poverty was disputed by the Minister of Labour and Social Affairs, the minister had to accept the outcomes of tripartite negotiation and pressure from trade unions and increase the poverty line to 50 per cent of the average salary. At the same time the cabinet approved an increase of the minimum wage. In June 1993 the National Council passed the bill on child allowances and family support that Meciar refused to sign, arguing that it would create a deficit in the budget. The Constitutional Court decided that the prime minister had to sign the bill or resign. This issue was solved by passing a new bill. At that time the role of the parliamentary opposition and the Committee for Health and Social Affairs in policy making increased. But still it seems that the main role in economic and social policy is held by the government and interest groups organised in the tripartite system.

The role of the Committee for Foreign Affairs has been growing, especially after Slovakia's admission into the Council of Europe and signing the Association Agreement with the European Union. Since some MPs were selected to represent the National Council in the Parliamentary Assembly of the CE from opposition parties, it may be concluded that in foreign policy more consent had been reached.

According to Western mass media it appeared that the ethnic issue was the main political concern in Slovakia. The proportion of laws passed disproves such appearance (see Figure 1). Hungarian political parties during 1993 organised several rallies where they protested against the delays of bills on the most controversial issues: using names and surnames, names of cities and alternative education. They also used their rights to send protest letters to the Council of Europe. Finally, in December, the Regional Council of the Association of Cities and Municipalities (organised in southern Slovakia) announced the establishment of a province with its own self-administration. This only increased tensions between Hungarian and Slovak politicians, even after the formation of new coalition government. This issue can still raise tension and conflict in the parliament.

With respect to policy making it seems that the main actors raising issues are quite clear. The government has the crucial role in policy making, despite limiting constitutional and political factors. Parliamentary parties, including opposition parties, also have an influential role in policy

FIGURE 1

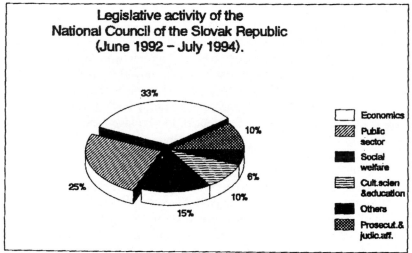

Department for Information & Analysis

formulation. Then, interest groups through the tripartite mechanism and affiliation to political parties (though it is not visible) can formulate an agenda and issues for the parliament. Finally, the role of international institutions, such as the International Monetary Fund and the World Bank should not be forgotten. Both cabinets in Slovakia had to balance the budget and to restrict some policies according to conditions set by these institutions.

CONCLUSION

The Slovak Parliament after the 1992 election has been shaped by three general factors. The first one is related to the pre-Communist parliamentary tradition and the Communist legacy; the former mainly influenced the constitutional design, while the latter is linked with the continuity of the old parliamentary rules, included in the Act on the Legislature's Procedures. The second factor is connected with the formation of the party system inside the parliament that has had two opposite currents; the fragmentation of ruling political movements, and the tentative stabilisation of the multi-party system. The third element stems from changes in internal structure, as there were some more experienced members and better organised committee structure and activities. The fourth important component is the impact of adopted political institutions; parliamentary democracy based on a PR electoral system with a threshold and a preferential list system produced the multi-party system and coalition government; the tripartite mechanism has determined links between the government and political parties; and the election law influenced representation orientated to political parties.

It could be argued that the above factors have produced new elements that gradually imposed limitations on the parliament. First of all, the stabilisation of political parties limited the freedom of individual members in voting, and a system of incentives started to function. Further, the establishment of the Coalition Council imposed new limits on the parliament. Moreover, the corporatist structures, mainly the tripartite mechanism, have shifted the orientation of interest groups directly towards government rather than to the parliament. Finally, the President of the Slovak Republic, despite limited constitutional powers, played a more important role when the government was in minority position.

Nevertheless, the National Council has retained the position of the 'central site' prescribed by the constitution. The parliament has had a crucial role in the formation of new political elites and parties, in the integration of political forces and in peaceful conflict resolution during the post-Communist transformation and building of the new Slovak statehood.

NOTES

1. The name of the parliament was changed in late 1992 to the National Council of the Slovak Republic.
2. The data from the Slovak parliament are part of a comparative research project on Institutionalisation of Parliamentary Democracy in Poland, Hungary, the Czech Republic and Slovakia carried out by the Department of Political Science of the University of Leiden. This project was made possible by financial support of the Dutch Organisation for Scientific Research (NWO). From November 1993 to January 1994 97 members of the National Council were interviewed according to their party membership.
3. See P. Tatar, 'Slovakia's New Constitution', *East European Reporter* 5, 5 (Sept.– Oct. 1992), pp.9–11.
4. The national elections took place on 30 September and 1 October 1994 and brought seven political groups; three coalitions, two parties providing a common party list for another political group and two single parties.

5. In the First Republic before the elections candidates had to sign a 'commitment', the promise that if they became deputies, they would vote according to their party's decisions. Otherwise the deputies could lose their seats in the parliament.
6. Source: *Data on Election Results of 1992 in the CSFR (Volby 1992 CSFR)* (FSU (Federal Statistics Office): Prague, 1992).
7. Source: *Report on the 1994 Election Results (sprava o rysledkock volieb 1994)* (Slovensky statisticky urad: Bratislava, 1994).

A Comparative Analysis of Institutional Development in the Romanian and Moldovan Legislatures

WILLIAM CROWTHER and STEVEN D. ROPER

In this paper, we compare the process of legislative institutionalisation in Romania and Moldova. We examine three broad factors which influence this process: the political culture and the institutional framework inherited from the previous regime, the policy environment and the internal organisation of the legislature. This line of research is important for three reasons. First, the literature on post-Communist legislatures has not attempted to compare the process of legislative institutionalisation. Peabody notes that generally few studies have attempted comparative analysis of two or more legislatures. Second, by examining the process of legislative institutionalisation, we explore the internal and external environment in which the Romanian and Moldovan legislatures function.[1] This provides us with an opportunity in which to examine the nexus between the legislature and the broader political system. Third, this research provides a unique opportunity in comparative politics to examine two countries that have, to a considerable degree, a common history and political culture but distinct political institutions.

HISTORICAL ANTECEDENTS OF THE ROMANIAN AND MOLDOVAN LEGISLATURES

Romania

In order to understand the current nature of these two legislatures, it is instructive briefly to review the historical context in which they have developed. The Romanian nation dates back at least to the period of Roman colonisation. The first Romanian states, Wallachia and Moldavia, were established in the fourteenth century. By the fifteenth century, the Ottoman Turks established a suzerainty over this region. The pre-eminence of the Ottoman Empire was challenged in the eighteenth century by both Russia and Austria. From 1821 until the outbreak of the Crimean War, Russia exerted primary influence in Wallachia and Moldavia. National independence came late to the region. Only in 1859 were the United Principalities of Wallachia and Moldavia recognised by the European

William Crowther is Professor in the Department of Political Science, University of North Carolina at Greensboro, USA, and Stephen D. Roper is Visiting Assistant Professor of Political Science, University of Missouri-Columbia, USA.

powers. Full independence followed the Berlin Congress in 1878. In March 1918, the Bessarabian legislature voted for union with Romania. In December of that same year, Transylvania adopted the Proclamation of Alba Iulia and became part of Romania. This period of 'Greater Romania' lasted from 1919 until 1940 when the areas of Bessarabia and Northern Bukovina were relinquished to the Soviet Union as part of the Ribbentrop–Molotov agreement. Later that year, Northern Transylvania was re-unified with Hungary, and Southern Dobrogea was given to the Bulgarians. Romania's population reflects the dynamic history of this region. According to the 1992 Romanian census, there are over 25 ethnic minorities in Romania. Ethnic Romanians comprise 89 per cent of the population while Hungarians constitute the single largest ethnic minority at just over seven per cent of the population.

The current legislative culture in both Romania and Moldova reflects their earlier political traditions. While the post-Communist legislatures of these two countries have existed for only four years, the Romanian legislature as an institution can be traced back to the Convention of 1858. Indeed, the basic structure of the current Romanian legislature is modelled on the structure first adopted in the 1866 constitution. Throughout the inter-war period, Romania had only two free elections (1919 and 1928), and the legislature became increasingly under the control of external influences.[2] The 1938 constitution granted the king the power to nominate half of the members of the Senate, and less than a month after the adoption of the constitution, all political parties were abolished.[3] Unlike many other Communist legislatures, the Romanian Communist legislature (Grand National Assembly) never developed democratic features. Even after several legislative reforms were enacted in the mid-1970s, Mary Ellen Fischer reports that the Central Committee was still the superior body.[4] Fischer notes that there was an extremely high turnover rate in the Grand National Assembly which thwarted attempts at reforms.

Moldova

Moldova, like Romania to its west across the Prut river, is inhabited primarily by a Latin language-speaking people whose presence in the region dates from the period of Roman colonisation. An independent Moldovan principality, including the territory of the contemporary republic, was first established during the fourteenth century. Bessarabia, the region between the Dniester and Prut rivers, constitutes the largest area in current Moldova. Bessarabia was annexed by Imperial Russia following the Russo-Turkish war of 1806–12. With the collapse of the Russian Empire, political leaders in Bessarabia formed a National Council (*Sfatul Tarii*) and voted on 27 March 1918 to unite with Romania. Moldova thus shares with Romania the political heritage of the inter-war years. In June 1940 Bessarabia was re-occupied by Soviet forces as a consequence of the Ribbentrop–Molotov agreement. The Soviet Socialist Republic of Moldova was formed on 2 August 1940 by joining Bessarabia with eight of the *raions* that made up the Moldavian Autonomous Soviet Socialist Region.

Moldova's population, which has long been more heterogeneous than that of Romania, was at the beginning of its independence approximately 64 per cent Moldovan, 14 per cent Ukrainian, 13 per cent Russian, 3.5 per cent Gagauz (a Turkic language-speaking people of Orthodox Christian faith who originated in Bulgaria) and two per cent Bulgarian.[5] Moldova's democratic transition was complicated from its inception by intense inter-ethnic conflict. By mid-1988 Moldovan dissidents had organised the Democratic Movement in Support of Restructuring (later re-christened the Moldovan Popular Front) to press for democratisation and redress for discriminatory practices imposed upon the titular population. The prospect of ethnic Moldovans gaining political power touched off an immediate response by Russian speaking minorities. Many supported Edinstvo (the Internationalist Movement for Unity), a pro-Russian movement whose strongest base of support existed in the cities on the left bank of the Dniester river, while non-Moldovans supported Gagauz-Halchi, which is the main organisation representing Moldova's Gagauz minority during the transition period.

LEGISLATIVE DEVELOPMENT IN ROMANIA

The Critical Choices of 1989 and 1990

The development of the Romanian legislature has been strongly influenced by a limited number of critical choices made during late 1989 and early 1990. The political environment in which these decisions took place was fundamentally conditioned by the nature of the Romanian revolution. Because of its role immediately following the revolution, the National Salvation Front (NSF) was able to establish the limits within which institutional decisions were made. The NSF was formed on 22 December 1989 in reaction to the demise of the Ceausescu regime. While the original members of its council included intellectuals, army officers and students, the most prominent among them were former Communist officials. Seizing the initiative during a period of extreme instability, the NSF proclaimed a provisional government. Ion Iliescu was named President of the NSF Council and interim president of the country. Petre Roman was named prime minister of the interim government.

On 27 December, the NSF Council issued a ten-point programme in which single-party domination was abolished and free elections were guaranteed.[6] Article 3 of the programme created an 11-member Executive Office within the NSF Council which was responsible for the exercise of power. Article 4 of the programme established 11 commissions within the NSF Council responsible for specific policy areas. The 14 commissions currently found in the Romanian legislature reflect the general policy areas of these 11 initial commissions.

Initially the NSF claimed that it was not a political party and that it would not nominate candidates for the April 1990 national election. However, by 23 January the NSF issued a statement reversing this decision. Leaders of the three historic parties of Romania protested against the decision, arguing that there could not be a fair election if the NSF both organised and participated in the election. The NSF Council agreed to hold discussions with leaders from various political parties in order to dispel any perception that it was attempting to monopolise Romanian politics.

As a consequence of this 'round table' discussion between NSF leaders and leaders of other political parties, the Provisional Council of National Unity (PCNU) was formed. The PCNU acted as a *de facto* legislative body until the elections were held. Approximately 50 per cent of the council's membership was drawn from the NSF, and the other 50 per cent of its membership represented the registered political parties.[7] On 14 March 1990, the PCNU issued a decree which postponed the election from April until 20 May. This decree also created a bicameral legislature comprised of a lower house (Assembly of Deputies) and an upper house (Senate). The decree mandated that the legislature would have 18 months in which to ratify a constitution and that within 12 months after the constitution was ratified, a new election had to occur.

While these critical policy decisions were issued by the PCNU, clearly the NSF Executive Office and President Iliescu were the primary sources of authority at this time. For example, the secret police was officially resurrected under a new name in March 1990 without legislative authority. Indeed, legislative authority for the creation of this organisation took almost a year after the legislature first convened.[8]

The 1990 Election

The electoral law passed by the PCNU was intended to be provisional. It was valid only for the 1990 election and provided for the simultaneous election of the president and the legislature. The 1990 Romanian election employed a combination of multi-member districts and proportional representation. Voters chose among party lists in multi-member districts. Forty-one electoral districts were established. There was no threshold barrier for parties to enter the legislature, and independent candidates only had to secure the endorsement of 251 eligible voters in order to be placed on the ballot. Each party list for the Assembly of Deputies and the Senate was determined by the local county electoral commission. The list of presidential candidates was established by the Central Electoral Bureau in Bucharest. The actual ballot contained the list of parties and the names of party candidates. The 1990 electoral system was based on a Belgian model in which so-called 'wasted votes' were aggregated at the national level. Unlike the 1990 presidential election in Moldova, the Romanian President was popularly elected. If no presidential candidate achieved an absolute majority in the first round of the election, a second round was to be held between the two candidates who received the most votes in the previous round. A candidate only needed to receive a majority of votes in the second round.

There were a total of 396 seats in the Assembly of Deputies and 119 seats in the Senate. Of the 396 seats in the Assembly of Deputies, 387 were contested. The remaining nine seats were distributed to minority political parties as established by Article 4 of the electoral law.[9] Seventy-three parties offered candidates for the Assembly of Deputies, and 60 parties offered candidates for the Senate in the May 1990 election (see Tables 1 and 2). There were a total of 5,344 candidates for the 396 seats in the Assembly of Deputies (7.4 per cent were elected), and 1,562 candidates for the 119 seats in the Senate (7.6 per cent were elected). Presidential candidate Iliescu won an overwhelming 85 per cent of the vote. Some observers have argued that the victory of the NSF is reminiscent of elections during the Communist period. Rady argues, with substantial justification, that the election of 1990 more closely parallels the elections during the inter-war period and reflects Romanian inter-war political culture.[10]

Even though the NSF won just over 66 per cent of the seats in the legislature, the distribution of commission seats held by NSF members averaged just over 60 per cent. The distribution of commission seats, however, was indicative of the importance that the NSF leadership attached to particular policy areas. While the NSF held only 54 per cent of the seats on the Ecology Commission, the party held over 73 per cent of the seats on the more important Central and Local Administration Commission. The NSF also held most of the leadership positions in the two chambers. The first President of the Assembly of Deputies, Dan Martian, was a member of the NSF, as also was the first President of the Senate, Alexandru Birladeanu.

Although the NSF held an absolute majority in the legislature and key portfolios in the government, finding consensus on economic matters proved to be difficult. Prime Minister Petre Roman and President Iliescu held different views as to the pace of economic reform. Roman wanted more privatisation and less government controls on the economy while Iliescu maintained that economic restructuring should occur slowly. Because of these emerging differences, Iliescu created a 'shadow government' inside the executive branch. He organised his own staff on the basis of the government ministries.[11] Most NSF legislators supported Iliescu's position, and therefore the real debate on economic reform occurred between the president and prime minister and not within the legislature.

TABLE 1
ROMANIAN PARLIAMENTARY ELECTION, 1990: ASSEMBLY OF DEPUTIES

Party	Vote %	Number of Seats	Seats %
National Salvation Front	66.31	263	67.9
Hungarian Dem Union Romania	7.23	29	7.5
National Liberal Party	6.41	29	7.5
Romanian Ecological Movement	2.62	12	3.1
National Peasants Party	2.56	12	3.1
Alliance for a United Romania	2.12	9	2.3
Dem Agrarian Party of Romania	1.83	9	2.3
Romanian Ecological Party	1.69	8	2.1
Romanian Socialist Democratic Party	1.05	5	1.3
Social Democratic Party	0.53	2	0.5
Democratic Group of the Centre	0.48	2	0.5
Democratic Party of Work	0.38	1	0.2
Party of Free Change	0.34	1	0.2
Party of Nat Reconstruction Romania	0.31	1	0.2
Party of Young Free Dem of Romania	0.31	1	0.2
German Dem Forum of Romania	0.28	1	0.2
Liberal Union 'Bratianu'	0.26	1	0.2
Romanian Dem Union of Romania	0.21	1	0.2
Total	94.92	387	100.0

Sources: Ariadna Combes and Mihnea Berindei, 'Analiza alegerilor', in Pavel Campeanu, Ariadna Combes and Mihnea Berindei (eds.), *Romania inainte si dupa 20 Mai* (Bucharest: Humanitas, 1991) and Alexandru I. Bejan, 'Prezentarea si analiza comparativa a rezultatelor alegerilor de la 20 Mai 1990', in Petre Datculescu and Klaus Liepelt (eds.), *Renasterea din Romania de la 20 Mai 1990* (Bucharest: Coresi, 1991).

TABLE 2
ROMANIAN PARLIAMENTARY ELECTION, 1990: SENATE

Party	Vote %	Number of Seats	Seats %
National Salvation Front	67.02	91	76.5
Hungarian Dem Union of Romania	7.20	12	10.1
National Liberal Party	7.06	10	8.4
National Peasants Party	2.50	1	0.8
Romanian Ecological Movement	2.45	1	0.8
Alliance for a United Romania	2.15	2	1.7
Dem Agrarian Party of Romania	1.59	-	-
Romania Ecological Party	1.38	1	0.8
Romanian Social Democratic party	1.10	-	-
Independent	-	1	0.8
Total	92.45	129	100.0

Sources: Combes and Berindei (1991) and Bejan (1991).

The 1991 Constitution

Following the election in May 1990, the primary task of the legislature was to draft a new constitution. The membership of the legislative drafting committee reflected the parties' strength in the legislature. Eyal argues that the most crucial issue confronting this committee was the distribution of power between the legislative and executive branches.[12] President Iliescu made it clear to members of his party that he wanted a strong presidency.

The draft that was adopted established a semi-presidential system based on the French model. Article 102 stipulates that the president and not the legislature nominates the prime minister, and it is the president who dismisses the prime minister. While Petre Roman's nomination as prime minister was approved by the legislature shortly after the 1990 election, the legislature was not consulted when Roman was dismissed by Iliescu in September 1991.[13] In addition, Articles 86 and 87 grants the president the right to consult with the government and participate in government meetings. The constitution also provides emergency powers to the president and the authority to propose referenda.

The Romanian constitution was overwhelmingly approved by the legislature. Over 81 per cent of the legislators voted for the constitution in November 1991. Significantly, however, almost all of the members of the Hungarian Democratic Union of Romania (HDUR) and the National Peasants Party-Christian Democrat (NPP-CD) voted against the constitution. The legislators of these parties felt that specific reference to 'separation of powers' needed to be included in the constitution. Moreover, these legislators felt that the constitution granted too much power to the executive.

While the president has been extremely influential in legislative areas, the government has also actively sought legislative authority. There are currently 21 government ministries in Romania. While Article 72 provides that the legislature may pass constitutional, organic and ordinary laws, the legislature has occasionally granted the government the right to rule by decree.[14] In addition, there are numerous examples of state bodies being created by the government without legislative authorisation. This practice of delegated legislative authority exists in most legislatures, including the United States. The difference is that the Romanian legislature has not developed the level of institutionalisation that is found in Western legislatures. Therefore, decrees which delegate legislative authority to state bodies acted to erode the Romanian legislature's power. While the PCNU initially maintained the French practice whereby members of the legislature could not hold government portfolios, the constitution currently allows members of the legislature to hold government positions. Some have argued that dual membership in the government has also weakened the legislature.

Unlike other European legislatures, there is little differentiation made between the Romanian lower and upper chamber. Title 3, Chapter 2 of the constitution establishes the general structure of the legislature. Each chamber contains a Standing Bureau of 13 members (one chairman, four vice-chairmen, four secretaries and four quaestors). The president of each chamber presides over their respective Standing Bureau. The president of each chamber is elected for the chamber's term of office (currently four years). The other members of the Standing Bureau are elected at the opening of each session in February.

There are 14 Standing Commissions in each chamber. Legislators are selected for the standing commissions by the chairperson of their legislative group based on proportional representation. While sessions of both chambers are generally public, commission meetings are closed.

The 1992 Election

With the constitution ratified, the next critical task for the legislature was to draft a new law for the September 1992 national election. The political landscape in Romania by early 1992 had changed substantially. Petre Roman had been replaced in September 1991 by former Minister of Finance Theodor Stolojan. Opposition parties had formed a coalition called the Democratic Convention in November 1991. In the local election in March 1992, the Democratic Convention won mayoral contests in Romania's largest cities, including Bucharest, Timisoara, Iasi and Brasov. Because of the success in the local election, the Democratic Convention decided to contest the national election. Also in March 1992, those NSF members who supported President Iliescu in his dispute with Prime Minister Roman left the party to form the Democratic National Salvation Front (DNSF).[15]

The electoral law enacted by the legislature in July 1992 substantially changed the 1990 procedures. Not only was the name of the Romanian lower house changed to the House of Deputies but the number of seats in the legislature was significantly changed. Using a 'representational standard', the number of seats in the House of Deputies was reduced from 387 to 328, and the number of seats in the Senate was increased from 119 to 143.[16] These alterations reflected a growing concern among DNSF legislators that the legislature would be more fragmented following the 1992 election.

Moreover, many of the new electoral rules appear to have been designed to protect the DNSF's control over the legislature. A three per cent electoral threshold was adopted for parties to enter the legislature, with the additional stipulation (likely because of the success of the Democratic Convention in the 1992 local election) that the threshold would be increased for coalitions.[17] In addition to the three per cent minimum, one per cent was added for each member of the coalition up to eight per cent.[18] Therefore, the Democratic Convention needed eight per cent of the national vote to enter the legislature. The number of electoral districts was increased from 41 to 42. Other changes were enacted which made it more difficult for independent candidates and representatives of the ethnic minorities to win election.

While the DNSF still garnered a plurality in the 1992 national election, the party failed to receive the absolute majority it enjoyed in 1990 (see Tables 3 and 4). Ultimately, the DNSF had to form a coalition government with several extremist parties including the Party of Romanian National Unity (PRNU), the Greater Romanian Party (GRP) and the Socialist Party of Work (SPW). Despite this coalition, members of the DNSF held almost all the government portfolios. Both the President of the House of Deputies, Adrian Nastase, and the President of the Senate, Oliviu Gherman, were DNSF members.

TABLE 3
ROMANIAN PARLIAMENTARY ELECTION, 1992. HOUSE OF DEPUTIES

Party	Vote %	Number of Seats	Seats %
Dem National Salvation Front	27.71	117	35.7
Democratic Convention	20.01	82	25.0
National Salvation Front	10.18	43	13.1
Party of Romanian Nat Unity	7.71	30	9.1
Hungarian Dem Union of Romania	7.45	27	8.2
Greater Romania Party	3.89	16	4.9
Socialist Party of Work	3.03	13	3.4
Dem Agrarian Party of Romania	2.99	-	-
Total	82.97	328	100.0

Source: Monitorul oficial al Romaniei, 257 (15 Oct. 1992), pp.2–13.

TABLE 4
ROMANIAN PARLIAMENTARY ELECTION, 1992: SENATE

Party	Vote %	Number of Seats	Seats %
Dem National Salvation Front	28.29	49	34.3
Democratic Convention	20.16	34	23.8
National Salvation Front	10.38	18	17.5
Party of Romanian Nat Unity	8.12	14	13.6
Hungarian Dem Union of Romania	7.58	12	8.4
Greater Romania Party	3.85	6	4.2
Socialist Party of Work	3.18	5	3.5
Dem Agrarian Party of Romania	3.30	5	3.5
Total	84.86	143	100.0

Source: Monitorul oficial al Romaniei.

While the actual number of parties represented in the legislature decreased after the 1992 election, the number of legislative groups increased from eight to ten. The legislature passed a decree stating that only parties with ten seats would be allowed to form their own legislative group. Therefore while the GRP and SPW were able to form separate legislative groups in the House of Deputies, these parties had to join other lists in the Senate because they failed to achieve the ten-seat minimum. After the 1992 election, the legislature decreed that it would not recognise individuals who switch party affiliation after taking office. In May 1994, the Constitutional Court declared that these two provisions in the Standing Rules were unconstitutional.

The percentage of incumbents who were returned to the legislature in 1992 was quite low. Based on calculations for the House of Deputies, the percentage of legislators for all parties who were returned was 22 per cent.[19] HDUR returned the single largest percentage of members at just over 41 per cent. This result is not surprising considering the low levels of public trust in the legislature. Following the 1992 election, the composition of the legislative commissions changed reflecting the DNSF's concern over the loss of its absolute majority. During the first legislature, even though commission assignments were based on proportional representation, the NSF was actually under-represented in commissions. In the current legislature, the DNSF is fully proportionally represented in the commissions. It thus appears likely that the DNSF decided to increase its representation on the commissions in comparison to that which it maintained in the previous legislature because it no longer possessed an absolute legislative majority. The number of DNSF legislative and commission seats is approximately equal, at 34 per cent. However, the DNSF holds 44 per cent of the seats on the important Industry and Work Commission but only 27 per cent of the seats on the Human Rights and Minority National Problems Commission.

The margin of victory for President Iliescu declined significantly in the 1992 election. Iliescu received just over 85 per cent of the first-round vote in 1990. In 1992, he received less than 48 per cent of the first-round vote and just over 61 per cent of the second-round vote. While DNSF opponents argued that this sharp decline indicated a lack of confidence in the DNSF and Iliescu, supporters argued that these returns reflected a more moderate and realistic view of Romanian politics.

Following the 1992 election, Iliescu named Nicolae Vacariou as prime minister. Vacariou was given the difficult task of heading a minority party cabinet. The DNSF was dependent on nationalist and leftist parties to secure its majority in the legislature. This coalition, however, became fragmented and three separate votes of no confidence were taken between 1993 and

1994. While these votes failed, they sent a clear signal that the legislature was not satisfied with the government. In March 1994, the Vacariou Government was reorganised. The opposition, however, argued that these changes were not substantial. Moreover, it appears likely that impetus for the reorganisation emanated from President Iliescu rather than Prime Minister Vacariou.

The Romanian legislature has so far failed significantly to institutionalise its legislative authority. While the opposition has attempted to increase the influence of the legislature both with respect to the president and the government, institutional features and the external political environment have limited its role. While the process of legislative institutional development has just begun, several critical choices have already been taken. These choices will affect the development of the Romanian legislature at least for the near future.

LEGISLATIVE DEVELOPMENT IN MOLDOVA

Critical Choices and the 1990 Election

As in Romania, the conditions in which preparations got under way for Moldova's first democratic election, to the republican Supreme Soviet, were far from optimal. By the autumn of 1989, governmental authority was already breaking down in Soviet Moldova, and ethnic mobilisation was in full swing.[20] The formerly dominant Communist Party became sharply divided between a reformist wing, headed by First Secretary Petru Lucinschi, and hard-liners who consolidated control over most of the Transdniestrian district and city administrations. The Communist Party reformers managed to control the formulation of the election law, which incorporated most of the demands made by the extra-party opposition.

The final version of the election law mandated that candidates had to be nominated from electoral districts in work collectives of 100 persons or from residents' meetings of 50 or more persons. The law stated that a nominee would 'normally' reside in the electoral district. This requirement, however, was interpreted loosely.[21] In keeping with normal Soviet practice, the republic was divided into single member districts (380 in all). A minimum of 50 per cent of the vote was required in order for a candidate to be elected. If no candidate achieved this figure, a run-off election was held between the two candidates with the largest percentage of the vote.

Open and generally fair political competition did occur during Moldova's first legislative election campaign in early 1990. Opposition candidates were given access to space provided in the republican Central Committee's newspapers to publicise their individual campaign platforms.

Furthermore, the weekly journal of the Moldavian Writers' Union, *Literatura si arta*, was used extensively as the unofficial campaign organ of the Popular Front of Moldova, the primary organisation of the anti-Communist opposition. In early February, this journal published the Popular Front's electoral platform which called for full sovereignty, a return to the use of traditional national symbols, private property, a free market and political pluralism.[22] By the February election date, the Popular Front's candidates were on the ballot in 219 of Moldova's 380 electoral districts.

Increased co-operation between the Popular Front and reform Communists was evident during this period. Collaboration extended into the electoral arena where one could find the names of ranking Communist Party members, such as Mircea Snegur, among the nominees of the Popular Front.[23] Competitive races were held in 373 districts.[24] In the 140 contests decided without a run-off (winning candidates having received more than 50 per cent of the vote), reformers claimed victory in 59 (42 per cent) contests. While 115 (82 per cent) of those elected were Communist Party members, many of these ran with the support of the Popular Front (*Literatura si arta* 1990a, 1).[25] With respect to ethnicity, first-round elections returned 91 (65 per cent) Moldovans, 21 (15 per cent) Russians, 18 (13 per cent) Ukrainians, seven (five per cent) Gagauz and three (two per cent) Bulgarians.[26]

The second round of elections, held on 10 March 1990, filled the bulk of the positions in the republican Supreme Soviet and proved decisive in the political life of Moldova. With the conclusion of the run-off election, a total of 101 (27 per cent) Supreme Soviet legislators were selected from the list supported by the Popular Front.[27] Reformers, however, calculated (correctly, as soon became evident) that with the added votes of deputies sympathetic to the Popular Front, 'democratic forces' would command more than half of the votes in the new legislature.[28]

The Moldovan Legislature

The 1990 election marked a significant step in Moldova's democratisation. Unfortunately, it failed to produce an effective legislature, and it reinforced inter-ethnic conflict in the republic. Soviet Moldova's first and only democratically elected legislature opened its inaugural session on 17 April 1990. Borrowing from the Soviet model, it maintained a presidium which carried out legislative functions when the larger body was not in session. Legislative leadership consisted of a president of the legislature and two vice-presidents elected by the legislators. The work of the legislature was carried out by 15 permanent commissions, each having legislative authority in specified functional areas. The commissions wrote legislation in their areas and then submitted it to the entire body for approval or amendment.

Members were elected to the commissions by the legislature. Four departments of state were also directly subordinated to the legislature. These included the Department of Privatisation, the Department of State for Statistics, the Department of State for the Protection of Natural Resources and the State Control Department.[29]

As occurred in other former Communist countries, difficulties almost immediately arose in Moldova concerning the relations between the newly established legislature and the executive branch. The head of state of Moldova is the President of the Republic. Under constitutional arrangements prevailing after the 1990 national election, the president (Mircea Snegur) was elected by the members of the legislature. New provisions were introduced in 1991 which called for the president's direct election by all members of the population over 18 years of age. At the same time, the position of the president with respect to the legislative branch was strengthened. The Government of Moldova was, and is, in an ambiguous position with respect to legislative–executive relations. It is made up of approximately 20 ministers, each in charge of a specific policy area (many parallelled by legislative commissions). The activity of the government is directed by a prime minister and two deputy prime ministers. Members of the government are proposed by the president but must be confirmed by the legislature before taking office.

The Moldovan legislature's early performance highlights the difficulty of democratisation after years of authoritarian rule. While the breakdown of political consensus, and of basic order, inside the legislature may have been inevitable, the speed with which it actually occurred appears to have been forced by ideologically motivated activists who immediately introduced emotionally charged issues into debate. This extreme approach to legislative activity, particularly by the new and inexperienced Moldovan legislators, led to rapid polarisation primarily along ethnic lines. Popular Front representatives, for example, entered a motion to rename the national legislature the *Svatul Tsarii* which they argued was in accordance with the national tradition. This motion failed after an extremely acerbic televised exchange between legislators, but a second and almost equally controversial motion restoring the pre-revolutionary Moldavian flag as the symbol of the republic passed. Furthermore, legislators selected a government composed almost entirely of ethnic Moldovans. In addition while ethnic Moldovans accounted for 69.6 per cent of the legislature, they received over 83.3 per cent of the legislative leadership positions.[30]

These early actions in the legislature had immediate negative consequences, providing representatives of the ethnic minorities with little hope that their interests would gain a fair hearing in Moldovan-dominated institutions. Inside the legislature, anti-reformers organised themselves into a legislative faction, *Sovietskaya Moldaviya*, and became increasingly obstructionist. Simultaneously, adherents of the Popular Front engaged in increasingly violent street demonstrations. Citing this behaviour as a threat to their physical safety, 100 opposition legislators walked out of parliament on 24 May 1990. Hence little more than one month after opening its first session, Moldova's legislature had collapsed into disarray.

Outside the Supreme Soviet, preparations were undertaken to resist actively what many Russian speakers considered to be discriminatory legislation. In early May, the minority-controlled city governments of Tiraspol, Bender and Ribnitsa refused to accept the legitimacy of measures passed by the new legislature, and these city governments passed measures suspending application of the law on the flag on their territories.[31] This initiated the devolution of power from republican to local institutions. In the southern region of Moldova, the Gagauz announced the formation of their own republic on 21 August 1990. Transdniestrian authorities followed suit on 2 September 1990, proclaiming the formation of the Transdniestrian Moldovan Soviet Socialist Republic.

Established in August 1991 in response to the anti-reform coup attempt in Moscow, the Republic of Moldova immediately faced a challenge to its sovereignty. As separatists consolidated their position in Transdniestria and the Gagauz region, nationalists inside the Moldovan legislature became increasingly militant, bringing intense pressure on President Mircea Snegur to restore order through force. In late March 1992, a state of emergency was declared and an effort was made to disarm units of the separatist militia. This attempt met with armed resistance, and by May 1992, Moldova had descended into full-scale civil war.

While conflict with the separatists failed to reunite the country, it did instigate a crucial legislative realignment. A growing economic crisis and the government's failure to carry through reforms had already undermined initially broad support for the Popular Front. Opposition leaders in the legislature seized the political advantage and turned reaction against the war into the focus of general dissatisfaction with Popular Front leaders. In August 1992 members of 'Village Life' (the legislative faction of the Democratic Agrarian Party) banded together with defectors from the Popular Front and delegates associated with the 'Accord' faction (later the Socialist Party) and elected Andrei Sangheli, a ranking member of the previous regime, as prime minister. Sangheli's government curtailed the influence of the Popular Front and improved minority representation in leadership positions. It promised more efficient economic management and a more moderate approach to the nationality question.

Inside the legislature, confrontation continued unabated between the anti-Communist and pro-Romanian forces. This confrontation centred around the Popular Front and the reform Communists, and less nationalist forces that comprised the core support for the Sangheli Government. This led to continued legislative deadlock and further fragmentation. By early 1993, the Popular Front was in complete disarray. Alexandru Moshanu, the pro-Popular Front president of the legislature, was replaced by Petru Lucinschi, a leader of the reform Communist forces.[32]

Key intellectual supporters defected from the Front and organised the 'Congress of the Intellectuals' in order to promote a more moderate nationalist agenda. The once dominant Popular Front's voting strength in the legislature was reduced to a mere 25 deputies. Even so, legislative leaders were unable to overcome the factional divisions that plagued the legislative branch. Badly needed legislative action on administrative reform and a new constitution failed due to the impossibility of constructing legislative majorities. Consequently, Moldovan leaders concluded that the existing legislative arrangement was no longer viable, and over the objection of pro-Romanian delegates, voted to dissolve the Soviet-era institution and hold early elections for a new legislature on 27 February 1994.

The 1994 Election

According to legislation enacted on 19 October 1993, Moldova's first entirely post-Communist legislature would be comprised of 104 legislators. It was hoped that this smaller body would be more manageable than the 380-member Soviet institution. Delegates were elected on the basis of proportional representation from closed party lists. A four per cent threshold for participation in the legislature was established, avoiding controversy concerning the separatist regions that otherwise could have blocked or negatively affected the elections.[33]

Campaigning focused on economic reform, competing strategies for the resolution of the separatist crisis and relations with both the CIS and Romania. An array of small parties (such as the Reform Party), mostly supported by urban professionals, campaigned for rapid marketisation and privatisation. Reform Communists such as the Socialist Party and the Agrarian Democrats called for a slower transition to capitalism. The Agrarian Democrats, the Socialist Party and Edinstvo argued for full participation in the CIS and taking as conciliatory an approach as possible to the separatist crisis. The Popular Front and National Christian Party campaigned for unification with Romania, while the more moderate Congress of the Intellectuals campaigned for Moldovan independence in the near term but for eventual unification.

The results of this election marked a sharp reversal from the politics of the early transition period. Nationalist and pro-Romanian forces were overwhelmingly rejected in favour of those wanting Moldovan independence and accommodation with ethnic minorities. Legislative power passed to the hands of the Agrarian Democrats, who won 43.2 per cent of the vote and 56 of the 104 seats in the legislature. Another 28 seats were won by the Socialist bloc which captured 22 per cent of the vote. The pro-Romanian parties suffered a severe setback. The bloc of Peasants and Intellectuals won 9.2 per cent of the vote and 11 seats, while the Popular Front Alliance won 7.5 per cent of the vote and nine seats. None of the other nine parties and blocs that fielded candidates topped the four per cent threshold required to enter the national legislature (see Table 5).

TABLE 5
MOLDOVAN PARLIAMENTARY ELECTION, 1994

Party	Vote %	Number of Seats	Seats %
Christian-Democrat Popular Front Bloc	7.53	9	8.6
Victims of the Communist			
Totalitarian Regime of Moldova	0.94	-	-
National Christian Party	0.33	-	-
Social Democratic Bloc	3.66	-	-
Bloc of Peasants and Intellectuals	9.21	11	10.6
Democratic Party			
Socialist Party	1.32	-	-
Edinstvo Movement Bloc	22.00	28	27.0
Women's Association of Moldova	2.83	-	-
Ecologist Party			
'Green Alliance'	0.40	-	-
Democratic Agrarian Party	43.18	56	53.8
Republican Party	0.93	-	-
Democratic Labor Party	2.77	-	-
Reform Party	2.36	-	-
Total	97.46	104	100.0

Source: Electorala '94: Documente si Cifre (Chisinau, 1994).

The Agrarian victory had clear policy implications. Agrarian spokesmen made clear their commitment to national independence but were more favourably inclined toward the CIS than their predecessors. They enjoyed more support from the ethnic minorities and better relations with Moscow. Progress in the realm of economic reform can be expected to be slow due to the Agrarians' cautious attitude concerning marketisation and privatisation. The reaction of the World Bank and International Monetary Fund to the new government was positive. These organisations praised Moldova's reform progress and approved of the Agrarians' proposed reform course.

These decisive results also had an immediate impact on the Moldovan legislature. The 1994 elections placed the Agrarians in control of an absolute majority in the parliament. They appear also to command the support of a strong majority in the population at large. Their success both reflects a commitment by Moldovans to the institution of the legislature (despite the early failures of that institution) and holds out considerable hope that the legislative branch will emerge as a more effective element in the political system in the near future.

COMPARING INSTITUTIONAL DEVELOPMENT IN ROMANIA AND MOLDOVA

The two new legislatures examined here have evolved in quite different directions even in the short period since their inception. It is our contention that this early period of development is critical to the entire process of institutionalisation. Decisions concerning patterns of institutional inter-action and links between constituents and legislators established in the initial period of a legislature's existence have a disproportionate weight in determining what follows.

What factors are significant in shaping differential outcomes in Romania and Moldova? We suggest that these factors can be grouped into three broad categories. *First*, inheritance, by which we refer to the initial institutional framework carried over from the previous regime, political culture and initial personnel. *Second*, the internal organisation of the legislature. *Third*, the policy environment, such as the character and gravity of issues facing the new legislators, and the nature of other key actors with which it interacts.

In each of these broad categories strong differences separate Romania and Moldova. The consequences of this divergence are important. *First*, the legislative institutions and traditions in these countries are quite distinct, as were the circumstances surrounding the formation of their post-Communist legislatures. Romania's legislature represents a unique fusion of inter-war and Communist legislative practices. To a certain degree, this mixture is true throughout eastern Europe. In Romania, however, the ineffectiveness of the Communist Grand National Assembly and the formal patterns of interaction both inside the legislature and between it and the executive were congruent with and in large part based on the previous legislative political culture. Whether it was the king or the Central Committee, political power during the inter-war and Communist periods was vested in institutions outside the legislature.

With no pre-Communist legislative tradition of their own, the Moldovan's only legislative history (except for the very brief *Svatul Tsarii* experience) was its shared inter-war history with Romania. This, however, was of limited utility. The legislature was in Bucharest, and Bucharest was indisputably the political capital of the Romanians, with its own distinct political culture and traditions. Moldova held its first democratic election under the auspices of the Soviet system. While indigenous democratic currents were evident in post-1989 Moldova, there was also a very strong strain of continuity with the culture and procedures of the Soviet period. Moldova's current legislature is deeply affected by the Soviet legislative tradition. Under Soviet practice authority was vested in the presidium, and the executive was expected to co-ordinate and guide legislative activities, while legislators served as a conduit for raising constituent concerns about executive activities. Elements of this tradition migrated into the post-Communist period both through the retention of institutional practices from the pre-independence period and through the socialisation of legislators. In Moldova, there was nearly complete continuity of personnel from the Soviet to the post-Soviet period. Legislators elected under communism continued to serve after the abolition of the Communist Party and the dissolution of the Soviet Union. The republican Supreme Soviet became the national parliament.

To understand better the functioning of these two legislative bodies and their differences, delegates to both parliaments were surveyed during the summer of 1992. In each case parliamentarians were asked to respond to written questionnaires consisting of approximately 50 questions concerning the organisation and working of the legislature, selected policy issues, and relations between different parliamentary groups. The results of this comparative parliamentary survey are presented in Tables 7 to 14 below.[34]

One of the obvious consequences of the differences in their respective transitions is found in the character of the Romanian and Moldovan legislators (see Tables 6 to 8). Romania's initial legislators were more likely to be professionals and more likely to have had university or post-university education. Romanian legislators were also more diverse in terms of age. In contrast, the Moldovan legislators were drawn more from active economic careers and were more likely to have had a polytechnic education than their Romanian counterparts. Moreover, Moldovan legislators tended to be in their forties. It should also be noted that once active as legislators, Moldovans are much more likely to maintain their previous professions than are their Romanian counterparts.

TABLE 6
AGE DISTRIBUTION OF ROMANIAN AND MOLDOVAN LEGISLATORS

Age	Moldova %	Romania %
20s	0.5	3.1
30s	23.9	21.4
40s	51.1	40.0
50s	21.7	25.9
60s	2.7	9.0
70s	-	0.6

Source: Comparative Parliamentary Survey

TABLE 7
LAST TYPE OF SCHOOL ATTENDED BY COUNTRY

School	Moldova %	Romania %
Other	10.1	1.7
Professional School	-	1.1
Technical School	0.5	2.0
Polytechnical Institution	19.1	8.7
University	54.8	64.1
Post-University	14.4	23.5

Source: Comparative Parliamentary Survey

TABLE 8
PROFESSION BEFORE ELECTION TO LEGISLATURE BY COUNTRY

Profession	Moldova %	Romania %
Not Applicable	25.8	18.1
No Response	-	
Professional	19.8	59.4
Researcher	15.4	8.5
Agricultural Leader	12.6	-
Administrative Leader	11.5	2.3
Political Leader	6.0	0.9
Manager	4.9	6.4
Worker	3.8	-
Private Owner	-	2.6
Other	-	0.9
Retired	-	0.9

Source: Comparative Parliamentary Survey

This contrast between the Romanian and Moldovan legislators can be extended to a broader discussion of the political culture in the two countries. It can be shown on the basis of attitudinal survey data that significant differences exist in legislative opinion concerning fundamental issues of political and social organisation. In Romania, politics has long been the domain of the educated elite. Since independence, Romania has adopted a unitary state structure in which all political decisions emanated from Bucharest. Political elites throughout the nineteenth and into the twentieth century made economic and social decisions which often alienated the masses. The peasant uprising in 1907 and its subsequent suppression served to demonstrate the extent of the gulf that separated elites and masses. The population's already deep distrust of central authority was further intensified by a particularly repressive Communist regime.

By contrast, Moldova is markedly parochial with a population of only approximately four million and a geography that can be traversed lengthwise by car in less than a day. No one is, geographically or socially speaking, far from the village. Social divisions between elites and masses are far less marked, and political alienation is significantly less ingrained, than in Romania. The impact of these very different centre–periphery relations are reflected in the attitudes of Romanian and Moldovan legislators concerning the distribution of resources between the national government and the localities (see Table 9). Moldovan legislators were much more likely to advocate the distribution of resources to localities than Romanian legislators.

TABLE 9
MEMBER ATTITUDES CONCERNING DISTRIBUTION OF TAXES BY COUNTRY

Distribution	Moldova %	Romania %
All to the Centre	-	1.4
Majority to the Centre	6.9	17.9
Equal Division	39.9	54.6
Majority to the Localities	49.5	24.1
All to the Localities	2.1	0.8

Source: Comparative Parliamentary Survey

TABLE 10
FREQUENCY OF CONSTITUENCY COMMUNICATION BY COUNTRY

Frequency	Moldova %	Romania %
Most Frequent	38.8	15.7
Moderate Communication	35.8	33.2
Most Infrequent	25.5	51.1

Source: Comparative Parliamentary Survey. These findings are based on a scale of constituency contact which was constructed from results of three separate questions on *frequency of contact by mail, in legislative offices and at other locations.*

This difference in perspective is also evident in legislators' attitudes toward their constituents. Romanian legislators contact their constituents far less frequently than their Moldovan counterparts (see Table 10). Furthermore, in Romania many of the legislative groups have objected to reforms designed to increase communication with the electorate. For example, legislators have protested at attempts at recording individual member votes. There is no specific source that provides constituents with information on how their legislator votes. This difference in constituency contact may be in part a product of geography. A second likely source of difference is the effect of the electoral system. Romanian elections are conducted in multi-member districts which are based on proportional representation. The Romanian party lists are decided in Bucharest and not in the local electoral districts. Legislators often do not live in the district that they 'represent'. The Moldovan electoral system in 1990 utilised single-member districts in which legislators were expected to reside in the district.[35]

Romanian and Moldovan legislators also differ in their perceptions of executive authority. Romanian legislators were much more likely to express the view that too much power was concentrated in the executive branch (Table 11). This result is hardly surprising considering differences in the political culture and recent political history of these two countries. The large number of Moldovan legislators who consider the legislature too powerful probably derives from their socialisation and expectations concerning political and administrative behaviour formed under Soviet rule.

This difference in perception regarding the proper balance in the legislative–executive relationship probably also results from the different definitions of legislative effectiveness in the two countries. A clear contrast between Romanian and Moldovan legislators emerged when they were asked to evaluate the activity of the legislature as a democratic institution and the efficiency of the legislature. Twice as many Romanian legislators consider the legislature's performance 'good' or 'very good' as compared to Moldovan legislators (see Tables 12 and 13). Nearly six times more Moldovan legislators consider their legislature 'very inefficient'.

TABLE 11

DISTRIBUTION OF FUNCTIONS BETWEEN THE LEGISLATURE AND THE
GOVERNMENT BY COUNTRY

Branch	Moldova %	Romania %
Excessive for Government	25.0	31.6
About Right	54.0	67.2
Excessive for Legislature	19.3	0.9

Source: Comparative Parliamentary Survey

TABLE 12

EVALUATION OF THE LEGISLATURE AS A DEMOCRATIC INSTITUTION BY COUNTRY

Evaluation	Moldova %	Romania %
Very weak	6.9	5.1
Weak	61.7	32.9
Good	30.3	57.6
Very good	1.1	4.5

Source: Comparative Parliamentary Research

TABLE 13

EVALUATION OF LEGISLATIVE EFFICIENCY BY COUNTRY

Evaluation	Moldova %	Romania %
Very Inefficient	30.5	5.6
Somewhat Inefficient	28.9	15.1
Somewhat Efficient	39.0	61.9
Very Efficient	1.1	16.5

Source: Comparative Parliamentary Survey

TABLE 14

ANALYSIS OF VARIANCE OF MEMBERS' EVALUATION OF DISTRIBUTION OF FUNCTIONS BY
EVALUATION OF LEGISLATIVE EFFICIENCY

Source of Variation	Sum of Squares	DF	Mean Square	F	Sig of F
Main Effects	23.41	3	7.80	2.75	0.04
Evaluation of Efficiency	23.41	3	7.80	2.75	0.04
Explained	23.41	3	7.80	2.75	0.04
Residual	507.59	179	2.84		
Total	531.00	182	2.92		

Source: Comparative Parliamentary Survey

TABLE 15
ANALYSIS OF VARIANCE OF MEMBERS' EVALUATION OF DISTRIBUTION OF FUNCTIONS BY
EVALUATION OF THE LEGISLATURE AS A DEMOCRATIC INSTITUTION

Source of Variation	Sum of Squares	DF	Mean Square	F	Sig of F
Main Effects	42.98	3	14.33	4.99	0.00
Evaluation of Legislature	42.98	3	14.33	4.99	0.00
Explained	42.98	3	14.33	4.99	0.00
Residual	520.02	181	2.87		
Total	563.01	184	3.06		

Source: Comparative Parliamentary Survey

This distinction, with Moldovan legislators taking a considerably more jaundiced view of their legislature, extends to other areas, including attitudes toward legislative groups' efficiency and inter-group co-operation. Statistical analysis of the Moldovan sample presented in Tables 14 and 15 indicates that legislators who are more critical of the legislature are significantly more likely to consider it too powerful as well.

A second set of considerations which affect the fate of the new post-Communist legislatures concerns their internal organisation. More research needs to be conducted in order to understand fully the impact of the commissions and leadership systems on these two institutions. While the current Romanian legislature is not highly developed as an institution, it has made greater strides in the direction of institutionalisation than the Moldovan legislature. This conclusion is suggested from the responses of legislators reported in Tables 11 and 12 above. Other data support this inference. Levels of participation in legislative activities, for example, are significantly higher among Romanian than Moldovan legislators. More Romanian legislators participate in the activities of legislative commissions and hold more leadership positions. This result is not surprising given that more Moldovan legislators continued to be actively engaged in their professions after election to the legislature than Romanian legislators, who were more likely to resign their positions once elected. Furthermore, 59 per cent of Moldovan legislators reported that they would not seek re-election, while only 15 per cent of Romanian legislators intended not to run again. These findings lead us to the conclusion that while the Romanian legislature is far from institutionalised, the legislature is a more professionalised institution than its Moldovan counterpart.

The third broad category that we suggest has affected the evolution of these two legislatures is the general policy environment in which they function. This includes both the character of the other principal institutional actors and the nature of salient issues in the political arena. Focusing solely on the internal environment of the legislative bodies themselves would lead to the erroneous conclusion that the Romanian legislature has been the more effective of these two institutions. This, however, is by no means the case. The dominant policy-making arena in Romania has been located in the executive branch. Since the emergence of the NSF as a movement, the Romanian executive has insulated itself from legislative influence and has maintained the initiative in policy making. But while the Romanian legislature has become increasingly complex internally, its internal development has not been translated into significant gains in external influence. Why has the internal development of the Romanian legislature not had a more decisive impact on its relationship with the executive branch?

As previously mentioned, the political culture in Romania strongly conditioned the critical choices of 1989 and 1990. The nature of the rapidly constructed post-Ceausescu provisional government was congruent with Romania's inter-war political culture. Moreover, crucial policy decisions made in 1989 and 1990 created a legislative environment conducive to executive domination. Unlike other legislatures in eastern Europe, there was one-party domination of the Romanian legislature for almost two and half years. In addition, the president of the country belonged to the ruling party. It is therefore not surprising that NSF legislators supported presidential initiatives and were content to allow the executive to dominate policy making.

By the time of the 1992 election, President Iliescu had established his superiority over the legislature and was able to manipulate the constitution in order to restrict legislative authority. While the opposition in the legislature became much stronger following the 1992 election, it was unable to alter significantly legislative–executive relations. As noted earlier, the changes in the government in March 1994 were executive rather than legislative initiatives. Perhaps the real test for the Romanian legislature will come when the opposition controls either the legislature or the executive. Until that time, the executive will continue to exert primary influence in policy-making.

Moldova's legislature, on the other hand, has been the site of much decisive political activity. The legislature has made crucial decisions on such issues as territorial independence, the separatist crisis, and economic reform. Faced with legislative deadlock, the executive branch, under President Snegur, took the legislators' inability to develop policy as an indication of a genuine lack of political consensus. Faced with these conditions, the executive generally assumed a passive stance rather than pursuing an aggressive extra-legislative political agenda. Moldova's less professionalised (and by the legislators' evaluation much less efficient) legislature thus has had a significantly greater affect in the years since independence due to the less aggrandising character of its executive partner.

A second factor determining this outcome was the existence of a much more complex issue structure in Moldova than in Romania. In both Moldova and Romania one finds a reform/anti-reform political cleavage. In Moldova, however, the Communist/anti-Communist cleavage is weaker and more defuse since many legislators, even strong reformers, were elected as Communists and because anti-Communist sentiments in the general population are markedly less intense than in Romania. Overlying this common interest structure, one finds in Moldova a third strong set of divisions based on nationality. First, majority (Romanian speaking) versus minority (Russophone) differences led to a breakdown in efforts to establish a broadly representative legislature. Complicating the situation, there were both pro- and anti-reformers and pro- and anti-Communists on each side of the linguistic divide. Second, as the political transition progressed, a new set of divisions emerged within the majority community between those identifying themselves as 'Romanian' nationalists and those identifying themselves as 'Moldovan' nationalists.

The impact of this welter of cross-cutting cleavages is obvious when comparing the stability of party affiliation in the two legislatures. By mid-1992, 88.8 per cent of Romanian legislators interviewed reported that they had not altered their political affiliations. Less than half (45.7 per cent) of Moldovan respondents retained their initial affiliation. Under these conditions of intense fragmentation in the Moldovan legislature, an initially strong executive/ruling party power structure collapsed. The executive was forced to seek alternative partners in the legislature. This necessity ultimately acted to increase the political salience of that body and invigorated legislative activity. Unlike his Romanian counterpart, President Snegur was ultimately forced to consult with the legislature. Thus, ironically, Moldova's own lack of internal cohesion created an external environment which proved favourable to the legislative branch.

CONCLUSIONS

In this paper, we have compared the institutional development of the Romanian and Moldovan legislatures by examining the impact of political culture and the pre-reform institutional framework, the internal organisation of the legislature and the policy environment. Current political realities combined with the previous political culture have produced markedly different legislative institutions in Romania and Moldova.

Tradition and custom, as we have attempted to show, exerted a strong influence over the critical early decisions of institution building and warrant close examination if we are adequately to understand the political patterns which follow. This is not to argue that politics is pre-ordained. Rather, we are arguing that tradition and custom affect the environment in which decision makers must operate. Ultimately, it is easier for decision makers to decide policy within certain social limitations than to change those limitations. We find that the Romanian legislature has achieved a greater degree of institutionalisation than its counterpart in Moldova. Delegates see it as more efficient, participate in legislative activities in greater numbers and are more likely to view their legislative activities as a primary career.

The internal organisation of a legislature is of central importance in its development, but the character of salient political issues and the constellation of other institutional actors also clearly play a role in determining the fate of the legislature. While the Romanian legislature is more professionalised, it possesses less influence in the formation of public policy than the Moldovan legislature. We suggest that this anomalous result derives both from the distinctly dissimilar executives and differences in the cleavage structure that underlies legislative politics in the two countries. This finding underlines the need to examine the external as well as the internal environments in which legislatures develop.

DOCUMENTS

Romania:

Monitorul oficial al Romaniei (Bucharest: Parlamentul Romaniei)
Digest of Central Laws of Romania (Bucharest: Coresi)
The Legislative and Institutional Framework for the National Minorities of Romania (Bucharest: Romanian Institute for Human Rights)
Partide politice (Bucharest: Rompres)
Romanian Legislation on the Constitutional Court (Bucharest: Monitorul oficial)
Romanian Legislation on Radio and Television Broadcasting (Bucharest: Monitorul oficial)

Moldova:

Monitor (Chisinau: Ministerul Justitiei)
Republic of Moldova (Chisinau: Foreign Relations Committee of the Republic of Moldova, 1992).

NOTES

1. Robert L. Peabody, 'Leadership in Legislatures: Evolution, Selection, and Functions', in Gerhard Loewenberg, Samuel C. Patterson and Malcolm E. Jewell (eds.), *Handbook of Legislative Research* (Cambridge: Harvard University Press, 1985).
2. Tismaneanu and Tudoran argue that the Romanian Government was largely democratic during the inter-war period. See Vladimir Tismaneanu and Dorin Tudoran, 'The Bucharest Syndrome', *Journal of Democracy* 4 (1993), pp. 41–52. Others, such as Rady and King have argued that the usurpation of power by King Carol essentially thwarted any attempts at sustained democracy during this period. See Martyn Rady, *Romania in Turmoil* (London: IB Tauris, 1992; Robert King, *History of the Romanian Communist Party* (Stanford: Hoover Institution Press, 1980).
3. Walter H. Malloy (ed.), 'Rumania', *Political Handbook of the World* (New York: Harper, 1939).
4. Mary Ellen Fischer, 'Participatory Reforms in Romania', in Jan F. Triska and Paul M. Cocks (eds.), *Political Development in Eastern Europe* (New York: Prager, 1977).
5. *Republic of Moldova* (Chisinau: Foreign Relations Committee of the Republic of Moldova, 1992), p.16.
6. *Monitorul oficial al Romaniei*, 4 (27 Dec. 1989), pp.2–3.
7. Bogdan Szajkowski, 'Romania', in Bogdan Szajkowski (ed.), *New Political Parties of Eastern Europe and the Soviet Union* (London: Longman, 1991), p.222.
8. Jonathan Eyal, 'Romania', in Stephen Whitefield (ed.), *The New Institutional Architecture of Eastern Europe* (New York: St. Martin's Press, 1993), p.31.
9. *Monitorul oficial al Romaniei*, 35 (18 March 1990), pp.1–11. Unlike other constitutions in this region, the Romanian constitution guarantees each ethnic-based political party one seat in the lower house. The number of ethnic-based parties represented in the lower house increased between the 1990 and 1992 elections from 12 to 14. For a more complete discussion see Robin Remington, Steven D. Roper and Luann Troxel, 'The Balkans', in Ian Bremmer and Ray Tarus (eds.), *Liberalism and Nationalism in Changing Post-Communist Societies* (Cambridge: Cambridge University Press, 1995).
10. Martyn Rady, *Romania in Turmoil* (London: IB Tauris, 1992).
11. Jonathan Eyal, 'Romania', in Whitefield (ed.), *The New Institutional Architecture of Eastern Europe*, p.132.
12. Eyal, 'Romania'.
13. Eyal, 'Romania', p.132.
14. Eyal, 'Romania', p.134.
15. At the second national conference of the DNSF held in July 1993, the DNSF changed its name to the Party of Social Democracy of Romania.
16. Michael Shafir, 'Romania's New Electoral Laws', *RFE/RL Research Report* (11 Sept. 1992), p.25.
17. Carey notes that the DNSF had wanted a four per cent threshold. If this standard had been adopted, the DNSF-led coalition would not have been able to form. See Henry F. Carey, 'The Art of Rigging Romania's 1992 Parliamentary Elections', *Sfera politicii* 10 (1993), pp.8–9.
18. *Monitorul oficial al Romaniei*, 68 (15 July 1992), pp.2–3.
19. This calculation does not take into account those members that did not run for re-election or who sought election in the Senate.
20. William Crowther, 'The Politics of Ethno-national Mobilisation: Nationalism and Reform in Soviet Moldavia', *The Russian Review*, Vol. 50, No. 2 (April, 1991), pp.183–203.
21. *Sovietskaya Moldaviya* (29 Nov. 1989), p.1.
22. *Literatura si arta*, 6 (8 Feb. 1990), p.2.
23. Snegur, a Central Committee Secretary since 1985, was appointed President of the Moldavian Supreme Soviet by hard-line party boss S.K. Grossu in July 1989. By early 1990, however, he had clearly associated himself with the Popular Front and its political programme.
24. *Moldova socialista* (1 March 1990), p.1.
25. *Literatura si arta*, 9 (1 March 1990) p.1.

26. *Moldova socialista* (1 March 1990), p.1.
27. This estimate is based on returns after the second run-off election held on 10 March 1990. *Moldova socialista* (27 Jan. 1990), p.1; *Literatura si arta* (15 March 1990), p.1 and *Moldova socialista* (17 March 1990), p.1. Nine more repeat contests were held on 22 April 1990. This round decided only two more contests. Elections were invalidated in four districts because less than 50 per cent of the electorate participated, and in three others because neither candidate obtained the necessary number of votes to be elected. A fourth round of elections was accordingly scheduled for 17 June *Moldova socialista* (28 April 1990), p.2.
28. Virgil Zafaievschi, 'Down with the Helmet, Up with the Cap', *Literatura si arta* 11 (15 March 1990), p.1.
29. T. Esinencu (ed.), *Republic of Moldova* (Chisinau: Editura Universitatis, 1992), p.25.
30. *Moldova socialista* (13 May 1990), p.1; *Moldova socialista* (26 June 1990), pp.2–3. .
31. For the central government's response to these actions see *Moldova socialista* (26 June 1990, p.1). On conditions in Bender see P. Ionel, 'Meetings During Work Time', *Moldova socialista* (4 May 1990), p.3.
32. *Moldova Suverana* (6 Feb. 1993), p.1.
33. In essence it was felt that if Transdniestria was composed of a single or several contiguous electoral districts, and if those districts did not participate in the elections, the region could claim to be unrepresented in the national legislature, and thus not bound by its decisions. On the other hand, drawing districts that broke up Transdniestria and combined parts of it with right-bank districts would have fuelled the Transdniestrian leaders' arguments that they were going to be forcibly assimilated, and hence fed the separatist movement.
34. The surveys were conducted by William Crowther in co-operation with the Institute of Sociology of Moldova and Informatix Lat. in Romania. In both cases questionnaires were distributed through the co-operation of parliamentary leadership. 188 responses were obtained in Moldova, and 357 in Romania. Funding for the Moldovan portion of the project was provided through a grant from the National Science Foundation.
35. For the 1994 election, Moldova adopted a system of proportional representation in which the entire country was one electoral district. It would be interesting to see if this change in the electoral system has had an effect on constituency relations.

The Early Legislative Process in the Russian Federal Assembly

THOMAS F. REMINGTON and STEVEN S. SMITH

The paper describes the establishment of legislative rules and procedures in the Russian Federal Assembly, the new bicameral parliament created under the 1993 Russian Constitution. The paper reviews the constitutional and electoral setting in which the new parliament formed, its organisational structure, and the elements of the legislative process. We discuss the consequences of the different bases of representation of members of the upper and lower chambers, particularly with respect to the development of parliamentary parties in the lower chamber and their role in its governance. We assess parliament's effectiveness in enacting laws and conclude with observations about the factors likely to affect the future development of the Federal Assembly.

On 11 January 1994, newly elected legislators convened in Moscow to open the first sessions of the Duma and Council of the Federation, the two houses of the Federal Assembly of the Russian Federation. The Federal Assembly replaced the Supreme Soviet and Congress of People's Deputies that were dissolved by presidential decree in September 1993. The members of the Federal Assembly, who as in the past are called deputies, were elected in December 1993, when the new constitution was ratified as well. The Duma is composed of 450 deputies, half selected on the basis of proportional representation and half elected in single-member districts. The 178-seat Council of the Federation is composed of two deputies elected from each of the 89 constituent regions of the Russian Federation (known as subjects of the federation – that is, the republics, oblasts and krais into which Russia is divided).

In this paper we provide an account of the legislative process as it emerged in the first year of the new Russian Federal Assembly.[1] Our purpose is primarily descriptive. We review the constitutional and electoral context of the new parliament, outline the organisational structure and procedure of the two houses, and describe the major steps in processing legislation. But we begin and end with observations about the factors that

Thomas F. Remington is Professor of Political Science at Emory University, Atlanta, Georgia, USA. Steven S. Smith is Professor of Political Science at the University of Minnesota, Minneapolis, Minnesota, USA. The research reported here is supported by a grant from the National Council for Soviet and East European Research, which does not bear responsibility for any of the content or findings of this paper.

shape the legislative process. The new constitution and elections produced a weaker parliament, at least in terms of formal powers, with stronger parliamentary parties, than the old Supreme Soviet. Both characteristics have greatly influenced the creation of a decision-making process within the parliament.

THEORETICAL PERSPECTIVES ON LEGISLATIVE INSTITUTIONS

Two theoretical approaches – often called organisation theory and social-choice theory – order most analysis of legislative institutions. Although they are usually called theories, neither perspective has generated a single dominant, specific theory of legislative institutions, so they are best labelled as perspectives or approaches. Organisation theory focuses on organisational or institutional adaptation to change in tasks and environmental conditions. Social-choice theory concerns the way in which goals or policy preferences, as well as existing rules, shape collective choices about policy and institutional arrangements. We view these perspectives as entirely compatible and see the factors emphasised by both perspectives as essential to understanding recent developments in Russian legislative institutions.

Nearly all of the factors identified by Olson and Norton in the introduction as critical to shaping the role and organisation of parliaments can be categorised under the broad headings of organisation and social-choice theory. Some, such as the character of the policy issues confronting a parliament, define the tasks and environments of a parliament. Others, such as the external electoral and party systems, define rules and shape the distribution of goals and preferences that influence the politics of a parliament.

To make our task manageable, we do not attempt to weigh the influence of the full set of factors affecting the Russian Parliament. After all, even on a cross-national basis, an assessment of the independent effects of all relevant factors is impossible. We try to gain some leverage on the subject by focusing on institutional change. Specifically, we concentrate on the differences in the internal structures and procedures of the old Supreme Soviet and the new Federal Assembly, with special attention given to parliamentary leadership, parties and committees. By doing so, we can narrow our focus to those factors that appear to be critical to the evolution of Russian parliamentary practice between 1990 and late 1994.

A span of four years may seem to be an unreasonably short period for assessing the factors underlying change in the Russian Parliament. A conclusive answer may require the passage of some time, but we believe that changes in parliamentary practice have already occurred that are so critical that they will figure prominently in future accounts of the evolution of a democratic parliament in Russia.

In our view, two forces suggested by these two general approaches explain much of the similarity and difference in Supreme Soviet and Federal Assembly parliamentary practice. First, substantial continuity in policy-making responsibilities, work-load, and societal turmoil lead us to expect continuity in the way the two parliaments organised themselves to process legislation. As organisation theory suggests, similar tasks and environment produce similar organisational forms. In the case of the Russian parliaments, this means continuity in the system of committees and working groups that serve as the primary means of evaluating and drafting legislation.

Second, the new constitution and electoral law created new rules for policy making and elections and produced a parliament with a substantially different mix of policy preferences. The social-choice perspective leads us to expect that changes in basic rules and preferences will produce changes in strategies and preferences about procedures. The most obvious consequence was that the role of parties or party-like factions was greatly enhanced in one house but not the other. The result is that parliamentary parties and committees form a decision-making process in the Duma that is quite different from that in the Council of the Federation.

We proceed by first reviewing the changes in the constitutional and electoral context that had important consequences for the operation of the two houses of the Federal Assembly. We close that section with more specific predictions suggested by those changes. Then we turn to the details of the structure and procedure of the two houses to determine whether the predictions were borne out in the first six months of the Federal Assembly's first session.

THE CHANGING CONTEXT

The breadth and depth of change in Russian politics in recent years rule out tidy explanations of the development of Russia's legislative institutions. Many features of the tasks, environment, political alignments, rules, and strategic context of legislators have been in flux throughout the period since 1989, when Soviet President Michail Gorbachev initiated reforms of legislative institutions at the union level. These reforms were followed by remodelling of the legislative institutions in the republics of the USSR, including the Russian Republic, which adopted its new legislative structure in 1990. When the USSR dissolved in late 1991, Russia gained full sovereignty. We begin with a brief outline of the changes that have occurred since 1990 and a summary of the changes in the conditions identified by the organisational and social-choice perspectives.

PARLIAMENTARY INSTITUTIONS, 1990–93

A transitional period in Russian legislative institutions began in 1990 with the creation of a 1,068-member Congress of People's Deputies and the 252-member Supreme Soviet, which was drawn from the Congress.[2] These institutions were created by amending the 1979 Russian Constitution. The deputies were selected for five-year terms by direct popular election in March, 1990, and convened as the Congress of People's Deputies nine times between May 1990 and March 1993.[3] The Supreme Soviet served as the working legislature. The Congress could reverse or direct the decisions of the smaller Supreme Soviet but the Congress met for only a few days each year and seldom delved into the details of everyday legislation, concentrating rather on constitutional and other major policy issues.

The Supreme Soviet was bicameral – each chamber had 126 deputies – but not in the usual sense. In fact, the legislative process of the Supreme Soviet might be described as 'collapsed bicameralism'. Most of the Supreme Soviet's work was done in joint session and most of the details of legislation were devised in joint committees. The two houses were led by a single presidium, or executive committee, which was headed by a chairman who was known informally as the 'speaker'. The presidium, comprising the committee chairs, devised the floor agenda, assigned legislation to committees, hired the staff of a large central apparat, and made a number of decisions in the name of the Supreme Soviet. The chairman presided over both the Congress and the Supreme Soviet. Succeeding Boris Yeltsin as chairman after Yeltsin's election as president, Ruslan Khasbulatov eventually came to use the resources of the chairmanship to centralise power within the Supreme Soviet and use that power on behalf of the conservative bloc of Communists and Agrarians. Party organisations did not materialise, although political factions and blocs were given certain formal rights by the rules.[4]

The old constitution was amended further in 1991 to provide for a separate, directly elected president. Boris Yeltsin was elected president in June of that year. But the constitution left quite ambiguous the distribution of government power between Congress and the president. Although the new constitutional provisions explicitly declared a separation-of-powers system, they also left in place the traditional Soviet-era precept that the legislature could decide any matter under the jurisdiction of the Russian Federation. The mixed provisions of the amended constitution, combined with the opposition majority that materialised after the demise of the Soviet Union, gave Yeltsin's opponents a means to block the president on any issue. Many of Yeltsin's supporters also concluded, in retrospect, that the single-member district system allowed the old-regime forces that still controlled local politics to dominate the 1990 elections.[5]

In this transitional period, the Supreme Soviet had a genuine policy-making role and a sizeable agenda, particularly after Russia claimed sovereignty over the republic's resources and policy. Even before the attempted coup against Gorbachev in August 1991, and the subsequent decree banning the Communist Party, the party's control over the elected, Yeltsin-led legislature was weak. After the dissolution of the Soviet Union in the autumn of 1991, the Russian Republic's legislative institutions gained responsibilities associated with statehood, including those in the foreign and defence policy arenas.

THE NEW CONSTITUTIONAL FRAMEWORK

In 1992 and 1993, a political deadlock developed between the opposition bloc of deputies who gained control of the parliament and the reformist group loyal to Yeltsin. The *impasse* prevented agreement on a new constitutional framework and eventually motivated Yeltsin to dissolve the parliament by decree in September 1993. He then made additional modifications to the constitutional draft that was under development and, by decree, ordered a referendum for the constitution for December. He also ordered simultaneous elections of deputies to the new Federal Assembly, which itself was to be created by the constitution that he hoped would be ratified. With the December elections and referendum, the constitution was declared ratified and the deputies to the parliament's two chambers were elected.[6]

The new constitution can be viewed as the work of the Yeltsin camp. It clarifies the responsibilities of the president, the government and the legislature. It provides for a dual executive (president and prime minister) and a bicameral Federal Assembly with a strong lower and weak upper chamber. Both the president and the government have the right to submit legislation to the parliament. The president appoints the prime minister (although not other ministers) subject to the approval of the Duma. If the Duma rejects the president's nominees for prime minister three times, the president appoints a prime minister, dissolves the Duma, and calls for new Duma elections.

Under the new constitution the president may issue decrees (*ukazy*) that carry the force of law until legislation is enacted that supplants the decree. Yeltsin's decrees have been quite important, extending to privatisation, banking reform and criminal procedure, although they have been issued with an invitation to the Federal Assembly to pursue substitute legislation. Not surprisingly, Yeltsin's decree-making power has been questioned by critics who charge that the president may not use the power to override existing law. If the president's interpretation of the power stands, the

Russian President will be able to modify the policy *status quo* without action by the parliament and then use the veto power to resist a legislative response, should the two houses be able to formulate one.

The government may be subjected to a vote of confidence in the Duma. If the Duma votes no confidence in the government, the president may choose to ignore the first such vote but must either dismiss the government or dissolve the Duma if the Duma votes no confidence a second time within three months. The prime minister may submit a motion of confidence to the Duma, which, if denied by the Duma, leads the president to decide whether to dismiss the government or dissolve the Duma.[7]

Legislation, with the exception of legislation falling in the unique jurisdictions of the two houses, originates in the Duma and, if adopted by the Duma, is then sent to the Council of the Federation.[8] The constitution obliges the Council of the Federation to act on Duma-passed legislation concerning budget, taxes, financial policy, treaties, customs and war. If the Council of the Federation approves the legislation or fails to examine it within 14 days, the legislation is deemed enacted, subject to the President's signature. If the Council of the Federation rejects the legislation, the two houses may form a conciliation commission to resolve differences. Any compromise legislation must be approved by the Duma. With or without a conciliation commission, the Duma may enact legislation after Federal Council rejection with a two-thirds majority vote. Vote outcomes, with the exception of veto overrides, are determined by a majority of the total number of deputies (not a majority of those deputies present and voting).

Within five days of final action by the Federal Assembly, legislation is sent to the president, who then has 14 days to sign or veto the legislation. A veto can be overridden only by a two-thirds majority vote in both chambers (two-thirds of the total number of deputies in each chamber).

ELECTORAL SYSTEM

The new constitution provides for a four-year term for the president and deputies of the Duma. However, the December 1993 referendum on the constitution made provision for a two-year term for the first Duma and Council of the Federation. The constitution does not fix a term for Council of the Federation deputies, who are described as 'one each from the representative and executive organs of state power' from each of the 89 regions of the Russian Federation. No term limit for Duma deputies is established. Presidents are limited to two terms.

The electoral system used in the December 1993 elections was established by presidential decree, but the new constitution provides that the electoral system will be established by law. For the Duma, the presidential decree provided for a mixed system of proportional representation and single-member districts. Half of the 450 seats were allocated proportionately to registered parties that received at least five per cent of the vote. The other half were elected in a single-stage plurality election in single-member districts. Individuals could be both party list and single-member district candidates, but were seated as single-member district deputies if selected by both means, allowing the party to advance lower ranking candidates on its list.

The party-list Duma seats are allocated on the basis of nationwide voting. This appears to have reflected a deliberate decision by Yeltsin's strategists to reduce the influence of regional elites on the outcomes. Nevertheless, as happened in the 1993 elections, the process encourages the election of many party groups to the lower house of the parliament and reduces the likelihood that any one party or bloc will muster a majority. The balance of proportional representation and single-member districts remains an issue among Duma deputies in their discussion of an electoral law for the next election.

Oddly, the electoral decree did not adhere to the constitutional draft on the selection of deputies of the Council of the Federation. The constitution requires that the two deputies from each region be selected from the legislative and executive branches of regional governments. Instead, the decree provided for the election of Council of the Federation deputies with a one-stage, two-winner plurality election in each of the regions. Future selection of Council of the Federation deputies is to be selected by regional governments under the constitutional constraint, although this remains a matter of controversy. There is serious discussion, particularly among Yeltsin supporters, about amending the constitution to provide for direct election of deputies in the Council of the Federation.

In the party-list voting for the Duma, parties opposing Yeltsin and government policies polled about 43 per cent of the vote (see Table 1).[9] Half of the opposition vote went to the Liberal-Democratic Party of Russia, led by Vladimir Zhirinovsky. Pro-reform parties garnered about 34 per cent of the party-list vote, with about half of that going to Russia's Choice, the party led by former Prime Minister Egor Gaidar. The actual balance of forces in the Duma was affected by the outcomes in the single-member district races, which offset, to some degree, the strong showing of the opposition groups in the party-list voting. There was great uncertainty, however, about the actual balance of political forces in the Duma following the election, because deputies from single-member districts were free to affiliate themselves with any faction or group and many changed their political affiliations between the elections and the first days of the parliament's session.[10] Around one-third of the district deputies chose to affiliate with one of the reform-oriented factions and 29 per cent affiliated with one of the opposition groups.

TABLE 1

RESULTS OF DECEMBER 1993 PARLIAMENTARY ELECTIONS

Party	Party List Vote % Affiliated	List Seats Received (450 seats)	District Deputies	Total seats	As % of Duma (April)
Reform parties					
RC	15.51	40	33	73	16.22
PRES	6.73	18	12	30	6.67
Yabloko	7.86	20	8	28	6.22
Dec	12.00	00	26	26	5.78
RDDR	4.08	0	0	0	0.00
Total	34.18	78	79	157	34.89
Centrist parties					
DPR	5.52	14	1	15	3.33
WOR	8.13	21	2	23	5.11
NRP	0.00	0	66	66	14.67
KEDR	0.76	0	0	0	0.00
BRNI	1.25	0	0	0	0.00
Civic Union	1.93	0	0	0	0.00
DiM	0.70	0	0	0	0.00
Total	18.29	35	69	104	23.11
Opposition parties					
APR	7.99	21	34	55	12.22
CPRF	12.40	32	13	45	10.00
LDPR	22.92	59	5	64	14.22
RP	0.00	0	14	14	3.11
Total	43.31	112	66	178	39.56
Against all lists	4.22				
Total	100.00	225	214	439	97.56

Notes:

RC = Russia's Choice

PRES = Party of Russian Unity and Accord

Yabloko = Bloc 'Yavlinskii–Boldyrev–Lukin' [the names of its three leaders]

December 12 = Liberal Democratic Union of December 12 (NB: did not put up a list as electoral association; formed in first week as a group comprising SMD deputies)

RDDR = Russian Movement for Democratic Reforms

WOR = Women of Russia

NRP = New Regional Policy (NB: did not put up a list as electoral association; formed in first week as a group comprising SMD deputies)

KEDR = Constructive-Ecological Movement 'Cedar'

BRNI = Future of Russia/New Names

DiM = Dignity and Charity

APR = Agrarian Party of Russia

CPRF = Communist Party of the Russian Federation

LDPR = Liberal Democratic Party of Russia

RP = Russia's Way (NB: did not put up a list as electoral association; formed in first week as a group comprising SMD deputies)

The partisan implications of the 1993 elections for the Council of the Federation were more difficult to assess than those for the Duma. Only 68 of the 171 winners of the 1993 elections were endorsed by a party and some of them were endorsed by more than one party. Of the 68, 40 were supported by Russia's Choice and the rest were distributed among other parties. The Liberal-Democratic Party of Zhirinovsky did not endorse anyone for the upper house.[11] However, the largest share of members in the upper chamber were chiefs of administration appointed by President Yeltsin and a substantial number held other regional-level offices or were directors of large (formerly state-owned) firms. The vast majority kept their positions, serving in the upper house on a part-time basis.

IMPLICATIONS OF THE NEW CONTEXT

The violent end to the previous parliament had a traumatic effect on Russia's political life. Neither parliamentarians nor president could be sure of public support – Yeltsin had been condemned by some of his supporters for his heavy-handed actions against the defenders of the White House, while the public had shown little sympathy for Khasbulatov and the other parliamentary figures who had led the armed uprising against the government. Both opposition and pro-Yeltsin forces, it appeared in December 1993, had reason to avoid confrontation and polarisation and to abide by the constitutional arrangements set in place by the December referendum. Yet, confrontation between Yeltsin and the parliament seemed likely, at least after an initial honeymoon period, if Yeltsin sought to use his decree power to further the process of economic reform. Similarly, the president's powers in the area of national security could not be readily checked by the parliament, as the war in Chechnia demonstrated.

The new constitutional framework and the outcome of the December elections and referendum lead us to several predictions about the organisation of the Federal Assembly.[12] First, and most obvious, we would expect the lower house, the Duma, to be party-oriented, although we expect greater policy cohesiveness among party-list deputies than among single-member-district deputies. At the same time, because no single party or coalition on either the left or the right held a majority in the Duma, we would not expect strongly majoritarian rules. Instead, we would expect a decision-making process that protected the procedural rights of all factions.

Second, we would expect the Council of the Federation to be far less party-oriented than the Duma and to have a far more regional emphasis. Council deputies were not elected on party lists and generally held positions of responsibility in regional governments. Consequently, council deputies would not be expected to be closely tied to party leaders or even to each other. If anything, we would expect the policy views of the members of the Council of the Federation to be tilted in favour of regional interests. This would be no small consideration because the distribution of responsibilities and taxing authority between the central government and regional governments remained quite uncertain at the end of 1993.

Third, we would expect both chambers to be reliant on a system of committees with substantial powers. The new parliament's agenda is just as large and diverse as the agenda of the transitional parliament, which had operated largely through a system of committees and joint commissions. Moreover, the absence of a cohesive majority bloc meant that there would not likely be a central party leadership capable of requiring compliant behaviour from any committee. However, the high salience of, and sharp divisions on most issues meant that little deference to committee recommendations could be expected on the floor of the Duma.

Fourth, we would expect the Council of the Federation, in comparision with the Duma, to have fewer sessions and committee meetings and to be more reliant on a few deputies and the staff to carry the legislative burden. The constitutional arrangement that requires the Duma to act before the Council of the Federation on most legislation places a heavier legislative burden on the Duma. And the nearly full-time responsibilities of the regional officials who comprise a large proportion of the Council's membership means that their attention would be diverted from Moscow affairs.

Fifth, we would expect that the presidium would be replaced by another kind of steering mechanism. The newly elected deputies would be expected to alter those features of the previous parliament for which a consensus for change existed among deputies. In fact, there seemed to be a consensus among nearly all political groups in the autumn of 1993 that the future parliament should prevent a powerful and manipulative chairman from abusing the powers of the presidium. On the other hand, several features of the decision-making process of the transitional Russian Supreme Soviet, most of which were copied from the Supreme Soviet of the Soviet Union, we expect to carry over to the Federal Assembly because they were subject to no criticism. These include multiple readings of draft laws, reliance on informal working groups and commissions to draft legislation, and seeking the approval of draft legislation from a wide circle of affected interests.

ORGANISING THE FEDERAL ASSEMBLY

The constitution specifies only a few features of legislative organisation and procedure for the two houses of the Federal Assembly. It provides for chairmen and deputy chairmen for the two houses, but does not specify either the number of deputy chairmen or method of selecting chairmen and deputy chairmen. The constitution authorises the two houses to form committees and commissions, which may conduct hearings. And it provides for a comptroller's office to monitor the implementation of the federal budget. Otherwise, the constitution authorises the two houses to adopt their own rules of procedure.

Preparations for the new Federal Assembly began before the ratification of the constitution. After the dissolution of parliament, President Yeltsin appointed a number of friendly deputies from the old parliament to a commission charged with preparing the rules and legislative agenda of the new parliament. Guided by the draft constitution and the electoral decree, the commission proposed draft rules for the two houses that differed substantially between one another and from the past rules with respect to the role of party factions (in Russian, *fraktsiia*, or fraction). Factions figured prominently in the rules proposed for the Duma, but they were not recognised in the rules of the Council of the Federation. Although the commission's draft rules were further modified in important ways before adoption in each chamber, the final versions retained the principles of a faction-dominated lower chamber and an upper chamber without factions.

The president's commission was strongly influenced by their reaction to the transitional Supreme Soviet and Congress, particularly the domination of the institution by its chairman, who exercised his power through the presidium. The proposed rules provided that the chairman's powers would be severely restricted, and there would be no presidium in either chamber. Members of the commission envisioned the new governing structures of the Duma as being 'horizontal' – based on agreements among the party factions – rather than 'vertical' – exercised through the chairman, the presidium and the committees. Consequently, they initially proposed that the steering body for the Duma be a council comprising the leaders of the factions.

Adoption of the Duma's rule took nearly three months. Opposition factions, which played no part in the presidential commission planning for the new parliament, deferred little to the commission's recommendations. Indeed, the Duma's new chairman, Ivan Rybkin, had been a leader of the Communist faction in the old Supreme Soviet. In contrast, the Council of the Federation, which was filled with many of Yeltsin's appointees to regional government and elected Yeltsin's favoured candidate, Vladimir Shumeiko, to the chairmanship, agreed quickly to a set of standing rules, adopting them in less than a month after first convening.

ORGANISING THE DUMA

By the end of its first six months of operation, the Duma developed both a strongly party-oriented system for leadership and co-ordination and a strongly committee-oriented system for the drafting of legislative details. On balance, particularly in contrast to the Council of the Federation, the party-related elements – factions and the Council of the Duma – have proven to be somewhat more important than committees in the chamber's decision-making process.

FACTIONS AND THE PACKAGE DEAL IN THE DUMA

Party factions began asserting claims to leadership positions in the Duma even before the first session opened. Faction leaders were able to assert these claims on behalf of deputies because they had substantially more influence over members than had faction leaders in the transitional parliament. Half of the deputies had been elected on the national party lists and a majority of those elected from single-member districts had been nominated by parties. On the opening day, deputies confirmed the official status of registered party factions and adopted the rule, proposed by the president's preparatory commission, that the principal governing body of the Duma be a Council of the Duma, composed of the heads of the party factions.[13]

The provisional rules adopted immediately provided that any electoral association which had elected deputies on a national party list could form a faction in the Duma, no matter how few members it had. Accordingly, the smallest, the Democratic Party of Russia, which had elected 14 members from its party list and only one from a district, enjoyed the same formal status as did Russia's Choice, the largest, which had elected 40 from its party list and another 27 in districts. Almost all deputies elected on party lists joined a corresponding faction early in the session. Nearly all other Duma deputies, those elected from districts, either registered with one of the eight party factions that had elected party-list deputies or formed their own 'independent' factions. Ultimately, three independent groups arose.[14]

A number of organisational questions arose immediately. How would factions be represented on the new steering body, the Council of the Duma – in proportion to their strength in the chamber or on a parity basis? What threshold would be required of the 'independent' groups to register and gain the same rights and privileges, including a seat on the Council of the Duma, as the party factions? Should party factions be empowered to expel a party-list member from the Duma for violation of party discipline? And, how should leadership positions – the chairmanship and deputy chairs of the chamber, committee chairs and deputy chairs, the chairmanship of the comptroller's office, and the chairmanship of the Human Rights Commission – be distributed among factions?

Complicating matters was the provocative style of Vladimir

Zhirinovsky, leader of the Liberal-Democratic Party of Russia, who repeatedly took the floor to pose extreme demands. Zhirinovsky's demagogic approach seems to have reinforced the deputies' interest in ensuring equality of rights for members and factions and not permitting excessive centralisation of power in parliament. This may help explain the relative ease with which the chamber agreed that the Council of the Duma would comprise factions on a parity rather than proportional basis, even though the rule tended to disadvantage the opposition forces composed of the Communist, Agrarian and LDPR factions.[15]

The second issue, the minimum size of membership required for a group to register, presented a thornier problem. Larger factions tended to prefer a higher threshold for registration, so as to keep the privileges associated with official status restricted to a smaller circle of factions. As anticipated, these privileges proved to be significant. A registered group has a representative on the Council of the Duma and therefore the opportunity to propose agenda items for the floor. An unregistered group interested in pressing for a particular decision must either work through sympathetic registered factions or committees or offer motions on the floor. A second advantage of registration is the privileged access to recognition enjoyed by registered groups in floor debate. As in the old Supreme Soviet and Congress, faction representatives, when speaking for their faction, can demand recognition ahead of deputies without faction affiliation. Thus, unaffiliated deputies usually have difficulty gaining recognition on the floor to offer motions. Another advantage is that only registered factions were able to claim committee chairmanships and other leadership positions in the grand bargain over the distribution of these posts in the first week of the session. Finally, certain material benefits are granted to registered factions – space, funding to hire staff and office expenses.

Even in the first days of the session, then, it was evident to the deputies outside the regular parties that faction registration was a critical step to influence within the Duma. A series of recorded votes was taken until a compromise figure of 35 was set between the high of 50 demanded by Zhirinovsky and the low of 15 demanded by some independents. Only one of the three independent groups met this threshold, the New Regional Policy group, which soon attracted over 60 members.

The third issue concerned the status of party-list deputies – the existence of an 'imperative mandate'. Proponents of the imperative mandate argued that party-list deputies had an obligation to adhere to the policy positions established by their factions. In fact, as the term implies, proponents believed that support for the faction was a necessary condition for continuing membership in the Duma. In their view, party-list deputies would undermine the purpose of party-list elections if they failed to vote with their parliamentary faction.

In the early stages of discussion of this issue, the leaders of Russia's Choice favoured the imperative mandate so as to increase party discipline. The position of Russia's Choice leaders may have reflected their experience during the transitional years when many early supporters of Yeltsin and reform drifted to opposition positions. In any case, the imperative mandate also was endorsed by LDPR, Communists, Agrarians and the Democratic Party of Russia. The concept was translated into a proposed rule that would have allowed party factions to remove from office any party-list deputy who violated party discipline. The expelled deputy's seat would then be filled by the next candidate on the list. The imperative mandate was finally rejected on a close vote.[16]

Individual factions have adopted their own formal rules on voting discipline, producing a diversity of practices. Some factions use a 'solidarity vote' procedure, with either two-thirds or simple majority vote within the faction needed to impose the expectation of a party-line vote on faction members. Most factions seem to tolerate defections on matters subject to a solidarity vote with stipulation that members carefully explain their position and that they do not directly and actively oppose the faction. Non-voting is often a convenient option for deputies in such cases. Members of nearly all factions claim that solidarity votes pertain only to 'matters of principle'. Some factions appear to have adopted a solidarity-vote rule as a defensive response to solidarity-vote rules adopted by other factions. Fearing that they would be disadvantaged in competition with more cohesive factions, some factions have backed into a solidarity-vote rule that might not have otherwise done so.

The fourth issue was the allocation of leadership positions among factions. Even before the final results of the December elections were known, faction leaders began negotiating over these positions, based on the assumption that no faction or bloc had a majority in the Duma. Because the factions had somewhat different substantive interests, faction leaders quickly discovered a grand compromise might be possible, although negotiations over details of the package deal continued for a week after the Duma's session opened.

The most important component of the package deal was the distribution of committee leadership positions. To accommodate factions' demands for positions, faction leaders agreed to expand the number of committees from nine, as initially proposed by the president's preparatory commission, to 23. This created more chairmanships and deputy chairmanships to spread among the factions and assured factions with special policy interests that a committee would address their concerns. However, the resulting array of committees produced overlapping jurisdictions.[17]

The faction leaders agreed on a bidding system for leadership positions. Each position was assigned a weight – for example, a committee chairmanship was worth more than a deputy chairmanship – and each faction was given 'chips' in proportion to the number of seats it commanded in Duma. Faction leaders could spend their chips to bid on positions. The typical result for a committee was a chair and deputy chairs from different factions.[18]

The package deal also balanced faction representation in the four deputy chairmanships of the full Duma. After the Agrarian Rybkin was elected to the chairmanship of the Duma, the post of First Deputy Chairman was assigned as part of the package agreement to Russia's Choice deputy Mikhail Mitiukov. Three other deputy chairmanships went to members of the Communist, Women of Russia and LDPR factions. A fourth position was eventually filled by a New Regional Policy member.[19]

The package agreement was approved by an overwhelming majority on 17 January and settled nearly all of the outstanding problems of matching faction demands with committee and leadership positions. The major exception were the demands of Zhirinovsky, who insisted that he chair and control either the Defence Committee or International Affairs Committee. Eventually, other faction leaders agreed to create a new committee, called the Committee on Matters of Geopolitics, which the LDPR was able to dominate.

Only two of the committees of the Duma were clearly dominated by one faction – Agriculture by the Agrarians and Geopolitics by the LDPR (see Table 2). Elsewhere, the package agreement succeeded in achieving a rough proportionality in faction strength in committees. Unregistered groups and deputies outside any organised group were awarded no leadership posts, although some of their members were elected by committees to sub-committee chairmanships and all were given committee assignments, as the rules require, largely by self-selection.

Plainly, then, factions are a central feature of Duma organisation. They are far more important than their predecessors in the Supreme Soviet and Congress of People's Deputies during the transitional period. The Council of the Duma provides for faction meetings in its regular schedule. Typically, factions meet twice a week, usually for two or more hours each time, and often hold special meetings. Deputies report that most factions conduct their meetings so as to allow open, wide-ranging discussion on all important policy and political matters of concern to their members. Nevertheless, as expected, the Duma is not a strongly majoritarian body because of the co-equal status of factions in the Council of the Duma.

TABLE 2
COMMITTEE MEMBERSHIP BY FACTION, 18 APRIL 1994

Committee	none	APR	LDPR	DPR	CP	WOR	RC	PRES	Yab	NRP	Dec. 12	RWay	Total
Agrarian	0	22	0	0	1	0	2	0	0	1	0	0	26
Security	0	1	3	2	1	1	5	1	1	3	1	1	20
Budget	0	4	4	1	2	2	8	4	3	9	6	0	43
Eco. Policy	0	2	2	1	2	1	3	1	2	4	3	0	21
Ecology	1	0	6	1	0	0	2	0	1	1	0	1	13
Federal Policy	0	1	1	1	2	0	3	2	1	1	0	3	15
Women/Family	1	1	1	0	2	3	0	0	1	0	1	0	10
Geopolitics	0	1	10	0	1	0	2	0	0	1	0	0	15
Info & Comms	0	1	2	1	4	1	4	0	2	1	0	0	16
Intl Relations	1	1	5	1	2	1	4	2	3	4	2	0	26
Local Govt	1	3	0	1	2	1	3	2	0	3	1	0	17
Nationalities	0	0	0	0	2	1	1	2	0	3	1	1	11
Pub. Orgs.	2	2	1	1	2	0	3	1	1	1	0	1	15
Defence	0	1	3	0	2	1	3	0	0	4	0	1	15
Ed., Cult., Sci.	1	1	3	0	2	2	6	1	2	7	2	0	27
Duma Org.	1	1	2	1	1	1	2	1	1	3	1	0	1
Natural Res's	0	4	2	0	1	0	1	1	0	1	0	0	10
Industry	1	0	8	1	3	1	2	3	1	8	0	1	29
Privatisation	1	2	3	1	3	0	7	1	2	2	1	0	23
CIS	1	1	1	0	2	1	0	3	2	1	0	0	12
Lab./Soc. Wel.	0	1	2	0	3	1	3	0	2	2	1	0	15
Legislation	0	2	1	1	1	1	4	2	2	3	3	2	22
Health	1	1	1	0	1	2	1	0	0	1	0	0	8
TOTAL	12	53	61	14	42	21	69	27	27	64	23	11	424
Chairmanships	0	2	5	1	2	1	4	3	2	3	0	0	23
Deputy Chairs	0	9	11	4	7	1	12	6	6	14	0	0	70

THE DUMA CHAIRMANSHIP, COUNCIL AND COMMITTEE ON ORGANISATION

The election and power of the Duma's chairman had great significance for deputies. Ruslan Khasbulatov, Yeltsin's successor as chairman of the transitional Russian Supreme Soviet, had turned the chairmanship into a base for great personal power. Duma factions agreed that the temperament and character of the chairman would be important. But the election of the chairman inevitably also tested the balance of political forces. The democratic forces' failure to elect one of their members revealed their comparative weakness. The better organised opposition bloc could not win either without support from a number of centrist deputies.

After a series of 'rating' votes (basically, straw polls to determine the relative strength of each of a series of nominees), Ivan Rybkin polled the largest number and eventually won the absolute majority required by a margin of one vote. Rybkin's voting record in the previous parliament, where he was a leader of the Communist faction, placed him solidly as a Communist loyalist. But he had run on the Agrarian Party's national list rather than that of the Communists, and he had built a reputation among political insiders as a straightforward, pragmatic and fair-minded politician.

The Duma's rules check the power of the chairman by requiring the chairman to work through the Council of the Duma to refer legislation to committee and set the chamber's agenda, by requiring the daily agenda to be approved by the full Duma and by allocating jurisdiction over the staff and operations of the Duma to a Committee on Organisation. The Committee on Organisation, chairmanship of which was given to a Russia's Choice deputy, also controls the material benefits granted to deputies, a power which had been used flagrantly by Khasbulatov to reward his friends and punish his enemies. 'Our task', the committee's chairman said in an interview, 'is to ensure that the apparat serves the deputies, and not the deputies the apparat'.

While the Council of the Duma is dominated by faction leaders, the rules specify that committee chairs participate without voting power and any deputy may attend its meetings. Nevertheless, all participants agree that decisions of the council are made by faction leaders by vote. Many committee chairs, who do not sit at the conference table with the faction leaders, do not attend council meetings on a regular basis because they have little voice in its deliberations.

THE DUMA COMMITTEE SYSTEM

The size of the Duma's 23 standing committees range from 43 on the Budget Committee to just seven on the Nationalities Committee (see Table 3). With the exception of faction leaders, all members are required to take one, but only one, committee assignment. In addition to the chair of each committee, all committees have three or four deputy chairs and many committees of sub-committees and thus sub-committee chairs as well. The relationships among chairs, deputy chairs, and sub-committee chairs vary widely across committees and probably are not well settled anywhere. In all cases, committees have adopted the common practice of Soviet- and transitional-era parliaments of using working groups to devise preliminary drafts of legislation.

The relationships of committees and their chairs to factions vary across committees and factions and are a source of some tension. Some committee chairs consider themselves rather independent of faction in matters falling under their committees' jurisdictions. In some cases, the chair's independence is the product of the deference faction members give him on the basis of his political stature or professional qualifications. But because their ability to report a bill out of committee requires that they accommodate differences within their committees, some committee chairs go to some lengths to distinguish their committee work from their duty to faction.

Generally factions do not dictate the behaviour of their members in committee. In fact, deputies from across the ideological spectrum described the relationship between committees and factions to us by distinguishing the political aspects of the legislative process from the process of drafting good laws. Some deputies and committee chairs report that faction politics was supposed to be, and to a large extent was, held separate from committee deliberation on bills, while political decisions, such as whether and when a controversial piece of legislation should be reported and what the shape of a compromise should be, were decided by the faction leaders in the Council of the Duma. Some committee chairs feel at a disadvantage because they do not have a vote on these questions in the Council, while others seem to accept the division between the political decisions of the Council and the professional policy work of the committees. In any event, the 'political' role of faction leaders and the Council of the Duma and the 'professional' sphere of the standing committees seems to be widely recognised.

The place of sub-committees and their chairs varies as well. In some cases, no sub-committees have been created and all work is reserved for the full committee and working groups. Where sub-committees have been created, deputy committee chairs, who gained their posts as a part of the early package deal, sometimes serve as sub-committee chairs. In other cases, sub-committee chairs were elected by the full committee membership. Currently, sub-committees do not seem to enjoy much autonomy. Full committee chairs control all committee staff and where sub-committees have had a chance to develop legislation, their work has been scrutinised by the full committee.

The designers of the Duma wished to deny its chair the autocratic control over the staff that Ruslan Khasbulatov came to exercise in the Russian Supreme Soviet. In the first place, the Duma and the Council of the Federation have separate staff arrangements, in contrast to the centralised staff under the collapsed bicameralism of the Supreme Soviet. Moreover, the Duma chairman's staff was to be restricted in size and the Council of the Duma was given no staff. Instead, responsibility for supervising the Duma's central staff is vested in the Organisation Committee, which does not have direct line authority in the processing of most legislation. Each committee (and faction) is formally authorised to hire staff experts, although these staffs remain quite small in comparison with other national legislatures with powerful committee systems. As a result, committee chairs have great discretion to hire committee specialists, although in practice some chairs share hiring decisions with deputy or sub-committee chairs.

In some respects, decision-making processes within committees have changed little from the process typical of the transitional years. As in the old Supreme Soviet, committees hold parliamentary hearings, although they must have the consent of the Council of the Duma. But the most important similarity with past practice is dependence on working groups and expert commissions for drafting the details of legislation. Some of these are formed to develop a draft law on a particular subject where the committee would like to initiate legislation. Others, by far more common, are expert groups which study legislation initiated by others (most commonly, the president, government, or a deputy) in order to reach consensus on revisions. The working groups are usually composed of executive branch officials, deputies, organisation representatives, and academic experts. As in the past, working groups help committees compensate for their lack of sizeable permanent staffs and the absence of a substantial library or research service. The groups commonly include deputies from the relevant committees of both houses, which facilitates co-ordination of the work of the two houses. Committee chairs decide which deputies and outside experts are appointed to working groups. The work of expert groups must be approved by the parent committee before it is circulated to other committees and the Council of the Duma.

PARTY-LIST AND SINGLE-MEMBER DISTRICT MEMBERS

The different bases of representation of Council of Federation members, party-list Duma members, and single-member district Duma members affect the way deputies deal with their constituents. Single-member district deputies report close ties with the voters of their districts and consider themselves obliged to serve their needs. For instance, a democratically oriented deputy from a district in the Urals works hard to find new international markets for the arms produced by a major defence plant in his city. Deputies from districts, as well as members of the Council of the Federation who represent sizeable province-level units, continue to respond to numerous requests for help of this kind. It is rare for constituent pressure to take the form of organised lobbying except in such cases as when a major local enterprise or organisation needs urgent relief. Deputies report that their constituency work rarely has much to do with their legislative activity.

District deputies often complain that the Duma's organisational structure favours party-list deputies over district-elected deputies, charging that the party factions seek to win national political capital through political grandstanding instead of passing laws that would benefit the needs of voters in particular districts. From their standpoint, they are burdened by having to visit their districts regularly and deal with their constituents' particular problems, whereas party-list deputies emphasise partisan politics, benefiting from the floor rights and other advantages that party factions enjoy in the Duma.

Party-list deputies do appear to spend more time in Moscow. However, party-list deputies have been aware of the potential advantages of building local organisations and reputations. In fact, some party factions have begun the practice of sending their members to particular regions of the country (often the regions from which a deputy has come) to meet with voters and perform constituency service.

ORGANISING THE COUNCIL OF THE FEDERATION

The Council of the Federation had little difficulty establishing standing rules. No clear party-based divisions, formal or otherwise, developed over rules. On the whole, deputies of the Council of the Federation seemed less intensely interested in the rules than deputies of the Duma. A decision-making process quite different from the Duma's process emerged. In the Council of the Federation, factions played no role in selecting committee chairs and members. No central executive committee exists. And the Council of the Federation meets infrequently, only a few days each month, leaving the day-to-day work to a few full-time deputies and the staff. But the Council of the Federation's processes are not only different from the Duma's, they are probably less fully developed as well. Because the Duma has been slow to move legislation, the Council of the Federation has not had much legislation to consider under the 14-day limit provided in the constitution. As a result, pressures to elaborate on its committee system or resolve procedural ambiguities were low during its early months.

Many, if not most of the deputies of the upper chamber were not endorsed by a party during the electoral campaign. A few were endorsed by more than one political party or association. As a result, there was little basis for party or faction organisation when the deputies arrived in Moscow in January. To be sure, like-minded deputies of the Council of the Federation do recognise each other, often have a history of working with each other and sometimes co-ordinate their activity, as they did in the election of a chair for the chamber. And some deputies openly associate with Duma factions and external political parties or associations. However, formal parties or factions have not formed, no partisan leaders are publicly recognised and parties and factions are not mentioned in the chamber's rules.

Like the Duma, the Council of the Federation did not seriously consider replicating the old presidium. But, unlike the Duma, the Council of the Federation chose not to create any executive committee. Instead, responsibility for bill referral, agenda and supervision of the central staff is placed in the hands of an elected chair. The chair's powers are not checked by or shared with any committee. In fact, the chair's power appears to be enhanced by the vacuum created by the part-time status of most deputies in the chamber. Shumeiko, in fact, has been the subject of some criticism for his creation of a large central staff and for his allocation of resources to committees and deputies. The infrequent sessions of the Council of the Federation have permitted Shumeiko to travel a good deal since his election as chairman. The paucity of legislation to be considered on the floor of the chamber leaves open the question of how willing the deputies will be to challenge the agenda recommended by Shumeiko.

Committee chairs and deputy chairs, as the rules provide, were elected by the memberships of their committees, with the chairs ratified by the full chamber. Committee chairs appear to have greater discretion than their Duma counterparts because of the need to act on some matters in the absence of many of their colleagues. But committee chairs suffer from the difficulty of mustering quorums to conduct business, not having assistance from other members to draft legislation and being less certain that their own handiwork will be supported on the floor. Committee chairs are authorised by the standing rules to hire staff, although budget allocations are a subject of tension between some of them and the Chairman of the Council.

The Council of the Federation has created fewer committees than the Duma – just 13. This appears to reflect two influences. First, partisan bartering over leadership posts was not associated with the creation of committees in the Council of the Federation, as it was in the Duma. Second, fewer demands for more committees were heard in the Council of the Federation because of the smaller size of the Council and the part-time status of its deputies.

Like committees of the Duma, the committees of the Council of the Federation conduct hearings. Moreover, Council committees work with working groups, usually shared with Duma committees, to draft the details or revisions of legislation. But no sub-committees have been created by the standing committees of the Council of the Federation. Participants report that attendance problems preclude active sub-committees and that little interest in sub-committees has been expressed. Besides, many deputies in the upper chamber appear to be so preoccupied with their responsibilities in regional government that they take little interest in committee business.

A large question about the upper chamber remains alive. Will the Council of the Federation become a full partner with the Duma in the making of public policy? The early signs are mixed.

Some members of the Council of the Federation are determined to make their chamber more than a reactive chamber whose agenda is set by the

Duma. In the case of the 1994 budget, the upper chamber asserted itself by approving a version of the budget before the Duma finished its work on the measure. Its action had no authoritative consequence, but it indicated that many Council of the Federation deputies wanted the Duma to know that they would influence the policy choices to be made. Earlier, the Chamber successively asserted, against initial Duma resistance, its right to recommend changes in Duma-passed legislation even though the Council of the Federation cannot formerly alter the legislation. The Duma has recognised the upper chamber's recommendations in its own rules. Furthermore, deputies of the Council of the Federation have exercised their constitutional powers a few times. The chamber frustrated Yeltsin by refusing to confirm his nomination for General Procurator. And it has denied confirmation to several of the candidates President Yeltsin put forward for the Constitutional Court.

In addition, many Council of the Federation deputies have involved themselves in legislation before the Duma finishes its work by joining working groups, holding hearings and, in a few cases, working on draft legislation. Some members say that they want the Council of the Federation to be a chamber of 'senators' rather than of 'governors' – reflecting the fact that they give higher priority to their parliamentary duties than their duties in regional government. Many of them have sought and gained floor votes on issues other than those concerning legislation directly before them, which reflects their eagerness to influence national public policy.[20]

Yet the Council of the Federation and its members have not taken much advantage of their constitutional right to introduce legislation in the Duma. Rather, they have waited on the Duma before taking formal action in nearly all areas of public policy. And the deputies who actively participate in working groups and hearings appear to be a minority of their chamber. It is not clear that incentives will be sufficient for them to continue their activity if they are not actively supported by their chamber.

The ambiguous status of the Council of the Federation has fed continuing discussion about the manner in which its deputies are elected. Some participants have an interest in further specifying how or who the legislative and executive branches of regional government select deputies. Others, found mainly in the Duma, are interested in a constitutional amendment that would provide for direct election of members of the upper chamber.

THE LEGISLATIVE PROCESS

The legislative process, especially in the Duma, is remarkably similar to the process developed in the union-level and Russian parliaments just before and during the transition years. As in the past, the process reflects an emphasis on the resolution of conflicts before legislation is considered on the floor. The process is outlined in Table 3. The major difference between the two chambers is that the Chairman of the Council of the Federation assumes most of the duties that are handled in the Duma by the Council of Duma.

TABLE 3

THE STANDARD LEGISLATIVE PROCESS IN THE STATE DUMA

1. Initiation and Consideration by the Council of the Duma
2. Referral to committee/ committees for preparation
3. Council of the Duma schedules bill for first reading
4. First Reading: Bill approved as basis for further work and returned to committee/committees
5. Committee receives and considers amendments to legislation; forms working group to develop revised version
6. Committee approves committee version of bills, prepares table of amendments recommended for approval and for rejection by chamber. Solicits conclusions of government.
7. Refers report to Council of Duma for scheduling on Chamber calendar
8. Council of the Duma schedules bill for second reading
9. Second reading: debate and votes on amendments and bill
10. Legal staff reviews text and copy is sent to Council of the Federation
11. Council of the Duma schedules third reading
12. Third reading: vote on bill, as amended
13. Law sent to Council of the Federation

The right to initiate legislation (that is, to introduce legislation in the Duma) is granted by the constitution to the president, the government, the legislative bodies of the regions, and the Council of the Federation and its members, as well as members of the Duma. At the time of writing, the right has been exercised mainly by the president, the government, and Duma deputies. Once introduced, legislation is referred to a committee by the Council of the Duma. The council may assign it to more than one committee, identifying a lead committee that is responsible for working with the other committee or committees. The committee prepares the bill for its first reading. When the committee considers the bill ready, the Council of the Duma schedules it for first reading. If the bill is approved on the first reading, it is returned to the committee or committees, which then consider amendments in preparation for a second reading.

It is important to note that deputies submit their proposed amendments immediately following the first reading. This allows the committee or committees handling the legislation to consider and report views on all amendments that the Duma will consider. Because amendments are disclosed at this early point in the process, bill opponents' options are more limited than they are in many legislatures.

The committee considers the amendments that have been submitted and the recommendations of outside experts. After preparing a report on the legislation, the committee in charge of the legislation brings the bill back to the Council of the Duma, which decides whether the legislation is ready to be scheduled for floor action. The council may choose to send the bill back to committee or to proceed to place it on the floor agenda for a second reading. The likelihood of majority support for the legislation appears to be an important factor influencing council members. Nevertheless, the council sometimes engenders the resentment of a committee chair in performing this agenda-setting function – recall that faction leaders but not committee chairs are voting members of the council. If the council decides to bring the measure to the floor, it also decides what amendments will be considered on the floor. Other amendments may, however, be introduced on the floor; no special rules are used which restrict members' rights to offer amendments.

The daily agenda proposed by the Council of the Duma is subject to amendment and vote on the floor. Debates over the agenda begin each day's session and often are the occasion for complaints about what is and is not brought to the floor. Members may offer amendments to the agenda, often in the form of a motion that a particular bill or topical issue be considered. The agenda debate usually lasts one hour. Once the agenda is approved, debate on the legislation proceeds as provided by the chamber's Standing Rules.

Consideration of amendments is stacked in favour of the committee's position under the rules. Before voting on individual amendments, the Duma first decides on one vote whether the committee's recommendation to reject certain amendments should be accepted. Only if this motion is defeated are the individual amendments opposed by the committee subject to a vote.

The Duma operates under a rule that a majority of all deputies (226 votes whether or not all seats are filled) is required to adopt a motion. The Council of the Federation adopted a rule favoured by Yeltsin (who wanted to make it difficult for parliament to act): a majority of the total number of seats in the chamber, 90 of 178, are required for a motion to pass. Because majorities in neither chamber are based on the number of deputies actually voting, a great deal of non-voting occurs among deputies who are present and would otherwise vote against a motion. (Establishing a high participation rating does not interest Russian deputies.) Low attendance in the Duma has been the subject of many complaints and suggested revisions of the Standing Rules.

Third reading is generally considered a *pro forma* action, although the 1994 budget was rejected at third reading on the first attempt. After adoption at third reading, a measure goes to the Council of the Federation.

The legislative process of the Council of the Federation is similar to the Duma's process, so we will not describe it here.

The rules permit repeated voting on the same motion. Often when a measure fails by a few votes of the required majority, the chairman calls upon members to take their seats and vote again. Passage of the 1995 budget bill on the first reading only succeeded, for example, on the thirteenth round of voting.

Methods of resolving differences between the two houses are not much different from those in other bicameral systems. If the Council of the Federation rejects a Duma-passed measure, the chambers may form a conciliation commission to work on compromise legislation. The work of the conciliation commission must be approved by both houses. However, if the Duma accepts the Council of the Federation's recommendations for changing a measure that the Duma passed originally, the Duma's actions are reviewed by the appropriate committee of the Council of the Federation and, if it finds the Duma's actions wholly consistent with the council's recommendations, it may so report to the Chairman of the Council of the Federation and the legislation is considered approved by the council.

The Duma demonstrated its ability to devise procedures for special purposes at an early stage. In the spring of 1994, the Duma adopted a resolution providing for a more elaborate procedure for considering the government budget than is provided in the constitution and the chamber's Standing Rules. The special budget procedures, which were not copied by the Council of the Federation, were designed to expedite consideration and avoid unnecessary delays in bringing the budget proposal to a vote, while also preserving enough time for adequate study and revision of the government's proposal.

This process had several key features. First, it was designed to move from a decision about aggregate budget numbers (the basic characteristics – total revenues, revenues from each of the subjects of the Federation, total spending, spending in broad categories) at the first reading to decisions on budget details at the second reading and thus to insulate the agreed totals against subsequent upward revision. Second, the Budget Committee was given the basic responsibility for setting general budget policy, while the committees with relevant jurisdictions could alter the details of the individual articles comprising the final document. Third, the Budget Committee and the Council of the Duma shared co-ordinating responsibilities – the Budget Committee on the substance of the budget and amendments and the Council of the Duma on scheduling. And, fourth, the full Duma could check the recommendations of the committees at three separate stages in the process – at first reading, when the Budget Committee reported its recommendations to the floor, and during debate on individual articles.

In practice, the Council of the Duma proved more pivotal to the 1994 budget process than the outline of the process suggests. At a few key points, the ability of Chairman Rybkin to bring together faction leaders in the Council of the Duma appeared to prevent stalemate over the budget. The 1994 budget experience indicates the willingness of the Duma to adopt specialised legislative procedures and use the Council of the Duma to overcome political obstacles to the enactment of a budget.

For the 1995 budget, the Duma enacted a different procedure, only to improvise again when the government presented its draft budget. Rather than accepting or rejecting the government proposal, the Duma voted to take it 'under advisement' and to form a reconciliation commission comprising government and Duma representatives to prepare the bill for the first reading. The commission's report then narrowly passed on a first reading and was returned to the government with instructions to present a new budget bill based on it.

CONCLUSION

As Table 4 shows, in the course of its first year of existence, the State Duma considered 211 draft laws, of which just over half had been submitted by deputies themselves and just under half by the government and president. Of these, the Duma had rejected 39 and the president another 15; 84 were enacted, but of these 84 laws 33 were acts ratifying international treaties, 16 more were measures with a temporary effect, such as laws authorising government spending for a quarter in the absence of a budget law, and 17 were sets of amendments to existing law, such as the criminal code. Only 14 were new federal laws; one, a new civil code, was generally considered a major achievement. Another 50 draft laws had passed a first reading and were on the agenda for 1995. The Duma's workload meanwhile was expanding rapidly. At the beginning of the 1995 session, the first deputy Chairman of the Duma, Mikhail Mitiukov, reported that some 438 pieces of draft legislation were expected to be proposed to the Duma in calendar year 1995. He expected, however, that only 67 would reach their third reading while the rest would still be under development. Moreover, he anticipated that about 80 per cent of the year's legislative agenda would be dealt with in the January–July session since the autumn would be taken up with the election campaign. The figures suggest that the Duma's ability to handle its legislative workload is limited, but growing: the Duma passed nearly as many laws in the October–December session as it had in the entire January–July session.[21]

The Duma's work is not confined to passing laws, of course. During 1994 it held 100 committee hearings. It had been in session 78 days of the year, and had considered a total of 626 matters. Thus only a few of the issues coming to the floor were directly related to laws. The Duma passed 41 resolutions (*postanovleniia*), which are legal acts of narrower scope than laws, and it had adopted 34 interpellations directed to government as well as 20 petitions and declarations.

Thus, although the legislative record was quite modest, the Duma, under the direction of the Council of the Duma, was able to moderate conflict and find a basis for agreement on a few divisive, complex issues. And the president was willing to accept these decisions even when he was clearly opposed to the result. But the existence of numerous veto points in the legislative process, together with the deep political divisions among deputies, impeded the Duma's ability to act on the severe social and economic problems facing the country. Moreover, the inattention of many members of the Council of the Federation to its work undermined confidence in its prospects as a full partner in policy making. Perhaps most important, the Federal Assembly's slowness to act gave the president an excuse to promulgate new decrees, some representing radical reform measures that stimulated loud protests from opposition deputies.

In most respects, the houses of the Federal Assembly have developed structures and procedures consistent with our expectations. The difference in the electoral systems used for electing deputies to the two houses, along with the distribution of partisans and policy preferences that emerged from the election, had significant and direct effects on the character of the parliamentary parties or factions and their role in the policy-making process. As expected, the Duma has become a far more party-oriented legislative body than the Council of the Federation. Yet, both houses, under the continuing pressures of an unstable political environment and heavy workload, adopted systems of committees and working groups, with some notable and predictable differences, that continue the practices of the past. And the two houses dropped the long-established Russian parliamentary institution of the presidium, although they found different substitute mechanisms. The Duma created a party-based executive committee to handle agenda setting and co-ordination functions and handed control over the administrative operations of the body to a separate committee. The Council of the Federation simply turned these responsibilities over to an elected chair.

Nevertheless, the new Russian Parliament appears to have overcome some of the problems that plagued its predecessor. So far, all parties have demonstrated a willingness to operate under the terms of the constitution and the standing rules of the two Houses of Parliament. Indeed, civil and even co-operative behaviour among deputies of opposite factions can be found on many committees and working groups. And many of the structural and procedural choices of the two houses appear to have established a good foundation for a the development of an effective policy-making role for the Federal Assembly.

TABLE 4

STATE DUMA LEGISLATIVE RECORD FOR 1994 (11 JANUARY– 23 DECEMBER 1994)

Total draft laws considered: 211

By whom introduced:
President   47
Government   46
Members of Duma   111
Constitutional Court   2
Supreme Court   1
Supreme Arbitration Court   3
Regional legislatures   1

Disposition of the 211 draft laws considered by Duma:
Passed by Duma: 116
Passed in 1st reading: 50
Passed in 2nd reading: 6
Rejected: 39

Presidential and Council of Federation action on 116 laws passed:
Signed into law: 84
Rejected: 15
Under consideration: 17

Nature of the 84 laws enacted:
Constitutional law: 1
New federal laws or codes: 14
Amendments to existing law: 17
Confirmation and implementation
  of a code: 1
Temporary acts (e.g. quarterly
  budget law):   16
Foreign treaty ratification: 33
Benefits for families of deceased
Duma members: 2

Other Duma activity:
Resolutions (*postanovleniia*):   41
Declarations (*zaiavleniia*):   12
Petitions (*obrashcheniia*):   8
Interpellations (*zaprosy*):   34
Hearings: 100

TABLE 5
SOCIAL AND POLITICAL COMPOSITION OF USSR AND RUSSIAN DEPUTIES, SELECTED LEVELS (IN %)

	Communist Party members	Manual Workers	Women
1. USSR Supreme Soviet (1970) (N = 1500)	72.3	31.7	30.5
2. USSR local soviets (1971) (N = 2 mln.)	44.5	36.5	45.8
3. USSR Supreme Soviet (1984) (N = 1500)	71.5	35.2	32.8
4. Russian Republic Supreme Soviet (1985) (N = 975)	66.6	35.8	35.3
5. USSR Congress of People's Deputies (1989) (N = 2250)	87.6	18.6	17.1
6. USSR Supreme Soviet (1989) (N = 542)	87.8	24.7	18.4
7. Russian Republic Congress of People's Deputies (1990) (N =1068)	86.3	5.9	5.4
8. Local Russian Republic soviets (1990) (N = 702,268)	49.1	24.9	35.0
9. State Duma of the Federal Assembly (December 1993) (N = 450)	10.0[a]	1.3	13.5

Note: Because categories overlap, figures add up to more than 100% in some rows.
a Figure refers to membership in the party faction of the Communist Party of the Russian Federation within the State Duma.

NOTES

1. Our account is based upon extensive interviews with deputies, staff and close observers of the Federal Assembly, along with study of the parliament's official documents and journalistic accounts. Most of the interviews were conducted on a not-for-attribution basis, so we do not cite participants by name except where they are quoted from published accounts. We have chosen not to cite anonymous interviewees because to do so would require great repetition with no useful information imparted to the reader.
2. On the pre-1990 Supreme Soviet, see G. Chiesa, with D.T. Northrop, *Transition to Democracy: Political Change in the Soviet Union, 1987–1991* (Hanover, University Press of New England, 1993); S. Minagawa, *Supreme Soviet Organs* (Nagoya, Japan, University of Nagoya Press, 1985); and P. Vanneman, *The Supreme Soviet: Politics and the Legislative Process in the Soviet Political System* (Durham, NC: Duke University Press, 1977). On the union-level reforms of the Gorbachev era, see T.F. Remington, 'Menage a Trois: The End of Soviet Parliamentarism', paper presented to Annual Meeting of American Association for the Advancement of Slavic Studies, Honolulu, November 1993; B. Kiernan, *The End of Soviet Politics: Elections, Legislatures and the Demise of the Communist Party* (Boulder, Westview Press, 1993); B. Kiernan and J. Aistrup, 'The 1989 Elections to the Congress of People's Deputies in Moscow', *Soviet Studies*, 43 (1991), pp.1049–64; M. McFaul and S. Markov, *The Troubled Birth of Russian Democracy: Parties, Personalities, and Programs* (Stanford: Hoover Institution Press, 1993); M. McFaul, *Post-Communist Politics* (Washington, DC: Center for Strategic and International Studies, 1993); R.T. Huber and D.R. Kelley (eds.), *Perestroika-Era Politics: The New Soviet Legislature and Gorbachev's*

Political Reforms (Armonk, NY: M.E. Sharpe, 1991); and V. Tolz, *The USSR's Emerging Multiparty System* (Washington, DC: Center for Strategic and International Studies, 1990). On the Russian Supreme Soviet during the 1990–1993 period, see T.F. Remington, E. Davidheiser and S.S. Smith, 'The Early Legislative Process in the Russian Supreme Soviet', paper presented at the annual meeting of the Southern Political Science Association, Atlanta, 5–7 Nov. 1992. Also see Y.M. Brudny, 'The Dynamics of Democratic Russia, 1990–1993', *Post-Soviet Affairs*, 9 (1993), pp.141–70. Also see P. Roeder, 'Varieties of Post-Soviet Authoritarian Regimes', *Post-Soviet Affairs*, 10 (1994), pp.61–101.

3. The deputies were selected from two types of districts: 900 geographically compact 'territorial' districts of equal size and 168 'national-territorial' districts that provided more representation to minority ethnic groups living in ethnic-administrative territories.

4. See T.F. Remington, S.S. Smith, D.R. Kiewiet and M. Haspel, 'Transitional Institutions and parliamentary Alignments in Russia, 1990–1993', in T.F. Remington (ed.), *Parliaments in Transition: The New Legislative Politics in the Former USSR and Eastern Europe* (Boulder: Westview, 1994), pp.159–80; and A. Sobyanin, 'Political Cleavages among the Russian Deputies', in Remington (ed.), *Parliaments in Transition*, pp.181–215.

5. On elections and regime change, see V. Bogdanor, 'Founding Elections and Regime Change', *Electoral Studies*, 9 (1990), pp.288–94; and H. Kitschelt, 'The Formation of Party Systems in East Central Europe', *Politics and Society* 20 (1992), pp.7–50.

6. Soon after the election, serious doubts about the validity of the reported results were raised in the Russian press by a team of political analysts headed by Alexander Sobyanin and were subsequently given wide publicity by a variety of political groups. The Duma officially approved the formation of a commission to investigate the validity of the charges. If Sobyanin's charges are correct, actual turnout was only 46 per cent, not enough to carry the new constitution. It is very difficult for outside observers to judge the validity of the charges because the central electoral commission has so far refused to allow independent observers access to the vote results or to publish a full tally of the results. Summaries of these charges were published in several articles in the Russian press. See, *inter alia*, V. Vyzhutovich, 'Tsentrizbirkom prevrashchaetsia v politicheskoe vedomstvo', *Izvestiia*, 4 May 1994; and Alexander Sobyanin and V. Sukhovol'skii, 'V korolevstve krivykh zerkal', *Segodnia*, 10 March 1994.

7. The joint responsibility of the President and parliament over the government puts Russia's system in the presidential-parliamentary category in the scheme defined by M.S. Shugart and J.M. Carey, *Presidents and Assemblies: Constitutional Design and Electoral Dynamics* (New York: Cambridge University Press, 1992). The French Fifth Republic system, in contrast, is considered a premier-presidential system in the Shugart–Carey scheme.

8. The constitution assigns certain responsibilities exclusively to the Council of the Federation, including approval of the use of Russian military forces outside the Russian Federation and confirmation of presidential appointees to high courts. In addition to confidence votes, the unique jurisdiction of the Duma includes confirmation of the president's nominee for prime minister.

9. Here and elsewhere, we use the term party to simplify an already complicated set of distinctions between types of political organisations. The electoral law provided that registered 'electoral associations' (*izbiratel'noe ob'edinenie*) that met a certain threshold of signatures could both nominate candidates in single-member districts and run candidates on party lists. Some of the electoral associations that ran candidates in the 1993 elections did constitute themselves as parties, while others, such as Yabloko, constituted themselves as 'blocs', and still others as 'movements'. For simplicity, we shall refer to all electoral associations as parties.

10. Elections were not held in Tartarstan and Chechenia in December 1993, and an insufficient number of candidates running invalidated the Council of the Federation election in Cheliabinsk. Consequently, a total of 444 seats in the Duma and 171 seats of the Council of the Federation were filled when the Federal Assembly convened in January. Tartarstan and the Cheliabinsk held elections later in the spring of 1994. The Central Electoral Commission refused to publish a full tally of election results, providing a list only of what it declared were the elected deputies, so the exact vote totals for party candidates in single-member district

races remain unknown, at least officially.

11. G. Belonuchkin (comp.), 'Federal'noe sobranie: Spravochnik' (Moscow: Panorama, 18 April 1994).

12. On east European electoral systems and parliaments, see J. McGregor, 'How Electoral Laws Shape Eastern Europe's Parliaments', *RFE/RL Research Report* 2 (1993), pp.11–18. Also see D. Nohlen, 'Changes and Choices in Electoral Systems', in A. Lijphart and B. Grofman (eds.), *Choosing an Electoral System: Issues and Alternatives* (New York: Praeger, 1994), pp.217–24; A. Lijphart, 'Constitutional Choices for New Democracies', *Journal of Democracy*, 2 (1991), pp.72–84; A. Lijphart, 'Democracies: Forms, Performance, and Constitutional Engineering', *European Journal of Political Research*, 25 (1994), pp.1–17; A. Lijphart, *Democracies: Patterns of Majoritarian and Consensus Government in Twenty-One Countries* (New Haven; Yale University Press, 1984); A. Lijphart, 'Democratization and Constitutional Choices in Czecho-slovakia, Hungary and Poland, 1989–91', *Journal of Theoretical Politics* 4 (1992), pp.207–23; A. Lijphart, *Parliamentary versus Presidential Government* (Oxford: Oxford University Press, 1992); A. Lijphart, 'The Political Consequences of Electoral Laws, 1945–85', *American Political Science Review*, 84 (1990), pp.481–96, and D.M. Olson, 'Political Parties and Party Systems in Regime Transformation: Inner Transition in the New Democracies of Central Europe', *American Review of Politics*, 14 (1993), pp.619–58; and T.F. Remington, 'Introduction: Parliamentary Elections and the Transition from Communism', in T.F. Remington (ed.), *Parliaments in Transition*, pp.1–27; and A. Stepan and C. Skach, 'Constitutional Frameworks and Democratic Consolidation: Parliamentarism versus Presidentialism', *World Politics* 46 (1993), pp.1–22. Also see M. Urban, 'December 1993 as a Replication of Late-Soviet Electoral Practices', *Post-Soviet Affairs*, 10 (April/June 1994), pp.127–58; and M.A. Weigle, 'Political Participation and Party Formation in Russia, 1985–1992: Institutionalizing Democracy?', *The Russian Review*, 53 (1994), pp.240–70.

13. Committee chairs were given the right of participation in the Council of the Duma, although without a vote.

14. The independent factions are New Regional Policy, with a heavy representation of state enterprise directors; Russia's Way, a group with a strongly nationalist and Communist bent; and the Union of December 12. The last had a predominantly reformist outlook and was close to Russia's Choice on substantive policy questions, but sought to establish a separate political identity for its members, most of whom were young, professional and concerned with maintaining strong district ties. By mid-1994, only seven deputies chose not to affiliate with a faction.

15. By the same token, it gave a strategic advantage to the representatives of the small parties in ensuring a hearing for their preferred issues.

16. The rule's most ardent defender was Zhirinovsky, who clearly intended to use it to strengthen his personal control over his party in the face of strains and defections among his followers. Interviews indicated that many deputies who were initially favourable to the rule were persuaded by Zhirinovsky's behaviour at the founding congress of his party – when he was elected 'leader for life' and the party agreed not to hold another congress for ten years – that the imperative mandate would give Zhirinovsky a disproportionate advantage in building a personal power base.

17. For example, three committees have direct responsibility for economic policy: the Committee on Budget, Taxes, Banks, and Finances, the Committee on Economic Policy, and the Committee on Property, Privatization and Economic Activity, which are chaired by deputies from different factions.

18. In the bidding process, factions checked each other's excesses by naming more or less radical deputies to the committee posts. If one of the reformist factions proposed a relatively radical figure as their choice for a particular committee, the opposition factions would propose a similarly hard-line figure for one of their preferred committees, and when the reformers proposed a moderate, so did the opposition camp. The Agrarians, who most observers agree operate more as a single-issue lobby than as a party, are worth special note. They concentrated their chips on the agricultural committee, over which it acquired overwhelming control (the chairman, first deputy chairman, and 19 more of the 26 members are from the

Agrarian faction). Consequently, few other leadership positions in the Duma were acquired by Agrarian Party members.

19. Zhirinovsky had demanded that he be given the fourth deputy chairmanship. Other factions, including the Communists and Agrarians resisted his demand, but had not been able to agree on an alternative candidate until June 1994.

20. Members have also increased their autonomy of the executive branch by passing an amendment to the Law on Status of the Deputy under which no deputy of the Council of the Federation can be removed from his job without the consent of the chamber. Since the largest share of members are chiefs of regional administrations in the subjects of the federation, most of them appointed by the president, this provision reduces their personal dependence on Yeltsin and thus reduces his leverage over them.

21. The figures on the Duma's record for 1994 and plans for 1995 are drawn from *Rossiiskaia Gazeta*, 26 July 1994; a report from the staff of the Duma distributed to deputies at the start of the new session in January 1995 ('Informatsiia rabote Gosudarstvennoi Dumy v 1994 (s 11 ianvaria po 23 dekabria)'; and the newspaper *Segodnia*, 14 Jan. 1994.

Institutional Development of the Parliament of Estonia

PEET KASK

The paper describes institutional development of the Estonian Parliament after the first elections in March 1990. A peak of institutional changes occurred during the first few months after the elections, often through painful learning from errors but often simply by copying institutions of developed democratic countries. A high quantity of new legislation has been demanded from the parliament, especially after Estonia restored its status as an independent state in August 1991. A second peak of institutional changes is related to the adoption of the new Constitution in June 1992.

A very important moment of the post-Communist transition is the first free parliamentary elections. Estonia had this opportunity on 18 March 1990 when still part of the Soviet Union. For Estonians, the elected Supreme Council achieved a place in history mainly for its achievements in helping to restore independence. (Independence was internationally recognised in August–September 1991.) Although the transition to democracy has been of somewhat lower emotional attraction to the public than the transition to independence, the development of the parliament itself is an immensely important element in the sequence of events of the post-Communist transition.

The sequence of the basic events in the transition is as follows: (1) liberalisation (in the Soviet Union); (2) founding of mass movements wanting regime change; (3) drafting and adoption of the election law; (4) the first elections creating the body of the parliament; (5) institutional development of the parliament: its rules of procedures, parliamentary parties, committees and speaker; (6) creation and development of political institutions outside the parliament: establishing parties, drafting and adopting the constitution; and (7) the second elections.

The main focus of the present study is the fifth of the seven elements listed above, but the other elements are discussed also, as far as they are related to the development of the parliament. The present paper relates to four different legislative assemblies in Estonia. The legislative body of the Soviet Estonia was *Ülemnõukogu* – the Supreme Soviet. After the 1990

Peet Kask is an adviser to the State Assembly of the Republic of Estonia. The author would like to acknowledge helpful discussions with Professor Seweryn Bialer at Columbia University, New York.

elections the legislative assembly was still called *Ülemnõukogu*, but was customarily translated into English as the Supreme Council. Only when a new parliament was elected in September 1992 (a year after state independence was restored), was its name changed to *Riigikogu* – the State Assembly. In the present paper, the Constitutional Assembly is also mentioned. It was distinct from the Supreme Council, existing in parallel with the latter from September 1991 until June 1992.

The parliament elected in 1990 did not occupy a void. The former Supreme Soviet had existed with its institutions, which had been very different from those of the democratic world. Still, many institutions were simply taken over from the Soviet era. During the subsequent evolution, many of them had to be abolished or transformed, and many completely new institutions had to be created.

In the following few paragraphs, external factors determining the development of the parliament, such as the party system, the electoral system, and the constitutional system, are briefly described. Thereafter we shall turn our attention directly to institutions of the parliament.

THE PARTY SYSTEM

Movements and the First Elections

Table 1 lists the movements which most shaped the political atmosphere before the 1990 elections. It is interesting to note that the Communist Party, being seriously divided on ethnic lines by the question of state independence, was a relatively inactive organisation in the election campaign. Its prominent members ran under other umbrellas, mostly under the Free Estonia movement or the United Soviet of Working Collectives. What remained of the Communist Party renamed itself on 28 December 1992, becoming the Estonian Democratic Labour Party.

Nobody was strong enough to win a clear majority in the parliament. In fact, the elections were essentially a referendum on independence, and the system of pro-independence movements was an omnifarious mosaic which hardly helped voters to draw a distinction between various pro-independence candidates. A number of candidates were supported by more than one movement (sometimes even against their will). In addition to this, party or movement labels did not appear on the ballots. No official data on the electoral success of different movements were issued. Perhaps the most adequate description of the electoral success comes through investigating the parliamentary parties formed after the elections.

TABLE 1
MOVEMENTS 1987–90

Movement name	When founded (*de facto*)	Typical activists (subjective description)	Typical activities (subjective description)
Popular Front	Apr. 1988	Intellectuals in their forties; various	Pro-democracy mass meetings with speeches and songs; electoral activities
Green Movement	May 1988	'Greens'	Anti-pollution and anti-Soviet Army activities
Intermovement	Spring 1988	Russian speakers afraid of changes	Mass meetings with red flags
United Soviet of Working Collectives	Nov. 1988	Russian speaking industrial nomenklatura	Anti-independence strikes; electoral activities
Citizens Committees	Feb. 1989	Radical Estonian nationalists	Registration of citizens of 1940 Estonia; elections to the Congress of Estonia
Land Union	May 1989 (as a movement)	Agricultural nomenklatura	Electoral activities
Free Estonia	Jan. 1990	Pro-independence nomenklatura	Electoral activities

Parties

Table 2 presents official data on the parliamentary election results of 20 September 1992. The four most successful lists of candidates were electoral coalitions of two or more parties. Movements had lost their importance; in fact, the third most successful list used only the name of the former most powerful movement but this trick produced little if any positive gain. Table 3 lists parties who have seats in the parliament or have achieved substantial electoral support. Most of them grew out of the former movements.

As a rule, parties are best known by their leader's name. Parties are small: the largest is the Centre Party with slightly over 1,000 members. Being a party member is not popular. This attitude is felt even among the members of the parliament: many members of parliamentary factions do not recognise themselves as members of respective parties. Most of the parties prefer synonyms of the word '*partei*' (party) in their name: '*erakond*' (= '*partei*') or '*liit*' (union, league).[1]

TABLE 2

PARLIAMENTARY ELECTION RESULTS, 20 SEPTEMBER 1992

Electoral parties or coalitions	Percentage of votes	Number of seats
Fatherland	22.00	29
Secure Home	13.60	17
Popular Front	12.25	15
Moderates	9.73	12
Estonian National Independence Party	8.79	10
Independent Royalists	7.12	8
Estonian Citizen	6.89	8
Greens	2.62	1
Entrepreneurs Party	2.39	1
The other lists and all independent candidates	14.6	10
Total	100.0	101

TABLE 3

PARTIES REPRESENTED IN THE STATE ASSEMBLY OR HAVING SUBSTANTIAL ELECTORAL SUPPORT

Party name	When founded (*de facto*)	Relation to former parties and movements	Number of seats (in Oct. 1994)	Electoral support (in Nov. 1994 EMOR data)
National Independence Party	Jan 1988	MRP-AEF	8	3
Royalists	Sep 1989	Popular Front	8	3
Rural Centre Party	Jan 1990	Popular Front	5	3
Liberal Democratic Party	Mar 1990	Popular Front	6	3
Entrepreneurs Party	Mar 1990	-	1	1
Social Democratic Party	Sept 1990	Founded as a coalition of smaller social democratic parties; Popular front	5	1
Land Union (as a party)	Mar 1991	Land Union (as a movement)	8	3
Centre Party	Oct 1991	Nucleus of the Popular Front	11	10
Coalition Party	Oct 1991	Free Estonia	8	13
Fatherland	Nov 1992	Founded as a coalition of smaller parties; Citizens Committees	12	6
Citizens League (a movement)	Nov 1992	-	2	3
People's Party of Republicans and Conservatives	Jun 1994	Founded as a splitter party of Fatherland	10	3
Rural People's Party	Sep 1994	-	0	17

THE ELECTORAL SYSTEM

The election law for the March 1990 Supreme Council elections was prepared and adopted in 1989 when the pro-reform leadership of the Communist Party (CP) controlled the Supreme Council. The ideological leader of the CP, Mikk Titma, who carefully controlled the drafting and ordered changes whenever he found it necessary. The drafters themselves were influenced by American-Estonian Rein Taagepera, a specialist on electoral systems. His book on the matter was published in 1989.[2]

The original proposal by the drafting group was the open list proportional representation system (similar to the Finnish law). However, the CP leaders would lose votes if they ran under the CP label. After negotiations between the CP and the drafting group a compromise was achieved on the single transferable vote (as used in Ireland and Malta). The constituency magnitude varied between one and five seats. At the last moment before adopting the law, the Communists amended the draft law by inserting a clause requiring candidates to run in their home district. It hurt the Popular Front because most of their prominent leaders lived in Tallinn or Tartu.

The Election Law of 1989 was written when the Constitution of the Soviet Union was still in effect. It was not applicable later without major changes. However, different parties had different and contradictory wishes on the new electoral system. A compromise was reached in April 1992 but it looked awfully complicated. The electoral system has elements from both the open and the closed list systems. (Within the open list, candidates are selected for seats according to the number of votes they personally received, while within the closed list, candidates are selected for seats by their party.) The voter votes for a single candidate who usually stands in a party's list. A portion of the seats is allocated in the territorial constituencies by the open list formula, but the remainder (in fact, majority) of the seats are allocated as compensatory seats through cross-country closed lists. The five per cent threshold is valid for any list, except if a candidate has personally collected a simple quota in which he or she is elected. The electoral system puts great power into the hands of the party leaders because the great majority of the seats are won by those who stand high in their party's closed list. In 1992 the most successful independent candidate had 5,007 votes (0.949 quotas) but was not elected, while three candidates were elected through party lists with less than 100 personal votes. According to an amendment of June 1994, candidates with less than 0.1 simple quota are not qualified for the distribution of seats in territorial constituencies.

CONSTITUTIONAL CHANGES

Within a few weeks of the elections the Supreme Council restored the name, the flag and the coat-of-arms of the Republic of Estonia, and the legislation of Estonia was separated from that of the Soviet Union. In August 1990, the Supreme Council stated that 'the ordering of the affairs of life does not follow the Constitution of the Estonian SSR any more'.

However, in reality rules did not change so quickly. Independence came in August 1991, and the state power was considerably restructured only after a new constitution was worked out and adopted in June 1992. Still, there were some constitutional changes which were carried out before June 1992 by the Supreme Council itself. For example, in November 1991 new rules on government formation and no-confidence vote were adopted. According to the old rules, each minister was approved or dismissed by a separate secret vote. Under the new rules, the government is approved by a single open vote of simple majority and dismissed by the absolute majority rule. The Constitution of 28 June 1992 was a great step towards a consistent law, and a clear choice in favour of a parliamentary system.

THE PARLIAMENT: DEVELOPMENT OF THE LEGAL RULES

When the members of the first post-Communist parliament in Estonia came to its first session in March 1990, most of them knew very little either about the rules and regulations of parliamentary procedures or their importance.

From 29 March until 28 June 1990, the Supreme Council followed the Temporary Working Regulations prepared by the presidium of its predecessor, with some minor amendments. The draft had obviously been prepared with good intentions, but the drafters had got their experience under other circumstances. By mid-May the problems related to the management and rules of the parliamentary process had become obvious to all members. For example, each week began with wasting an hour or two of the plenary session on setting the agenda for the week. The plenary discussions on drafts of laws and resolutions also resembled a great but unproductive drafting group because the committees responsible for preparing materials for the floor were not given time for their meetings. Negotiations between the parliamentary party leaders led nowhere or produced valueless agreements – as one could expect in conditions when most of the MPs were members of two different parliamentary parties at the same time. Voting rules on 'proposals' (on moves or amendments) were irrational, for they had been designed to express unanimity of the people (and suppress dissent) but not to avoid deadlock in decision making.

On 28 May 1990, the Supreme Council created a seven-member drafting group to prepare new Standing Orders. Their draft produced a lot of discussion and so many amendments were proposed that the speaker, who was afraid of possible procedural deadlock, asked MPs to agree with the committee's decisions and not to demand votes on the floor. The MPs co-operated with him and so the Standing Orders of the Supreme Council (*Ülemnõukogu Reglement*) were adopted on the last day before the summer holidays.

THE MEMBERS

In 1988, when many political movements were created, artists, writers and scientists were the most active people in politics. When they were elected to the parliament, many of them told their colleagues that they would leave politics as soon as independence was achieved. There was a noticeable lack of lawyers and economists in the Supreme Council.

The MPs' prestige was high straight after the elections, but declined gradually as the real consequences of the changes turned out to be very different from the high expectations of the people. By the end of 1991 it had become customary for humorists to make mocking jokes about Members of Parliament. The long-run dynamics are well expressed by the support index for the parliament measured by EMOR polls (percentage of supporters minus that of opponents), see Table 4.

TABLE 4
SUPPORT INDEX TO THE PARLIAMENT (EMOR POLLS DATA)

Time	Mar 90[1]	Aug 90	Sep 90	Oct 90	Nov 90	Dec 90	Jan 91[2]
Support index	–	56	–	43	51	54	84
Time	Feb 91	Mar 91	Apr 91	May 91	Jun 91	Jul 91	Aug 91
Support index	75	48	45	38	24	–	–
Time	Sep 91[3]	Oct 91	Nov 91	Dec 91	Jan 92	Feb 92	Mar 92
Support index	58	27	37	22	-7	-23	-16
Time	Apr 92	May 92	Jun 92	Jul 92	Aug 92	Sep 92[4]	Oct 92
Support index	-9	-21	-17	–	-39	–	–
Time	Nov 92	Dec 92	Jan 93	Feb 93	Mar 93	Apr 93	May 93
Support index	-10	-32	-30	-20	-15	-28	-2
Time	Jun 93	Jul 93	Aug 93	Sep 93	Oct 93	Nov 93	Dec 93
Support index	-8	–	-6	-10	-11	-19	-14
Time	Jan 94	Feb 94	Mar 94	Apr 94	May 94	Jun 94	Jul 94
Support index	-12	–	-16	-22	-23	-16	–
Time	Aug 94	Sep 94	Oct 94	Nov 94			
Support index	-15	-15	-28	-20			

Notes:
1. In March 1990 – elections to the Supreme Council. Support index was not measured before August 1990, but was obviously very high.
2. In January 1991 – the Soviet Union military attacks in Vilnius and Riga.
3. In August and September 1991 – the state independence was widely recognised.
4. In September 1992 – elections to the State Assembly.

In September 1992 40 out of 105 members of the Supreme Council ran for a seat in the new parliament and only 20 were re-elected. Table 5 represents groups of members of the State Assembly according to their previous profession.

TABLE 5

PREVIOUS PROFESSION OF THE MEMBERS OF THE STATE ASSEMBLY ELECTED IN 1992

Previous profession	Number
Journalists, writers, architects, artists, musicians	25
Historians, philosophers, philologists	13
Lawyers, political scientists, sociologists	13
Specialists in economies and banking	12
Engineers	9
Specialist on agriculture	7
Natural science specialities	7
Pastors	3
Physicians	3
Others	9

PARLIAMENTARY PARTIES (FACTIONS)

According to the Temporary Working Regulations adopted on 2 April 1990, every member of the Supreme Council could be a member of up to two parliamentary groups at a time. The idea of the designers of the rule was to allow members of party groups to participate in some other groups, formed, for example, on a territorial basis.

The outcome of this rule was total confusion, however. Some members were independent of groups while some others belonged to a single group or two different groups. Leaders of all groups wanted to participate in inter-group negotiations, but negotiations could not succeed as there were too many leaders and most if not all of them could represent only their personal opinion. The Standing Orders adopted in June 1990 allowed any person to be a member of a single faction only.

In April 1990 the government was formed without any formal agreement between parliamentary parties. In the long run it turned out to be a minority government supported mostly (but not always) by the Popular Front parliamentary caucus. Party discipline was regarded in a negative light. Factions had nearly the lowest legal status one can imagine. Leaders of factions got no extra payment. Factions got no equipment. Both the presidium and later the Board of the Chairmen of Supreme Council decided not to provide factions with staff either. Seats in the house were allocated in order of constituencies.

After the 1992 elections the situation went to the other extreme. A permanent majority coalition was established prior to the first meeting of

TABLE 6
FACTIONS OF THE SUPREME COUNCIL, 1990–92*

Faction name	When created	Size when created	When disappeared	Relation to movements and parties	Relation to earlier factions (number of members coming over)
People's Centre Faction	Aug. 1990	15	Mar 1992	Popular Front	–
Independent Democrats	Aug. 1990	14	Jan 1992	Free Estonia	–
Social Democrats	Aug. 1990	9	Sept. 1991	Popular Front; Social Democratic (Independence) Party	–
Rural People's Faction	Sept. 1990	7	Apr. 1991	–	–
Rural Centre Faction	Sept.	7	Jan. 1992	Popular Front; Rural Centre Party	–
Liberal Democrats	Aug. 1990	6	June 1991	Popular Front; Liberal Democratic Party	–
Greens	Aug 1990	6	Aug. 1991	Green Movement	–
Christian Democrats	Aug. 1990	6	Jan. 1992	Citizens Committees; Christian Democratic Party	–
Virumaa	Aug. 1990	7	Aug. 1991	–	–
Communist Faction	Sept. 1990	7	Apr. 1991 Apr. 1991	Communist Party of the Soviet Union	–
Co-operation	Sept. 1990	7	Aug. 1991	–	–
For Equal Rights	Sept. 1990	6	Aug. 1991	United Soviet of Working Collectives	–
Republicans	Apr. 1991	6	Sept. 1991	Republican Party	Countryside People's (3)
Land Union	Dec.	6	(continued)	Land Union	Independent Democrats (5)
Union of Agrarian People	Jan. 1992	6	Sept. 1992	Union of Agrarian People	Rural Centre Faction (3)
Fatherland	Jan	14	(continued)	Fatherland electoral coalition	Christian Democrats (5) Liberal Democrats (4)
Centre Faction	Mar 1992	18	(continued)	Popular Front; Peoples Centre Party	Peoples Centre Faction (9) Greens (3)
Moderates	Mar 1992	7	(continued)	Social Democratic Party; Rural Centre Party	Social Democrats (5) Rural Centre Faction (2)
Citizen Reconciliation	Aug. 1991	10	Sept. 1992	–	Viruland (5)
Co-operation and Equal Rights	Sept. 1991	10	Sept. 1992	–	For Equal Rights (5) Communist Faction (4)

Note: * Data from Priit Järve, Estonian Academy of Sciences the State Assembly. It lasted for two years, until October 1994. The opposition was practically excluded from decision making. The voting machinery of the majority coalition was called 'road roller' by the frustrated opposition members. Factions have permanent staff now, and the leadership receives payment. The threshold number of members required to form a faction was established at seven, but was subsequently lowered to six. Privileges of factions do not substantially depend on their size; there is a noticeable tendency to establish small rather than large factions.

TABLE 7

FACTIONS OF THE STATE ASSEMBLY, 1992–(1995)

Faction name	When created	Size when created/Size on 10 Oct. 1994	Relations to parties	Relations to earlier factions
Fatherland	Oct. 1992	30/12	Fatherland; Liberal Democrats until Feb. 1994	Faction existed in the Supreme Council
Centre Faction	Oct. 1992	15/11	Centre Party	Faction existed in the Supreme Council
Moderates	Oct. 1992	12/12	Social Democrats; Rural Centre Party	Faction existed in the Supreme Council
National Independence Party	Oct. 1992	10/8	National Independence Party	–
Coalition Party	Oct. 1992	8/8	Coalition Party	–
Land Union	Oct. 1992	8/8	Land Union	Faction existed in the Supreme Council
Independent Royalists	Oct. 1992	8/8	Royalists	–
Estonian Citizen	Oct. 1992	7/ disappeared	Estonian Citizen League	–
Liberals	Nov. 1993	6/6	Liberal Democrats	Liberal Democrats in the Supreme Council (faction disappeared in June 1991)
Independents	Dec. 1993	6/7	–	National Independence Party (3)
Free Democrats	Apr. 1994	6/6	–	Centre Faction (5)
Rightists	June 1994	9/10	Party of Republicans and Conservatives	Fatherland

Tables 6 and 7 list factions in the Supreme Council and the State Assembly, respectively. The average duration of factions founded in August and September 1990 was 13 months. One can observe that two major rearrangements of factions occurred in the Supreme Council. After Estonia's independence was achieved in August 1991, Russians fully rearranged their factions. Within a short period, from December 1991 until March 1992, four Estonian factions disappeared and five were created, which is related to the fall of the first (Edgar Savisaar's) government in January 1992. In the State Assembly, however, only one faction has disappeared but a lot of them have lost members.

COMMITTEES

The Supreme Council created 12 standing committees (Table 8). Two of them, the Justice Committee and the Budget and Economy Committee were obviously more heavily involved in legislation than the others.

TABLE 8
STANDING COMMITTEES OF THE SUPREME COUNCIL, 1990–92

Committee name	Number of members (8 Nov. 1990)
Justice	14
International Affairs	12
Budget and Economy	11
State Defence	9
Rural Life	9
Social	8
Environment	8
Ethics	8
Journalism	8
Ethnic Relations	7
Science, Education and Culture	6
Public Affairs Reform	6

In April 1990, the committee chairmen were elected by the whole parliament, and the committees' memberships decided through negotiations of the Members of Parliament with the committee chairmen. Many MPs were members of different committees. Initially, there were no regular meeting times allocated to the committees, but whenever the plenary meeting had a break to allow committees to meet, all of them met at the same time. Therefore the committees too often had no decision-making power because of the lack of a quorum. After the Standing Orders reform in June 1990, each MP could be a member of only a single standing committee. Also, the committees got a fixed time for their meetings and power to elect their chairmen. In December 1990 the Supreme Council relaxed the quorum requirement for regular meetings of standing committees from a half to a third. The list of standing committees was changed after the September 1992 elections (Table 9). Legislative bills are now more evenly distributed than previously, but the distribution is still uneven.

TABLE 9
STANDING COMMITTEES OF THE STATE ASSEMBLY, 1992–(1995)

Committee name	Number of bills supervised (5 Oct. 1992 – 1 Sept. 1993)	Number of members/ members of the government coalition (31 Dec. 1993)
Justice	47	9/5
Economy (and Agriculture)	46	11/7
Constitutional Law	39	8/5
Budget and Taxation	23	11/6
Social	18	10/5
International Affairs	14	12/5
Culture	7	11/5
Rural and Regional Policy	3	10/5
Environment	3	5/3
State Defence	2	10/5

THE SPEAKER AND THE BOARD OF CHAIRMEN OF THE PARLIAMENT

Until March 1991 the Supreme Council was managed by its presidium (*Ülemnõukogu Presiidium*), a collective head of state with its own legislative power. In March 1991 the Board of Chairmen (*Juhatus* which is a synonym of *Presiidium*) of the Supreme Council was established separate from the presidium. It consisted of the speaker, the two deputy speakers and the chairmen of all standing committees. The board had to deal with technical problems related to the day-to-day business of the parliament; the presidium had allocated too little time and attention to these problems. The board was chaired by the Speaker of the Parliament.

In plenary meetings the speaker's power is delimited by the Standing Orders. From June 1990, '[t]he chairman of the meeting cannot discuss the content of the question from his chair. In order to speak from the rostrum he has to transfer the chair to a Deputy Chairman'.[3] During the early months the political support of the Speaker Ülo Nugis was not overwhelming: he opposed Prime Minister Savisaar, and both of them had the committed support only of different minorities. The Temporary Working Regulations and the Standing Orders served as the speaker's shield against attacks from his political opponents. 'I am a bureaucrat and I act according to the Standing Orders', was his favourite statement whenever protests were voiced. This way, the principle of the neutrality of the speaker was often expressed. (In terms of the political market, the speaker should help MPs to bargain by themselves, and therefore he should not have the means to influence the outcome of the free bargaining process). This principle is well known and enjoys a high legitimacy among MPs, even though sometimes the real life differs from the ideal one.

Since the 1992 elections, the Board of Chairmen of the State Assembly consists of three members only: the chairman (that is, the speaker), and the two deputy chairmen. The deputy chairmen are elected together, each voter having a single vote. Consequently, one of them represents the opposition. The Board of Chairmen of the State Assembly make their decisions by consensus.

THE SIZE OF THE CHAMBER

During the Soviet era, the Supreme Council of the Estonian SSR had 285 seats. The size of legislative assemblies in the democratic world tends to be approximately equal to the cube root of the number of the population.[4] A 285-member parliament was too large for Estonia's 1.6 million population. Before the 1990 elections it was decided to reduce the size of the Supreme Council to 101 regular seats plus four seats for the Soviet Army. The State Assembly elected in September 1992 has 101 seats.

THE WORKING TIME

During the Soviet era, the Supreme Council was a body of amateurs. It gathered for very short regular sessions only twice a year. The Supreme Council elected in March 1990 was designed to become a parliament of professionals. Members were not allowed to hold positions elsewhere.

According to the Temporary Working Regulations of April 1990, the Supreme Council would have regular meetings each week from mid-January until mid-June and from September until mid-December. Monday to Wednesday, 17 hours a week were reserved for the plenary meetings.

In June 1990 the Supreme Council made changes to its working hours. Each fourth week was freed from plenary meetings. Members used that week to spend in their home districts. During the subsequent three weeks there was a plenary meeting each day Monday to Thursday, totalling ten hours a week. The Supreme Council could change its regular working time by a two-thirds majority. The Council often used to prolong its meeting when the question under discussion was considered important.

On 12 December 1991, the Supreme Council decided to allocate three more hours a week for plenary meetings. The reason was a lengthy line of undiscussed bills waiting for a slot in the agenda. The drafters of the Standing Orders of the State Assembly were not satisfied with the practice of rigid planning of time and decided to use an open ended meeting once a week. Eight hours per week are directly allocated for plenary meetings (on Mondays from 11 am until 1 pm, on Tuesdays and Thursdays from 10 am until 1 pm), plus on Wednesdays meetings start at 2 pm and end only when discussions on the government's bills have been completed.

THE AGENDA

During the Soviet era, the Supreme Soviet had full formal power to set its agenda itself. In practice, however, the agenda was set by the leadership of the Communist Party who used the Presidium of the Supreme Soviet as its agent.

The formal rules did not change much after the March 1990 elections. According to the Temporary Working Regulations, the agenda of the week (the session) was to be adopted by absolute majority vote (that is, a majority of the elected members had to vote Yes). The draft agenda was presented by the presidium, but each member of the parliament had the right also to make proposals.

It took usually an hour or two of discussion before the agenda was adopted. The drafting group of the Standing Orders was not satisfied with this waste of time. According to the Standing Orders of June 1990, the presidium had to distribute the draft agenda for the week at the end of the last meeting of the previous week, and only parliamentary parties and committees could propose amendments to the agenda. At the same time, the Presidium was required to present all drafts of laws or other documents to the chamber within two weeks of introduction, together with its own recommendations in relation to these bills.

There was still too much misunderstanding of the new rules. Therefore, soon after the second working group on the Standing Orders was created in the autumn of 1990, it presented very exact rules on compiling the agenda. According to the amendments to the Standing Orders, from 8 November 1990 the weekly agenda setting was divided into three distinct parts. First, the Supreme Council decided how to proceed with new bills. Second, matters which had been on the agenda of the previous week but had not been handled then were unconditionally transferred to the new agenda. Third, bills referred to committees reappeared on the agenda when the respective committee had finished its work or at the due date of the committee report. Sometimes protests were raised in relation to the second or the third part of the agenda.

In November 1990, the Supreme Council established the rules of speedy discussion of urgent questions. Urgent questions could be placed on the agenda by a simple majority vote at any time during a plenary meeting.

During the subsequent months, most of the legislation was channelled through the use of the urgency procedure. Urgency rules were too often used only because of the long line of normal bills. In summer 1992, the drafters of the Standing Orders of the State Assembly abandoned the urgency rules.

THE QUORUM REQUIREMENTS AND THE VOTING RULES

The Supreme Council of the Soviet era was designed to be a show-place to express unanimity of the people. Two-thirds of the elected members had to be present for formal decision making. (Before the 1990 elections the administration usually arranged that products, in short supply in ordinary shops, were sold in the parliament building. Of course, this shop was closed to the public.) In order to adopt any decision, at least a majority of the elected members of the parliament was required to vote Yes. (Usually all those who were present voted Yes.) To amend the constitution, two-thirds of the elected members had to support the amendment.

The same rules were transferred into the Temporary Working Regulation of 2 April 1990. Under these rules, it was rational behaviour on the part of opponents to co-operate and leave the floor before the final vote of the bill they opposed. Abstention from the quorum was a more powerful weapon against the bill than voting Nay. Russian-speaking deputies who opposed Independence often collectively marched out of the chamber.

In the Temporary Working Regulations the quorum requirements and the voting rules for committee meetings were not specified. However, according to the general customary rule of the time, any meeting was thought to lack power to take decisions if a majority of the persons who had to meet were not present.

The Standing Orders of June 1990 introduced an important institutional change: it reduced the size of the required quorum and in many cases bound voting rules to the number of members who actively participated in voting. For the plenary meeting of the parliament, the quorum requirement was dropped. However, to adopt a simple law, a resolution or a declaration, the majority of the elected members of the parliament still had to vote Yes. In committees, the quorum of at least a half was required. This was reduced to a third on 12 December 1990.

According to the Standing Orders of the Supreme Council of 28 June 1990, the vote was secret if a third of the deputies present so applied. On 18

March 1991, the Standing Orders were amended by the clause giving Members of Parliament access to the results of the open roll calls from the computer memory. (Previously, only the speaker had free access to these data.) On 5 September 1991, secret voting was abolished except in cases of personal nominations and dismissals of high-ranking state officials.

By the constitution adopted in June 1992, the simple majority rule was extended to the adoption of simple laws. Now only the constitution and some other laws specified by the constitution are protected by qualified majority rules.

THE STAGES OF THE LEGISLATIVE PROCESS

Between 2 April and 28 June 1990, the legislative process was regulated by the relatively laconic Temporary Working Regulations. How to proceed was often decided during the process, and some traditions developed as unwritten amendments to the written rules. During this early period, the legislative process consisted of the following stages:

1. The draft law was presented to the speaker.
2. Usually the presidium discussed the bill before the Supreme Council did so. Usually the bill was also given to a standing committee, called the leading committee, in respect of the bill.
3. The leading committee discussed the bill.
4. When the agenda of the week of the Supreme Council was discussed, the presidium or any member could propose that the bill appear on the agenda. The Supreme Council voted on the agenda.
5. During the *first reading* of the draft law, the sponsor of the bill made a presentation of up to 30 minutes. A committee representative could speak for 20 minutes. They were asked questions by the members.
6. From the first reading on, Members of Parliament could propose amendments. Amendments were discussed in the leading committee.
7. During the *second reading* (and also during the third reading if one was decided to be necessary) Members of Parliament could also speak, for ten minutes each, in the order of their requests to speak. It became customary to vote on amendments when the discussion was finished. At the very end of the second (or the third) reading the vote on the bill was taken.

Most of the acts the Supreme Council adopted in spring 1990 were not laws but declarations and resolutions. They were not discussed in separate 'readings'. Usually, an *ad hoc* committee was formed to edit the drafts before the final vote.

The rules were variously refined. The time when specific processes occurred were more clearly defined. The actions which took place during the different stages were more precisely regulated. The most important stages were given a specific time period.

The Standing Orders of 28 June 1990, and, more precisely, the amendments to them adopted on 8 November 1990, established the time when the Presidium had to present bills to the floor for decisions on their further treatment. According to the rules, the bills had to be distributed to the members prior to the weekend before the reading. The members could propose amendments until the end of discussions. Gradually, the Supreme Council adopted the practice that, before discussions, the members got the written list of proposed amendments. From 7 November 1991, before a roll call on any amendment, the leading committee has to express its opinion on the amendment.

The Standing Orders of the State Assembly of 5 October 1992 further improved the clarity and distinctiveness of the stages of the legislative process. For example, proposed amendments must be distributed to Members of Parliament a day before the discussion. Also, before the vote on a proposed amendment to a draft law, the author of the proposal, the sponsor of the draft law and the representative of the leading committee have the right to comment on the amendment. Other members have an opportunity to speak only during an earlier stage when the bill and all amendments are discussed together. Only the Constitutional Assembly used the practice, similar to the British Parliament, of discussing each amendment separately, immediately before the vote on it.

A third reading takes place only in the case of some important draft laws: always when the constitution or the State Budget is discussed, and on special demand in the case of ordinary bills. In the Supreme Council, a parliamentary party or a standing committee had the right to order the third reading of any bill. It was a minority right in order to allow repeating the roll call on some important amendment, or to win time for negotiations before the final vote. In the State Assembly the third reading can be ordered by a faction only if its move is not opposed by the leading committee.

CONSTITUENCY RELATIONS

Constituency relations have hardly been regulated by any rules. It is stated in the Standing Orders that during the residual time not allocated for the plenary or committee meetings 'members work in their constituencies or carry out tasks given by the Supreme Council or its committees'. The parliament has also paid for the transportation of members between Tallinn and their constituencies.

Some Members of Parliament arranged (usually irregular) office hours to meet with voters. A vast majority of the problems raised at these face-to-face meetings concerned people's living conditions. During the first years of the elected Supreme Council people still believed that the members of the Supreme Council could help them to get an apartment. Public discussions with an MP on interesting issues of the day have been more often enjoyed by both sides of the meeting.

CONTENT OF PUBLIC POLICY

Until the autumn of 1991, the dominant policy issue was the restoration of state independence. People were often physically involved in the political process. On 23 August 1989, more than one million people stood on the road from Tallinn to Vilnius to create the Baltic Chain, a human chain of about 500 kilometres in length, in order to express their desire for freedom. On 3 March 1991, 82.9 per cent of the adult population participated in the referendum on independence, and 77.8 per cent of them supported it. In the regions of strong ethnic Estonian domination the support was nearly 100 per cent. Still, the radical Estonian nationalists opposed the decision to arrange the referendum and the National Independence Party even boycotted the vote – on the ground that the Soviet-era immigrants could attend it.

After the restoration of independence, the question of who will be citizens appeared to generate the highest emotional charge. By decisions made on 6 November 1991, and 26 February 1992, only citizens of the pre-1940 Republic of Estonia and their descendants were acknowledged as citizens, while the Soviet-era immigrants and their descendants had to pass a language test and a one-year waiting period in order to get citizenship. This decision excluded more than 80 per cent of Russians from the constitutional referendum in June 1992 and presidential and parliamentary elections later in September. There were no Russians elected to the State Assembly. On 21 June 1993, the State Assembly adopted the Law on Aliens which would allow the government to refuse residency permits to non-citizens, but this decision caused excitement among the diplomatic corps, and the president vetoed the law. The law was amended, as proposed by the experts of the Council of Europe (most of the Soviet-era civilian residents got a right to residency permit), and adopted anew on 8 July.

The second issue which has distinguished movements and shaped the party system is de-communisation. After the 1992 elections the descendant of the Communist Party is not in the parliament. However, some movements and other parties have been founded with a higher than average percentage membership of former *nomenklatura* while at the other extreme some parties do not accept former Communists among their members and have attempted to disfranchise elite Communists in elections.

The third political issue on which parties diverge is the manner of privatisation. The former *nomenklatura*, the new rich and the descendants of the old owners of 1940 have different and contradictory interests. Also, the equalising voucher strategy of privatisation has been used by some parties to win political support.

The importance of the socialism-liberalism dimension is increasing. Savisaar's government faced serious shortage-of-supply problems in the winter of 1991/92 and inclined to control the distribution of goods, for which he was continuously criticised from the right. The shortage-of-supply problem was finally solved by introducing Estonian currency (in June 1992) and keeping the state budget balanced. However, Mart Laar's government has been accused of 'extreme Thatcherism', for example for his no-customs-barriers policy which has caused headaches for domestic agricultural producers, and for his development policy 'on account of pensioners'.

Some issues of democratisation have also been of considerable interest. From the end of 1991 until mid-1992 people were quite active in supporting the institution of direct presidential elections. The extent of the power of the president was the hottest issue in the Constitutional Assembly. The parliamentary election law is often criticised for its complexity and for giving too much power to party leaders.

CONCLUSION

The development of political institutions after the first post-Communist elections in Estonia has the following characteristics. First, political movements which were important before the first election formed a basis for the first parliamentary parties. Movements lost their importance, but parties were usually founded as a result of splitting or reconstituting a movement, or as an extension of a parliamentary party, or both. The first disciplined government coalition was formed straight after the second election. Four years after the first election the membership of parties is still measured only in hundreds per party.

Second, changes in the constitutional law were slow during the first one and a half years after the first election. However, after recognition of state independence the Constitutional Assembly (distinct from the parliament) was formed which drafted a new constitution. Ten months after restoration of independence the constitution was adopted in a referendum.

Third, within the first year after the first election the written rules of conduct of parliamentary procedures were worked out and improved considerably. Later changes have been rare and the need for them has been less urgent than during the first months of the democratic transition.

Fourth, the election system was radically revised before the second parliamentary election. Even though this second election law caused louder criticism than the first one, only minor amendments to the second law followed prior to the third election.

Fifth, and finally, in Estonia the political development has been relatively successful: Estonia has succeeded in avoiding severe political dead-locks, such as conflict between the president and the parliament which characterises a number of post-Communist states. One reason for this was strong emotional support from among the population for MPs and political changes initiated by the parliament which lasted for about 20 months after the elections (but only four months after the restoration of independence). There are some other reasons for the successful development, too: the model of democratic society was relatively well known to Estonians both from their own history and from close connections to Finland.

NOTES

1.   This phenomenon is known in the other post-Communist countries as well, see D.M. Olson, 'Political Parties and Party Systems in Regime Transformation: Inner Transition in the New Democracies of Central Europe', *The American Review of Politics*, 14 (Winter 1993), p.641.
2.   R. Taagepera and M.S. Shugart, *Seats and Votes: The Effects and Determinants of Electoral Systems* (New Haven and London: Yale University Press, 1989).
3.   *Riigi Teataja*, 1990, Nr. 2, Art. 33: 'Eesti Vabariigi Ülemn'ukogu Reglement', § 10 (6).
4.   Taagepera and Shugart, *Seats and Votes*, pp.173–83.

From Soviet to parliament in Ukraine: The Verkhovna Rada During 1992–94

STANLEY BACH

The collapse of the Soviet Union and the declaration of Ukrainian independence occurred during the term of the deputies of Ukraine's national legislature, the Verkhovna Rada, who were elected in 1990. It fell to these deputies, who were chosen under a system that the Communist Party continued to dominate, to begin the process of transforming the Rada from a largely powerless body into a functioning parliament during a period of intense controversy over the direction and pace of both political and economic change. This transformation was further complicated by uncertainty and disagreement about the constitutional relations among the Rada, the president, and the prime minister and his cabinet of ministers.

The process of electing a new Rada began in early 1994 and resulted in a wholesale change in the Rada's membership, some changes in its internal organisation and a significant shift in the locus of political power. One of the first concerns of the newly-elected deputies was to encourage the formation of a more stable and formal system of parliamentary parties or factions. Not surprisingly, however, the Rada remained an institution in transition, both in its internal organisation and procedures and in its place in Ukraine's evolving constitutional structure.

During March 1990, 450 deputies were elected to the Verkhovna Rada, which was then known in English as the Supreme Soviet of the Ukrainian Soviet Socialist Republic. During March–August 1994, there were new elections to the same unicameral assembly that, during the intervening time, had become in translation the Supreme Council of the Republic of Ukraine. The Rada remains an institution in transition from Soviet to parliament. As

Stanley Bach is a Senior Specialist in Legislative Process, Congressional Research Service at the US Library of Congress, Washington DC.

This is a revised and condensed version of a paper first prepared for a 1993 conference in Kiev on 'Parliaments, Prime Ministers, and Presidents: Relations Among Branches of Democratic Governments', sponsored by the East–West Parliamentary Practice Project and the European Bank for Reconstruction and Development. Revised versions were presented at the 1993 Annual Meeting of the American Political Science Association (subsequently appearing in *Congressional Studies Journal*, 2 (1994), pp.73–94), and in Prague at a 1994 'Research Conference on the New Parliaments of Central and Eastern Europe'. The author wishes to thank the many deputies and officials of the Verkhovna Rada who provided most of the information and insights on which this paper is based, and also Katherine Chumachenko, Nick Deychakiwsky, Orest Deychakiwsky, Stuart Goldman, Christina Maciw, Jurii Maniichuk, Francis Miko, Thomas Remington and Steven Woehrel for their very helpful comments or other assistance. Nothing in this paper is to be construed as representing a position of the Congressional Research Service or the Library of Congress.

the Supreme Soviet of the Ukrainian SSR, it was the highest constitutional organ of government, but in fact it exercised no significant political or governmental power as a legislative body. As individuals, its leaders may have been influential; the Chairman of the Supreme Soviet was the *de jure* head of state. As a parliament, however, it hardly even managed to maintain the facade of democratic forms, meeting for two annual sessions that lasted only as long as was necessary to ratify decisions made elsewhere in Kiev or Moscow.

After the disintegration of the Soviet Union, the Rada began to assert itself as a more serious and independent actor in Ukraine's policy-making process. Whether its leaders and members truly are committed to transforming it into an effective national parliament and whether they can succeed in doing so remain open questions, even after the selection in mid-1994 of new parliamentary leaders by an overwhelmingly new corps of deputies. What is certain is that, with the demise of the Soviet Union and the Communist Party as the *de facto* sources of power and policy, the opportunity for this transformation exists if the Rada has the will and capacity to seize it. What follows is a baseline report on the condition of the Verkhovna Rada as an institution at the end of 1992 – its membership, structure, procedures, and resources – and on some of the immediate consequences for the Rada of the 1994 elections.

THE VERKHOVNA RADA AS AN INSTITUTION IN 1992

Even before the 1994 parliamentary elections, the Rada was no longer a static institution. At the same time that it was beginning the extraordinary task of creating a new corpus of national law for Ukraine, it also was becoming more cognizant of the need to re-create itself. In fact, some of its members were trying to transform it into something it was not intended to be when they and their colleagues had been elected. They were constrained, however, by a membership and organisation that newly independent Ukraine inherited from the many decades of its Soviet experience, an inheritance that would not be easy to change.

Membership

In 1990, deputies were elected to five-year terms in the Rada from single-member districts in relatively open and even competitive elections, but elections that nonetheless took place in the context of continuing Communist Party dominance. Roughly 3,000 candidates ran for the 450 seats. In almost three-quarters of the districts, no candidate received a majority of the votes cast in the first round of voting, resulting in a run-off election between the top two candidates with only a plurality of votes being required for victory. (In either round, a majority of the electorate had to vote for the election to be valid.) Although the elections did not qualify as completely fair and free, voter turnout was 84.7 per cent in the first round and 78.8 per cent in the second, and opponents of the political *status quo* won more than one-quarter of the seats in the Rada.[1]

On the other hand, the newly elected corps of deputies continued to be dominated by members of the Communist Party and the *nomenklatura*. At the time of their election to the Verkhovna Rada, approximately 375 of the 442 MPs elected were formal or candidate members of the party (although some also were, or later became, supporters of Rukh or other pro-democratic groups).[2] The deputies reportedly included a majority of the 25 or so regional (*oblast*) Communist Party secretaries. Eighty-seven deputies were officials of government ministries at the national, regional, or local level, and 51 were employed by Communist Party organs. Seventy-five MPs were directors of industrial or agricultural enterprises, and 16 were active-duty military officers.[3] Thus, most of the deputies were closely linked to what became the old regime when, in December 1991, Ukraine declared its independence from a disintegrating Soviet Union.

The 'class of 1990' was overwhelmingly male – there were 13 female deputies – and only 68 of 422 deputies serving in late 1992 were 40 years old or younger. More than 200 deputies were more than 50 years of age. This age distribution would not be surprising in an established parliament, but it did not augur well for the openness and flexibility in thought required by deputies who found themselves serving in a political and economic context that was significantly different from the one in which they were elected. Almost 400 deputies had completed some form of higher education. But in contrast to the more common pattern in established parliaments, the largest occupational group were MPs designated as 'engineers'; more than 100 deputies so described themselves.

Most striking and important is the fact that only 21, or five per cent, of the deputies still serving in late 1992 were lawyers. This dearth of legal expertise was recognised by senior deputies and officials of the Rada as a serious deficiency. Few deputies had professional training and experience that made them likely to bring to their service in the Rada an understanding of a democratic law-making process and the requisites of effectively drafted laws.

The occupational backgrounds of deputies also were noteworthy because most of them continued in their occupations while serving in parliament. Roughly 190 of more than 420 deputies were full-time MPs; the others combined their parliamentary work with some other employment. So by the Rada's own estimate, more than half of the deputies participated in parliamentary activities only sporadically and occasionally. In 1992, the

Verkhovna Rada even adopted a monthly schedule that accommodated and actually may have encouraged this situation. It allowed deputies to spend most of their time in their constituencies, continuing to engage in other more remunerative professions, and visiting Kiev only for the one week of plenary sessions each month.

Thus, the working Verkhovna Rada was not even half the size of its formal membership. Since the deputies had been elected to an assembly that was not expected to place very heavy demands on their time, attention, or intellect, most of them undoubtedly never had any intention or expectation of being full-time MPs. Then, however, they found themselves members of a body facing far heavier demands. And even if they may have been inclined toward a full-time professional commitment to elective politics, they had no assurance that they would survive the next parliamentary elections, especially when the shape of the election law that would govern those elections, the political parties that would contest them, and even the likely date for the elections all remained unknown.

It is not surprising, then, that so many deputies devoted only part of their time to the Rada. In consequence, activist and reformist MPs may have enjoyed a degree of influence out of proportion to their numbers, especially on the Rada's permanent commissions. On the other hand, this situation also may have had several deleterious institutional effects. First, much of the extraordinary workload of the Rada had to be assumed by less than half of its members. Second, deputies who had made no real commitment to parliamentary service had less need to be concerned with and responsive to the interests of their constituents. And, third, the part-time deputies were unlikely to be well informed when they came to Kiev to cast their votes in plenary sessions. The ability of the Verkhovna Rada to transform itself from Soviet to parliament must remain severely limited until deputies are expected and enabled to devote most or all of their time to parliamentary service.

Structure

The transitional condition of the 1990–94 Verkhovna Rada also was evidenced by the weakness of parliamentary party groups in organising the deputies and their activities. Most deputies were not formally affiliated with any party or similar organisation, and deputies who did belong to the same party did not even sit together. Seats in the plenary session hall were assigned to deputies by regions and then in alphabetical order within each regional group.

From November 1992, deputies acknowledged membership in nine officially registered political parties and movements, but only two of them had even a dozen deputies among their formal members. Larger numbers of

MPs were associated with looser parliamentary coalitions. By one count, there were 47 groups of deputies in March 1993, although some were ephemeral, many were poorly organised, and individual MPs could and did belong to more than one of them.

Although precise numbers are elusive, one count identified 49 deputies as having been associated with Rukh in December 1992; 39 were more or less allied in the 'Congress of National Democratic Forces' and a roughly comparable number were affiliated together in 'New Ukraine'.[4] Only Rukh, which claimed the support of 27.7 per cent of the deputies after the 1990 elections,[5] had existed one year earlier and had any significant grassroots organisation; the others may be thought of as 'hydroponic' parties, lacking structures that rooted them in the towns, villages and farms of Ukraine's several regions. Ironically perhaps, the largest and initially most cohesive group within the Verkhovna Rada was the group of formally unaffiliated deputies who were the most committed supporters of the old regime. After the 1990 elections, they were known informally as the 'Group of 239', reflecting the fact that they constituted a majority of the Rada's entire membership.

The lack of effective and durable party structures within the Verkhovna Rada deprived the parliament of the organisational benefits that parties contribute to most other national parliaments. For example, the weakness or absence of parties in the Rada left otherwise ill-informed deputies, especially part-time deputies, without the very helpful general policy guidance and specific voting cues that parties offer their members, even in legislatures such as the US Congress where party unity is not nearly absolute. It also left the electorate without party labels as convenient devices for simplifying their voting decisions. The experience of virtually all democratic parliaments argues convincingly that a stronger and more clearly defined party system would be a prerequisite for a more productive and accountable Rada.

By contrast, the Verkhovna Rada did have a well-articulated committee system in the form of 24 'permanent commissions', each of which had legislative responsibility for one or more defined policy area. Some of the commissions had conventional responsibilities – such as those on foreign affairs, social policy and labour, health, education and science, and defence and state security. Others reflected Ukraine's unique experiences and conditions – for example, the Commissions on State Sovereignty, on Inter-Republic and Inter-Ethnic Relations, and on the Chernobyl Catastrophe. In mid-1992, the commissions ranged in permanent membership from seven to 27 deputies, but such numbers are misleading; more significant were the much smaller numbers of full-time commission members.

Most of the members on ten of the commissions were full-time deputies.

On the other hand, there were only four full-time deputies among the 26 members of the Commission on Planning, Budget, Finance, and Prices. Taken with the Commission on Economic Reforms and the Commission on the Development of Basic Branches of the National Economy, the three commissions that appear to have had primary responsibility for efforts to reorient the Ukrainian economy had to rely on only 20, or barely one-quarter, of their 77 official members. Although these numbers tell us nothing about the quality of work that full-time commission members contributed, they certainly suggest that critically important commissions were severely handicapped by inactive and inattentive members.

Something else that distinguished the Verkhovna Rada from more well-established parliaments was its procedure – or lack of procedure – for assigning deputies to the permanent commissions. In effect, each deputy elected in 1990 was able to select the one commission on which he or she wanted to serve, though the Chairman of the Rada may have influenced some deputies' choices. Such self-selection had the obvious advantage of allowing MPs to work on the issues that concerned them the most, for personal or political reasons, which should have encouraged their participation in commission work. And perhaps these assignments did not seem very consequential at a time when most deputies still were responsive to Communist Party leadership. However, self-selection also may produce some commissions that lack sufficient regional diversity and others – for instance, commissions with responsibility for matters such as the 'Agro-Industrial Complex' – that are populated by deputies with a special, perhaps constituency-based, interest in their work. The result can be commissions that are unrepresentative of the entire assembly.

The lack of a robust parliamentary party system combined with self-selected commission memberships made it imperative that the Verkhovna Rada have some mechanism for central co-ordination. That mechanism was the presidium, a steering committee composed of the Rada's chairman and two Deputy Chairmen, who were elected in plenary session, and the chairmen of the 24 permanent commissions, who were nominated by the Chairman of the Rada and then ratified by plenary vote. The presidium was empowered to schedule the two annual sessions of the Verkhovna Rada, but its fundamental official responsibility and power was over the agenda for plenary meetings.

Procedures

Between 1992 and 1994, most major legislation for newly independent Ukraine originated with the Cabinet of Ministers. In principle, the right to initiate legislation was not limited to the cabinet or to the deputies, chairman, presidium and permanent commissions of the Verkhovna Rada itself. Under the Ukrainian Constitution, the president, the Constitutional Court and other bodies including the Ukrainian Academy of Sciences all retained the formal authority to present legislative drafts to the Rada. In practice, though, the government defined the legislative agenda generally as well as the framework of the specific proposals the Rada considered. It was relatively unusual for individual deputies to propose their own legislation and even more unusual for their proposals on priority matters to receive serious consideration.

This state of affairs is generally characteristic of most democratic systems – the United States being a partial exception to the rule – and especially so under the kind of critical conditions that the Rada faced during this period. Particularly on economic legislation, the parliament relied on initiatives from the president and then from the prime minister and the Cabinet of Ministers. In the autumn of 1992, the Verkhovna Rada went so far as to grant the prime minister and cabinet the authority for six months to legislate on many economic questions, with these laws to take effect unless the Rada disapproved them within a ten-day period. This authority went considerably further than the authority President Kravchuk had been exercising to issue decrees that implemented, or at least did not contradict, existing law. The controversy that erupted in May 1993 over whether to renew this grant of emergency authority, or whether the Cabinet of Ministers should be more subordinated to presidential control, created a crisis in the Ukrainian political system that remains unresolved and that reflects the ambiguous allocations of power under Ukraine's current patchwork constitution.

When a bill was presented for the Rada's consideration, its chairman or one of his two deputies referred it for review by one of the 24 permanent commissions. Most proposals were sent to only one commission, but referral to two or more commissions was possible; for example, the Commissions on Foreign Affairs and on Defence and State Security both considered the START treaty. In conducting this review, the commissions did not normally hold public hearings – space limitations were cited as one reason – but there was some limited radio or television coverage of commission meetings. It was common practice for ministry officials and advisers to the commission, as well as its staff, to participate. The commission could debate and vote on specific amendments to the bill. But it also was common practice for a commission to decide conceptually on how a bill should be revised, and then leave it to staff to transform the concepts into formal legislative language. This practice should not have been surprising in view of the deputies' own lack of technical expertise, nor is it unique to the Verkhovna Rada. It does have the effect, however, of giving considerable power to unelected parliamentary officials who inevitably exercise some discretion in deciding how a general concept ought to be implemented.

After the commission completed action on the bill, the presidium had the authority to schedule it for consideration by the Rada in plenary session. Herein lay a primary source of the presidium's formal power and informal influence as a collective body. The presidium prepared a potential agenda for the one week of plenary meetings that took place each month. In light of the enormous workload the Rada faced, however, this agenda often far exceeded the amount of business that the parliament conceivably could transact. More important, therefore, the presidium also drafted daily agenda resolutions for the Rada to approve. In principle, it was free to amend or reject the proposed agenda, but such a thing rarely if ever happened. From time to time instead, the presidium presented an agenda with several options, leaving it to the deputies to decide by vote which alternative they preferred.

With the Rada expected to meet in plenary sessions only one week per month and with a legislative workload that would have overwhelmed even the most experienced and energetic legislators, the presidium's agenda decisions gave it impressive influence, if not effective control, over the fate of legislation. The presidium could expedite action on bills it favoured, just as it could postpone, perhaps indefinitely, those it opposed. In turn, this power should have given it great leverage to influence commission decisions. More often than not, the presidium appears to have followed the guidance of Chairman Pluishch. In the future, however, the presidium's agenda powers, if unchanged, could strengthen the hand of a new generation of commission chairmen. If the presidium acts to promote the interests and preferences of its members, as such a body is likely to do, each chairman can make persuasive arguments to the other members of his commission (and to other Rada deputies) that their legislation is unlikely to be taken up for plenary action unless it satisfies the chairman's preferences.

The Rada's process for plenary action also served to enhance the influence of its permanent commissions. There were two distinct stages to this process. The debate on first reading typically began with a 15–30 minute statement by the minister concerned with the bill, who was followed by the chairman or another member of the permanent commission that had reviewed it. Other deputies wishing to speak – on average for ten minutes each – notified the chairman or the secretariat. The result was a list of potential speakers that was available to the chairman, who was given (or assumed) some latitude in deciding who would be allowed to speak and in what order. The time available to each speaker as well as the total time for the debate on first reading were set in advance, in theory at least. The chairman proposed these time limits for the Rada's approval. Reportedly, however, the chairman was known to either expand or contract debate time at his own discretion.

During this debate, deputies could propose amendments to the bill but there were no votes on them at this stage. Instead, at the conclusion of the debate on first reading, amendments were referred to the appropriate permanent commission for its study and recommendations. Before the plenary debate on second reading, when deputies did vote on the amendments, the secretariat produced a document that presented each amendment, the related provision of the bill, and the committee's recommendation for approving or rejecting the amendment or adopting an alternative amendment instead. In unusual circumstances, additional amendments could be proposed during the debate on second reading; such amendments also would be evaluated by the commission before being voted on during a debate on third reading.

Typically at the end of the debate on second reading, the bill was passed by majority vote and signed by the chairman for presentation to the president. Under the law on the presidency, the president then had ten days in which he could veto the bill in its entirety or with his recommendations for amendments. President Kravchuk exercised this power only once during late 1992. In that case, he returned the bill with his proposed amendments that were reviewed by the appropriate commission in preparation for plenary votes during a debate on third reading. The Rada approved or disapproved the amendments individually and by majority vote, and then re-submitted the bill for the president's signature. Alternatively, the Rada could re-affirm its support for a bill it had passed, acting again by simple majority vote, in which case it was considered to be enacted. The ability of the president to propose amendments with his veto created opportunities for compromise that do not exist under systems that allow presidents only to accept or reject bills in their entirety. On the other hand, the Rada's power to override a presidential veto by majority vote could be expected to reduce severely parliamentary incentives to compromise.

Resources

After independence, the Verkhovna Rada slowly began the process of creating for itself the resources it required to become an effective national parliament. There were serious deficiencies to be addressed, though for some purposes it already had a well-developed support structure.

In January 1992, that structure was divided between the administration and the secretariat, both of which reported to the presidium. The administration was responsible for parliamentary finances and accounting, buildings and restaurants, and health and medical services for deputies and staff, as well as transportation and other logistical and housekeeping services. And these services were elaborate, largely because of the party property that had come under parliamentary control. The administration managed the Rada's own day-care centres and also provided housing in Kiev for all deputies. It owned and managed two hotels in central Kiev and maintained a resort in the Crimea. To supply its facilities, the administration even had its own food production plant. All told, more than 3,000 employees worked in the various units of the administration.

Offsetting these facilities and support services were some notable weaknesses in the Rada's resources, such as the staff, space, and equipment it provided its deputies. Each deputy received a cash allotment for hiring staff, but it was sufficient in late 1992 only to employ one person at an average wage (or several people on a part-time basis). Perhaps one reason was the lack of office space to house additional staff; some office space was provided to the 190 to 200 full-time deputies but not to the others, which did nothing to discourage absenteeism. Furthermore, MPs were not provided with any computers for their own use. Deputies who wanted access to the Rada's automated information systems had to go to their commission offices where they might find a networked personal computer.

More directly relevant to the Rada's legislative activities was its secretariat, with a total staff of roughly 300 persons that had expanded rapidly since the 1990 elections. The secretariat was divided into a triad of service units. Among its other responsibilities, the Documentary Services Unit published the proceedings of the Rada's plenary sessions as well as periodic and annual compilations of new laws. The Organisational Services Unit included a department that responded to public requests and complaints. Other groups were responsible for recording plenary and commission sessions and otherwise supporting the Rada's plenary sessions.

Of most interest are three units within the Legal and Scientific Services triad. First, the Legal Department, with a staff of 13 lawyers, was the only concentration of legal expertise that the Rada had created for itself. These lawyers served as general legal advisers to parliamentary leaders; they could also provide legal advice and legislative drafting assistance to the permanent commissions. Second, the Computerised Information Systems Centre had developed a relatively elaborate array of databases and automated information services. It received bills electronically from the Council of Ministers, and maintained a database of existing (post-independence) laws and a separate database of pending legislation that recorded successive changes in each bill. Other databases displayed electronic voting results, government statistics, and biographical information on Ukrainian legal and policy specialists whom the Rada could consult. The centre also provided the Rada with access to various foreign news sources and databases. Third, the Rada supported a unique institution in the form of a privately funded Council of Advisers comprising senior political advisers from the United States, western Europe, and Japan. The Council's multi-national staff provided complementary services, including an impressive capacity to translate documents into and from Ukrainian.

In addition, each of the permanent commissions had its own staff or 'secretariat', ranging in size from six to 17. In total, the commission secretariats employed 216 people, 66 professional and 150 administrative; the presidium fixed the size of each commission's staff. The policy-relevant staff assistance available to any of the commissions was limited. The lines of authority over the commission staffs were ambiguous; they were described as serving two masters. They had been components of the centrally controlled secretariat, but now were supposed to be more accountable to the various commissions. Nonetheless, the secretariat continued to attempt at least a co-ordinating role – among its Legal and Scientific Services was a Department of Coordination between the Secretariats of Commissions – and it actually may have had a more directive role in practice.

The most serious deficiency in the Verkhovna Rada's support structure was the lack of policy analysis that was prepared at its request and was responsive to its needs. Commission secretariats were small and the Rada's central secretariat provided no research and analysis services other than those of its Legal Department. And although the Rada also sought advice from university faculty and research staff at the institutes of the Ukrainian Academy of Sciences, this too was a limited resource on which to draw. One problem was the lack of trained policy research specialists. Another was the lack of a political tradition in which competing policy alternatives are openly advocated and compared. A third was the lack of policy-relevant information. Especially so long as many members of the Rada remain part-time deputies, the need for research and analysis, whether centralised or dispersed among commissions or parties-to-be, will remain acute. Until this need is met, the Rada remains at risk of being a captive of the ministries and their presumptive policy expertise.

THE 1994 ELECTIONS AND THEIR AFTERMATH

The Rada that has been described here adjourned for the last time on 25 February 1994. During the next three months, a new parliament was elected and began to organise itself. The preceding description is written mostly in the past tense because the new Rada will decide what aspects of its structure, procedures and resources it will preserve and what it will replace. In an established parliament, no one election is likely to be followed by fundamental institutional changes; most of what has been will continue to be. But not enough time has yet passed to know how, and how much, the Verkhovna Rada is changing. In some respects, the newly elected Rada marks a sharp break with the past. In other respects, it may witness attempts, successful or not, to preserve or even return to the past. The direction that the Rada ultimately chooses to take could well determine the prospects of the democratic transition in Ukraine.

Since independence, Ukraine had lacked a clear sense of direction in economic policy and had failed to reconstitute the political regime to, among other things, clarify the respective constitutional powers of the parliament, the prime minister and the president. The 1994 elections succeeded in that the results did 'appear to have reflected the will of the electorate'.[6] In terms of governance, however, there is reason to question whether these elections will prove to be truly transformative, either for the Rada as an institution or, more generally, for the economic order or the political system of Ukraine.

The Election

As in 1990, the new parliamentary elections took place in 450 single-member constituencies. However, this had not been a foregone conclusion. Some reformers had pressed for a new system of proportional representation, while those already in power and supporters of the recreated Communist Party favoured the existing electoral law. All evidently had made the same political calculation: that supporters of what was becoming known as 'the party of power' were much better organised across the country and were able to field many more well-known candidates, giving them much better chances of winning elections in single-member districts than the large number of often competing and poorly organised opposition parties. Several compromise proposals for mixed systems were suggested, but the Rada ultimately decided in November 1993 to preserve the existing electoral system. To some unknowable degree, therefore, the election was over before the first votes were cast.

The first round of parliamentary elections was even more inconclusive in 1994 than it had been in 1990. Only 49 of 450 deputies, half of them party candidates, were elected in the voting which took place on 27 March; 289 more were chosen in run-off elections that were held early in April. An additional 55 seats were filled by repeat elections in July and August, still leaving 57 seats to be contested during a third round of elections in November. Although this process was tortuously slow and cumbersome, the 338 deputies elected in March–April were sufficient to constitute the simple majority quorum needed for most purposes and the two-thirds quorum required for the Rada to act on what it construes to be 'constitutional' legislation.

A wholesale change has taken place in the membership of the Verkhovna Rada. Data are available only on the 338 deputies elected during March and April, only 56 (or 16.6 per cent) of whom were re-elected incumbents, and they constituted 29.8 per cent of the 188 incumbents who sought re-election. Notwithstanding the replacement of almost 90 per cent of the entire corps of 450 deputies, however, there is some evidence of continuity in the kinds of people who have been elected. Only 12 of the 338 elected deputies are women, and fully two-thirds of the 338 are at least 41 years old. In short, the new parliament does not appear to be dominated by a new generation that has come of age – politically, at least – since the USSR began to disintegrate.

Reorganising the Rada

One of the first concerns of the new parliament was to encourage the development of a more stable and formal system of parliamentary parties or factions. Adopting proportional representation would have encouraged the development of party organisations and stronger party discipline among deputies elected to the Rada. As it was, however, the spring 1994 elections were not organised or dominated by political party organisations. Only 11 per cent of the candidates were nominated by a party or bloc of parties, though they constituted 26.3 per cent of those elected. The other successful candidates were put forward by workers' collectives or voters' petitions in roughly equal numbers (120 and 129 respectively).

The Communist Party nominated 59 deputies who were elected; no other party nominated more than 12.[7] Many more deputies were affiliated with, though not nominated by, parties, so within days of the April elections, as many as 13 parties were credited with representation in the Rada. By far the largest delegation was that of the Communist Party with 86 deputies; only three others were thought to have more than a dozen members in the new parliament. There remained fully 170 deputies, exactly one more than half of the 338 elected, who had not been nominated by an officially registered political party nor who claimed a formal party affiliation.[8]

This situation created the prospect of a highly fragmented assembly that could have been immensely difficult to organise, politically and institutionally. Only two days after the new parliament convened, therefore, the new deputies adopted new regulations on parliamentary party factions.[9] To receive official recognition, each faction must have at least 25 members, who can include deputies who support a party programme without being formal party members. Groups of deputies also may form factions on a cross-party or 'non-party basis', presumably to benefit from the resources and other advantages that accrue to organised factions and their members. And to encourage stronger factions, deputies are prohibited from belonging to more than one of them, in contrast with the practice that had prevailed during the preceding Rada.

Under these regulations, positions on standing commissions and parliamentary delegations are to be distributed proportionately among the factions, which evidently also are assured opportunities to participate in committee and plenary debates. In addition, a 'Coordinating Council of Deputies Groups (Factions)' is to advise on the agenda and activities of the Rada and its committees. Perhaps just as important, the regulations suggest that staff, space and equipment are to be distributed among the factions, probably to the severe disadvantage of any unaffiliated deputies.

Not surprisingly, therefore, by 27 May 1994, most of the elected deputies had coalesced into nine parliamentary factions, six of which barely met the threshold requirement.[10] (See Table 1, which does not reflect the results of the July–August repeat elections.) This factional structure is likely to remain fluid for some time to come, and the minimal size of most of them suggests that at least some may have been born of convenience and without much more to hold them together than the advantages accruing to factions under the new regulations. On the other hand, two or three larger alliances or blocs, however fragile, may be forming. Some observers speak in summary terms of a division between the 'Left' or the 'Communists' on the one hand, and the 'Democrats' or 'National Democrats' on the other; others claim to see a third, 'Centre', group associated with some of the previous leaders of the Rada.

TABLE 1
PARLIAMENTARY FACTIONS IN THE VERKHOVNA RADA, AS OF 27 MARCH 1994

Communists of Ukraine	86
Centre	38
Agrarians	33
Rukh	27
Inter-Regional Group	27
Reform	27
Yednist (Unity)	26
Derzhavnist (Statehood)	26
Socialists	25
Unaffiliated	23

Source: Markian Bilynskyj, 'Ukrainian Parliamentary Commissions Formed', *Update from Ukraine*, US–Ukraine Foundation, 10 June 1994.

The new locus of power within the Rada was demonstrated by the election as chairman of Oleksandr Moroz, leader of the Socialist Party faction and formerly the leader of the Communist deputies in the pre-independence Supreme Soviet. Moroz received 171 of the 322 votes cast, defeating Vasyl Durdynets who had been the First Deputy Chairman of the Rada before the 1994 elections. In this election, the Communist, Socialist, Agrarian and Unity factions generally opposed the Centre, Reform, Rukh and Statehood factions, though factional unity was less than complete. The emerging coalescence of political forces was suggested by the fact that the Rukh leader, Vyacheslav Chornovil, withdrew as a candidate for chairman to the obvious benefit of Durdynets, who had been one of the most prominent leaders of the parliamentary majority that Rukh had opposed so vigorously before the recent elections.

Soon thereafter, the Verkhovna Rada formed 23 standing commissions, the same number that had functioned before the March–April elections, with the seats and chairmanships distributed roughly proportionately among the factions. Each faction and the unaffiliated deputies received at least one chairmanship, with the three largest factions each securing at least three. Nonetheless, complaints about insufficient consultation among the factions in assembling the slate of chairmen and in selecting the Rada's two deputy chairmen may presage a degree of polarisation and a lack of comity among deputies that could seriously hinder any attempts at consensus-building.

Although some deputies wanted to reduce the number of commissions, the politics of the moment may well have created different but reinforcing reasons not to do so. Commission seats and chairmanships were one resource that Moroz and his new majority coalition could use to reward allies and consolidate their control. And those who opposed this Communist/Socialist coalition could look on their commission positions as their most potent remaining source of influence in the Rada. Perhaps for this reason, many 'democrats' in the Rada successfully advocated increasing from three to four or five the number of sub-commissions per commission, 'the reasoning being that the more subcommissions there are the more diffuse power will become to the disadvantage of the Left'.[11]

Allowing for the vagaries of translations, most commissions of the new Rada carry titles identical or similar to those of their predecessors. (See Table 2 for a list of commissions in the 1994 Rada.) In several instances, however, changes in the committee system seem to reflect a better sense of institutional needs. For example, the workload that had been carried by the former Commission on Planning, Budget, Finance and Prices now appears to be divided between separate Commissions on the Budget and on Banking and Financial Affairs. Also, what had been the Commission on Mandates and Ethics of Parliamentary Members has been recast as the Commission on Regulations, Deputies' Ethics and Working Conditions, a change that may reflect a greater emphasis on the Rada's resources, infrastructure and standing orders.

TABLE 2

PERMANENT COMMISSIONS OF THE VERKHOVNA RADA, AS OF 26 MAY 1994

Agro-Industrial Complex, Land Resources, and the Social Development of the Village
Banking and Financial Activities
Basic Branches of Industry and Regional Development
Budget
Chernobyl
Culture and Spirituality
Defence and National Security
Ecological Policy
Economic Policy and the Administration of the National Economy
Fight Against Organised Crime and Corruption
Foreign Affairs and Relations with the CIS
Fuel and Energy Complex, Transport and Communications
Health, Motherhood and Childhood
Human Rights, National Minorities and Interethnic Relations
Legal Defence of Freedom of Expression
Legal, Political and Judicial Reform
Legality and Law and Order
Nuclear Policy and Nuclear Safety
Regulations, Deputies' Ethics and Working Conditions
Science and Education
Social Policy and Labour
State-Building, the Work of the Radas and Self-Administration
Youth, Sport and Tourism

Source: Markian Bilynskyj, 'Ukrainian Parliamentary Commissions Formed', *Update from Ukraine*, US–Ukraine Foundation, 10 June 1994.

Other changes in committees evidently reflect the emergence of new issues or the increased salience of 'old' issues that now merit formal recognition within the committee structure. There continues to be a commission on Chernobyl, but now there also is a separate Commission on Nuclear Policy and Nuclear Safety that should be well situated to address more generally the risks associated with Ukraine's continued reliance on dangerously unsafe nuclear reactors. Similarly, the new Rada has created a Commission on the Fight Against Organised Crime and Corruption, presumably to address an old problem that has taken a new and much more visible form. And the former Commission on Human Rights has been recreated as the Commission on Human Rights, National Minorities and Interethnic Relations. Whether this also represents a change in responsibilities, the change in name clearly signifies the east–west regional divide in Ukraine and the accompanying political differences between ethnic Ukrainians and ethnic Russians.

THE VERHKHOVNA RADA AS PARLIAMENT

The election of Moroz as Chairman of the Rada was not the only indication that, like Lithuania, Poland and Hungary, for example, Ukraine was experiencing the return of at least some elements of its 'old guard'. On 16 June, the Rada elected Vitaly Masol as prime minister by a vote of 199 to 24, with the support of President Kravchuk. Masol had been prime minister under the Soviet regime, during 1987–90. And soon thereafter, Kravchuk was defeated for re-election by former prime minister Leonid Kuchma, whose previous claim to fame had been his management of the Soviet Union's largest missile factory. So the triumvirate of Kuchma, Masol and Moroz, taken with the majority of the 'left' in the Rada, hardly constitute evidence of a democratic transformation in the political leadership of Ukraine.

As for the Rada itself, its future as a democratic parliament will depend not only on further internal, institutional change, but also on the resolution of at least two related questions affecting the fundamental design of Ukraine's political system – questions that Ukraine must address before it can finally adopt a definitive new post-Soviet, post-independence constitution.

What is to be the distribution of power between levels of government and within the national government? Should Ukraine transform itself into a federal state and the Rada into a bicameral institution in order to take account of the ethnic and cultural diversity, and the different historical experiences, among regions of the country? Giving greater constitutional or statutory powers to regional and local governments should reduce the Rada's workload, but also its ability to promote consistent national policies. And should Ukraine move toward presidentialism or parliamentarism? Either path is open, given the current confusion over the allocation of powers and responsibilities among the parliament, the president, and the prime minister and his Cabinet of Ministers. How Ukraine ultimately resolves both questions will reshape the underlying political and institutional context in which the Verkhovna Rada functions and, consequently, the criteria by which Ukrainians and scholars alike will evaluate its capacity and performance.

NOTES

1. Commission on Security and Cooperation in Europe (CSCE Commission), *Elections in the Baltic States and Soviet Republics* (Washington: US Government Printing Office, 1990), pp.113–36.
2. CSCE Commission, *Elections in the Baltic States and Soviet Republics*, p.133; and T. Kuzio and A. Wilson, *Ukraine: Perestroika to Independence* (New York: St. Martin's Press, 1994), p.125.
3. Council of Advisers to the Verkhovna Rada, *Briefing Information on Ukraine's Structure of Government and Parliament* (Kiev, manuscript, 1992). The data cited here do not reflect the results of special elections to fill the 28 seats that were vacant from 1 December 1992. Somewhat different figures, but to the same effect, are presented in Kuzio and Wilson,

Ukraine: Perestroika to Independence, pp.125–6.

4. Council of Advisers, *Briefing Information*.
5. Dominique Arel, 'Voting Behavior in the Ukrainian Parliament: The Language Factor' (Manuscript, 1993), p.6.
6. Commission on Security and Cooperation in Europe (CSCE Commission), *Ukraine's Parliamentary Election* (Washington, 1994), p.1.
7. International Foundation for Electoral Systems (IFES), *Ukraine's New Parliament* (Kiev and Washington, 1994), p.15.
8. IFES, *Ukraine's New Parliament*, p.14. With the Ukrainian party system in such a state of flux, any such data should be treated with caution. For example, somewhat different figures appear in the *RFE/RL Daily Report* for 12 April 1994, and in CSCE Commission, *Ukraine's Parliamentary Election*, p.24.
9. *Regulation on Deputies' Groups (Factions) in the Verkhovna Rada of Ukraine*, 13 May 1994.
10. Roman Woronowycz reports slightly different figures in 'New Ukrainian Supreme Council registers eight deputies' factions', *The Ukrainian Weekly*, 29 May 1994, p.3.
11. Markian Bilynskyj, 'Ukrainian Parliamentary Commissions Formed', *Update from Ukraine*, US–Ukraine Foundation, 10 June 1994, p.2.

parliaments in Adolescence

PHILIP NORTON and DAVID M. OLSON

Applying the research framework outlined in the introduction, this paper finds that in
the new democracies of central and eastern Europe borrowing from the old regime
rather than from Western expertise is predominant in constitution making and that the
policy activity of the new parliaments is shaped predominantly by external influences.
The fluid nature of political parties and limited pressure group activity facilitate policy
activity at the expense of 'responsible' party government. Policy attributes are shaped
by the stance toward the old regime. A process of institutionalisation is apparent, with
greater activity, committee specialisation and organisational sophistication.

Institutionalisation, as Richard Rose has noted, takes time, 'a decade or
more to demonstrate a regime's commitment to the rule of law and to
changing control of government in response to changes in electoral favour'.[1]
In the development of liberal democracy in the countries of central and
eastern Europe, parliaments may thus be described as being in their
adolescent stage. What generalisations can we draw from the experience of
the first five years or so of their existence about their birth, development and
place in their respective polities?

In our introduction, we identified a framework for analysis, constructing
our research questions under two principal headings: those of constitution
making and legislative impact. In seeking to determine legislative impact,
we distinguished three independent features: the external environment,
internal characteristics and policy attributes. From the case studies in this
volume, it is possible to provide some initial answers to these questions.

NEW CONSTITUTIONS

Constitution makers have a number of sources on which to draw in
completing their task. What were the principal sources for the constitution
makers in the new democracies? Was it the experience of established liberal
democracies or indigenous political culture and practice?

For those wishing to create democratic systems of government, the
experience of existing democratic systems would appear to offer a rich
source of material. As we noted in the introduction, Western countries have
been keen to offer advice and expertise. Yet what emerges from the studies

Philip Norton is Professor of Government at the University of Hull, UK. David M. Olson is
Professor of Political Science at the University of North Carolina-Greensboro, USA.

in this volume is the emphasis on the political culture and practice of each country in shaping its constitution and its institutions. William Crowther and Stephen Roper provide a particularly pertinent illustration of this in their comparative analysis of the Romanian and Moldovan legislatures, the former representing 'a unique fusion of interwar and communist legislative practices' and the latter being affected primarily by the experience of Soviet control, producing a notable continuity in structures – the republican supreme soviet becoming the national parliament – and in personnel. As Crowther and Roper note, though the precise mixture in Romania is unique to that country, it is not altogether dissimilar to the mixture in other east European legislatures.

Indeed, this carrying over from earlier regimes is perhaps the most consistent and obvious feature to emerge from these pages. This is not to say that Western experience was not drawn on, or at least called in aid, in determining some of the features of the new systems, a point brought out by Peet Kask in his analysis of Estonia, but the paucity of references to such borrowing from elsewhere is as noteworthy a feature of this volume as references to past practice of the country or countries under review.

That this has been such a feature of the new democracies can be explained by two characteristics that have distinguished the transition from Soviet rule to democracy in central and eastern Europe. The first has been the speed of change. Given the tempo of change in central and eastern Europe at the end of the 1980s, there was little time to dwell on foreign experience. Constitution makers had to move quickly, not least given the popular expectations generated by the end of Soviet domination.

The second explanatory characteristic has been that each country has witnessed a transition from one legislature to another. During the period of Soviet hegemony, the occupants of the Kremlin recognised the need to have a parliament in each of the satellite countries. The legislature in each case was, in Michael Mezey's typology, a minimal legislature[2] but nonetheless a legislature, meeting in order to give assent on behalf of the citizenry to measures of public policy placed before it.[3] When the Soviet yoke was withdrawn, the constitution and institutions of each country did not disappear with it. There was a legislature in place whose practices and structures could be drawn on. This thus distinguished the new European democracies from other countries where a democracy succeeded a military, autocratic or defeated regime where typically there was no parliament and hence no immediate past practice on which to draw in establishing a parliament.

It is the combination of these two features – the speed of change and institutional continuity – that make constitution making distinctive in the new European democracies.[4] The formation of parliaments in these democracies has been shaped by the indigeneous political culture and past practices. In the context of parliament building, past practices are particularly important. The different political cultures have been especially important in determining the policy attributes of the legislatures.

This is not to say that the experience of established liberal democracies may not be important. The new democracies are still in their early years. Most have incomplete constitutions, working with partial revisions of the Communist-era document. We would hypothesise that as the new democracies develop there will be a greater opportunity to draw on the experience of established systems and that such an opportunity will, in varying degrees, be taken. Indeed, as the new democracies develop they may witness some borrowing from one another.

LEGISLATIVE IMPACT

What emerges from our study of the external environment and the internal characteristics of the new parliaments in terms of their capacity to affect public policy is the extent to which the political systems in which they operate can be characterised as being in a formative stage. The relationship between the legislature and the executive stipulated by the constitution has generally constituted an invitation for conflict between the two, a conflict facilitated by the absence of constraints that characterise Western political systems.

External Constraints

Constitutional Structure

The constitutions of the new democracies vary. There is no consistent practice, for example, in choosing a unicameral or bicameral parliament. Some, such as the Slovak Republic, have a unicameral legislature, while Romania has opted for a bicameral legislature. The Czech Republic has a unicameral legislature on a temporary basis. In so far as a pattern can be observed, it follows that which has been noted in the rest of Europe and elsewhere, with unicameral legislatures existing in countries with small populations. With the exception of Ukraine, the larger countries of central and eastern Europe, such as Poland and Russia, have bicameral legislatures.

However, in so far as generalisation is possible, the most notable feature of the constitutional arrangements in the new democracies is the failure to opt decisively for a presidential or a parliamentary system of government. Former republics of the USSR have tended to favour a presidential system and the countries of central and eastern Europe have leaned more towards a parliamentary system. However, the extent to which each system leans towards a parliamentary or presidential system varies considerably. Perhaps the most remarkable feature is the number of countries that have some form of hybrid, or 'premier-presidential',[5] system. One study of 27 political systems of eastern Europe and the former Communist republics, published in 1994, listed one-third as hybrid, or 'semi-presidential', systems.[6] Even in some systems listed as presidential or parliamentary, the relationship between the president and the parliament is not as clear-cut as the ascription may suggest.

Though there appears to be a clear commitment to the concept of parliamentarianism in most of the new democracies – wanting a freely elected and deliberative assembly to determine the law – the experience of Soviet control has also instilled a wariness of conferring power in a single body. The result, especially in central Europe, has been a parliament with important powers, but powers tempered to a greater or lesser extent by powers vested in a president. Most but not all of the new democracies covered in this volume have opted for a popularly elected president, thus conferring on the Head of State a democratic legitimacy and a powerful political constituency independent of the legislature. Where this popular election has been conjoined with the power to choose the Head of Government, then we have a hybrid system with a presidential leaning; where the Head of Government is not chosen by the president, then we have a hybrid system with a parliamentary leaning.

Whichever type of hybrid exists, the separate election of the president is perhaps most crucial in creating the potential for conflict between the legislature and the executive. The more powers that are then conferred on the president, then arguably the greater the potential for conflict between the two.

The fact that there is a potential for conflict does not necessarily mean that conflict will be realised. For most of the history of the Fifth French Republic, relations between the president and the National Assembly have not been marked by conflict. Yet the early history of the new democracies has typically been marked by some degree of struggle between the parliament and the executive. This we attribute to the existence of multiple parties and the absence of constraints that exist in mature democracies.

Party Systems and Electoral Campaign Structure

The electoral systems introduced in the new democracies have varied, but the preference – other than in the former republics of the USSR – has tended to be for some form of proportional representation with a threshold requirement. The threshold for a single party to achieve membership in the parliament is usually three, four or five per cent.

Multi-party systems are a clear feature of the new democracies. Yet the most important characteristic for the purposes of our analysis is the fluid state of most of those party systems. The parties themselves have typically – though not always – had to be formed from nothing and had to campaign in competition with other parties in an environment not used to such activity. The culture has not always been a congenial one. The concept of competing for votes and members, and allowing electors the opportunity to switch from one party to another, is not one that politicians reared in the Soviet era have found easy to grasp.[7]

Freed from the shackles of commitment to one party, many voters have had difficulty making a choice. The same applies to parliamentarians. As we have seen from various of the contributions to this volume, the membership of parliamentary parties is sometimes fluid. Some parties are formed after the parliament has met. Some members move from one to another, engaging in what has been termed 'political tourism'. Throughout the first term of the pst-Communist Sejm in Poland, as Maurice Simon records, 'a variety of parliamentary clubs and circles were established and either persisted, changed their names, or ceased to exist, thus reflecting the continuous turmoil in the political arena'. In the Ukrainian Verkhovna Rada in 1992–93, there were nine officially registered parties but, as Stanley Bach reports, one estimate put the number of groups of deputies at 47, 'although some were ephemeral, many were poorly organised, and individual MPs could and did belong to more than one of them'.

Links between party groupings in a parliament and party leaders and organisation outside the parliament are also not well developed. In the Bulgarian case, as Georgi Karasimeonov notes, the relationship is marked by friction. There is not necessarily any sense of commitment to the party as a whole and, indeed, in some cases the 'party' itself constitutes little more than a body formed within the parliament. Members of Parliament may not want to vote with other party members, especially where the party grouping is hastily formed for convenience (in order to meet the regulations governing the formation of such party groups), and may not feel they have to, given typically the absence of any well-developed party discipline. Political parties thus do not serve as a constraint on the behaviour of Members of Parliament to the extent that they do in most Western systems.

The absence of developed parties militates against a responsible party system. That is, there is no one party or established collection of parties that electors can hold responsible for the actions of government. This is exacerbated by the separate election of president and parliament. In the event of conflict or stalemate, which of the two does the electorate hold responsible?

Interest Groups

There is evidence in some countries of organised groups having some links with political activity. As Darina Malova and Danica Sivakova show in their paper, contact between organised interests and political actors is a feature of political life in Slovakia. The number of organised interests has increased enormously since 1989 and different means are employed in seeking to influence public policy. Labour and employer organisations are especially well organised and active, but many other interests have learned how to exert influence. The picture that emerges is one of a range of organised interests developing links with government, parties and Members of Parliament.

However, there is little evidence of such links developing in other systems. The Slovak experience appears to be the exception rather than the rule. Rather, what emerges from the contributions to this volume is that interest groups are developing in the new democracies but have not yet developed clear links with political actors. Links with parliamentary parties are either not apparent (that is, we have no information about them) or are known to be weak or non-existent. Jana Reschová and Jindriska Syllová report that, though most members of the Czech Parliament registered some interest outside parliament in 1992, the links between interest groups and parliament are not well established. A similar picture emerges from Hungary, compounded by the reluctance of government to sanction the integration of groups into governmental and parliamentary processes.[8] In other systems, the limited development and impact of groups has to be inferred from the absence of information about them. Links between organised interests and parliaments, be it through parliamentary parties or individual parliamentarians, are not so well developed as to be discernible to observers.[9]

The absence of such links have important implications for parliaments and parliamentary behaviour. Political parties provide a weak anchor for parliamentarians. Interest groups in most of the new democracies appear to offer no anchor at all for members of the new parliaments. They provide few or no voting cues and sometimes little or no pressure to pursue particular issues with government.

Where interest groups are numerous, specialised and in conflict with administrative agencies, then we would expect parliamentary activity to increase and for that activity to follow a recognisable pattern. Where there is a virtual absence of interest group activity, then we would expect the activity of MPs to be shaped by other influences. Under Soviet rule, there was one single cue-giving body. Now, there appears in many cases to be an absence of developed cue-givers, thus allowing Members of Parliament to be active, but not necessarily in a patterned or predictable manner.

Internal Characteristics

A number of internal characteristics reinforce the 'irresponsible' nature of the political system. The principal characteristic is one already touched upon: the fluid nature of parties within the parliament. We mentioned in the introduction that too many parties, and too little organisation, will tend to fragment the legislature, depriving it of any internal ability to organise itself. Certainly, party within the new parliaments tends to be fragmented and members variously willing to move from one party or party group to another.

Militating against a developed party system is the high turnover of members. What emerges from the contributions to this volume is that the continuity in membership from one parliament to another appears to have been remarkably low. This may have its beneficial side, in that one consequence may have been the disappearance of many of those whose commitment was to the old regime, concomitantly bringing in people with new interests and different experiences, but it also has had the effect of denying the opportunity for members to build up experience in parliamentary practices and to develop a collective ethos.

A third characteristic contributing to the 'irresponsible' nature of the party system appears to be the weak link between the Member of Parliament and the constituent. In some countries, notably Poland, there is evidence of considerable constituency activity, and evidence of *some* constituency activity in some of the others (Hungary, the Czech Republic and Russia),[10] but constituency relationships do not feature significantly and consistently in the contributions to this volume. There appears to be a lack of contact in many cases. 'Under the old regime, members were expected to serve as a link between their constituents and the leadership at the centre. Under the new regime, these activities, at least for the time being, seem to be somewhat less in evidence.'[11] The electoral systems do not necessarily encourage contact and in some cases the deputies do not reside in their districts. Our evidence suggests that where contact does occur, the voter will often go to the deputy as a supplicant.

Nonetheless, we can point to a degree of institutionalisation in the new parliaments. There is a greater degree of professionalism, with more staff, greater resources (including – as in the case of the Ukrainian Parliament – computer technology), and the use of committees. The use of committees is a notable feature. All the parliaments covered in this volume have established permanent committees, supplemented in some cases by special or provisional committees. The number of permanent committees ranges from ten in the case of the Czech Republic to 24 in the case of both Poland and the Ukraine.

The committees are established by law or by standing orders and have an established place in the legislative process. Indeed, the committees are primarily responsible for the initial preparation of a bill or for considering it and preparing a report for the chamber. This distinguishes them from a number of Western legislatures, especially those operating in Westminster systems, where bills are considered first in plenary session. There is some empirical evidence that the referral of bills to committee, prior to deliberation in the chamber, enhances the policy affect of legislatures.[12] A number of the committees, notably but not exclusively those in the Czech and Slovak parliaments, are also vested with powers to require the submission of evidence. The power of the Slovak National Council to require ministers and civil servants to attend committee meetings is enshrined in the constitution.

The committees in the new legislatures meet regularly and the contributions to this volume draw out the activity of those committees. Maurice Simon's paper on the Polish Sejm provides especially valuable data on both the number of meetings and the work completed by the committees. Committee meetings increased in number under the old regime, but then increased markedly after 1989. During the first Sejm of the post-Communist period, the 24 permanent committees met 2,132 times. They issued 82 *disiderata* (requests to agencies to undertake particular actions) and 304 opinions (interpretations of particular rules or activities), the Committee on Health issuing the largest single number of *disiderata* and the Committee on Deputy Rules and Affairs issuing the largest number of opinions, followed by the Committee on Foreign Affairs.

Each deputy is almost invariably given a committee assignment. In some cases, all deputies serve on at least one committee. In others, the usual practice is for most deputies to be assigned to at least one committee. In the case of Hungary, for example, 288 out of the 386 members in the First Parliament had committee assignments. In some instances, some members serve on several committees, but the practice of limiting committee memberships (usually to one committee) appears now to be a common feature.

The chamber is more important than used to be the case under the old regime and is in session more often. Attila Ágh shows that, in Hungary, the First Parliament supplemented regular sessions with long winter and summer sessions, with plenary sessions occupying no less than 378 days between May 1990 and April 1994. Chamber sessions are employed not only for the consideration of legislation but also variously – as in the case of the Russian Duma and Polish Sejm – for interpellations (questions to government), resolutions and petitions. As Thomas Remington and Steven Smith show, the Duma was extremely active in its first year of existence, considering 211 draft laws. In 1994, it considered 626 matters and, as part of this consideration, passed 41 resolutions, adopted 34 interpellations and 20 petitions and declarations. These figures pale into insignifance alongside those for the first post-Communist Sejm in which 773 interpellations were registered. Deputies also asked 508 questions, receiving 295 oral and 213 written responses.

There is also greater institutionalisation in terms of party groupings and membership. Despite 'political tourism' and the high turnover of members, many parliamentary parties are established and resources flow to them as a result of constituting organised groups within the parliament. Some deputies have been returned to successive parliaments. We have seen in the preceding pages the extent to which the legislative process is used by parliamentarians, in some cases to block measures and in others to initiate them. Indeed, as we shall see in our consideration of policy attributes, active participation in the legislative process, especially at an early stage, is a notable feature of the new legislatures.

We can thus see institutional development taking place, and we would expect that to continue, with a greater drawing than before on the practice and expertise of other legislatures.

Policy Attributes

The policies pursued by the legislatures vary considerably. This is explicable in terms of the policy circumstances. The most important variable shaping the policy of the legislatures is the stance of the dominant legislative parties towards the old regime. In some cases, the focus has been on removing all vestiges of the old regime and seeking to recreate features of the pre-Soviet system, doing so at the expense of more pressing economic problems. Where the attitude towards the Soviet era has been less antagonistic, the emphases have been different. The policy emphasis has also changed as new parties have been elected to power.

Involvement in terms of the policy stages also differs. Where the executive has achieved a dominance in executive–legislative relations, the legislature looks to the executive to propose measures. Legislatures generally in the new democracies look to the government to propose economic policy and to bring forward the budget. However, the often weak hold of parties has meant that political parties have yet to serve as a fully effective conduits for the transfer of power from legislature to executive. Consequently, legislators retain some capacity for independent action in the legislative process. As we have seen in the case of Hungary, many legislative amendments originate not from opposition deputies but from members of the parties forming the governing coalition. The circumstances of the new democracies create particular opportunities for introducing measures, the sweeping away of the old system offering almost a clean slate on which to write. As Georgi Karasimeonov writes

> the short experience of postcommunist legislatures leads to the conclusion that for a certain time to come they will be much more active in setting the policy agenda and initiating new bills than legislatures in established democracies. This is a result of the gigantic tasks of changing the old system and secondly of the desire of parliament to keep its primordial role as the major policy maker.

We thus witness most legislatures being involved in the early stages of the legislative process (Ukraine is among the exceptions), with committees, factions or individual members introducing and sometimes achieving passage of bills. Of the 211 bills introduced in the Russian Diet in 1994, 111 originated with individual members. It is clear from the figures presented by Remington and Smith that a number of those proposed by individual members were passed by the Duma (since the total number approved by the Duma was 116), though not all bills passed by the Duma were approved by the Council of Federation and the president. The data, though, are sufficient to demonstrate the activity of members in the initiation of legislative measures. In the first post-Communist Sejm in Poland, 26 bills were introduced by committees, of which 14 were adopted and only one withdrawn or rejected; the rest failed to complete the legislative process.

The involvement at early stages is more pronounced than in Western systems, with the exception of the United States. The legislatures in most cases thus veer more towards Mezey's category of legislatures with strong, rather than modest, policy-making power. Even so, there is a clear generalisation to be drawn from the evidence presented in this volume. The government may not be responsible for most of the measures introduced, but most of the measures it introduces are passed; whereas most of the measures introduced by individual members (or factions) are not passed. The 90 per cent rule does not yet operate, but from the evidence presented we can generalise that the movement in the new democracies is in that direction.

SUPPORT

How, then, have the legislatures of the new democracies been viewed by citizens? Competition for election to the legislatures has generally been keen and turnout in elections has been high. As the paper by Georgi Karasimeonov shows, turnout in the first free election in Bulgaria, in June 1990, was 91 per cent. Surveys show that support for legislatures is widespread, spanning all social groups.[13]

However, that support is not constant. It varies from country to country and over time.[14] We have seen that in countries such as Hungary, Bulgaria and Poland, support for the legislature is declining rather than increasing. This is reflected in the survey data reported in the papers and may also be inferred from a decline in voter turnout. The turnout in the 1994 elections in Bulgaria, though still high at 84 per cent, was seven per cent lower than in 1990.

This is not dissimilar to experience in many Western countries and, as with the findings from Western experience, may be a consequence of dissatisfaction with economic performance – that is, of variables largely beyond the control of the legislature. The evidence presented in this volume suggests (but is insufficient to do more than suggest) that legislatures may also be autonomous actors, their actions serving to undermine rather than bolster support, through exhibiting conflict or behaviour that attracts a negative response from voters. The evidence from Hungary, presented by Attila Ágh, suggests that the parliament may be both a cause of dissatisfaction (the behaviour of elected members) and a consequence (popular attitudes towards the government).

If (and, given limited data, it is important to stress that it is a big if) legislatures are able by their actions to influence levels of popular support, then it is possible to hypothesise that legislatures may serve to impede the decline through facilitating the emergence of a responsible party system. The more political parties are organised both within and outside parliament, and have an established, cohesive and continuing parliamentary membership, then the greater the capacity for voters to hold a body or bodies to account for measures of public policy passed by the parliament. The institutionalisation of legislatures facilitates the development of organised parties, organisation being necessary to maximise the use of resources, committee assignments, and procedures to block or pass measures.

CONCLUSION

The new parliaments of central and eastern Europe exist in political systems that are characterised in many cases by fragility and conflict. The parliaments are still in a formative stage, their capacity to determine policy outcomes being limited in many cases by an independent executive and by the growing strength of political parties. Some, such as the Moldovan legislature, are not highly developed as insitutions. They are buffeted by forces largely beyond their control. Popular support remains but is declining rather than increasing

Yet the parliaments are also vital to the new democracies. No democracy can exist (or at least has existed) without one. The parliament is the means – or, in systems where the president is elected separately, one of the means – through which citizens can express their preferences. The parliaments have proved important actors in the new democracies. They have served as magnets for political parties and arena in which parties articulate their views. 'The institution of parliament thus allows for the articulation of political differences, and so provides for the "parliamentarianisation" of conflict. In a direct sense it re-routes political battles from the streets into the chamber(s) of parliament.'[15] The parliaments have proved to be more independent in determining public policy than most legislatures in established Western systems. In some cases, they have served as the site for the resolution of major national issues.

We can discern the process of institutionalisation. They are acquiring the 'legislative effectiveness, organisational articulation and rule abiding patterns' that, according to Geoffrey Pridham, form part of the process of parliamentary institutionalisation.[16] We can also see some evidence of parties, pressure groups and constituency relations developing and the emergence, to a greater or lesser extent (depending on the country), of a 'responsible' party system.

How, then, to summarise the position in which the parliaments find themselves? A line from Dickens has been variously quoted to demonstrate the challenges facing certain legislatures at certain times. It may be especially appropriate in this context. For the parliaments of the new democracies of central and eastern Europe 'these are the best of times, these are the worst of times'. Whether the best pushes out the worst remains to be seen. Initial indications, based on patterns of institutionalisation, are not discouraging.

NOTES

1. R. Rose, 'Dynamics of Democratic Regimes', in J. Hayward and E.C. Page (eds.), *Governing the New Europe* (Cambridge: Polity Press, 1995), p.87.
2. M. Mezey, *Comparative Legislatures* (Durham NC: Duke University Press, 1979).
3. P. Norton (ed.), *Legislatures* (Oxford: Oxford University Press, 1990), p.1.
4. See D. McSweeney and C. Tempest, 'The Political Science of Democratic Transition in Eastern Europe', *Political Studies*, 41, 3 (Sept. 1993), pp.408–19, for a discussion of other variables contributing to 'a distinctively *East European* route to democracy' (p.417).
5. M.S. Shugart and J.M. Carey, *Presidents and Assemblies: Constitutional Design and Electoral Dynamics* (Cambridge: Cambridge University Press, 1992).
6. T.F. Remington, 'Introduction: Parliamentary Elections and the Transition from Communism', in T.F. Remington (ed.), *Parliaments in Transition* (Boulder CO: Westview Press, 1994), Table 1.1, pp.13–15.
7. This is illustrated by the experience of Norton. Speaking about British party politics to a visiting delegation of Russian parliamentarians in 1994, he mentioned that both main parties in Britain had seen a decline in their membership over the years. One of the parliamentarians

queried this: 'How can that be?' he asked. 'Do you not have sanctions against members leaving parties?'

8. See also G. Ilonszki, 'Parliament and Parliamentarians in Hungary in a Comparative Perspective', in A. Ágh (ed.), *The Emergence of East Central European Parliaments: The First Steps* (Budapest: Hungarian Centre of Democracy Studies, 1994), p.247. The problem is further compounded by the fact that interest group representation is not considered by Members of Parliament to be compatible with the nature of the parliament and their freedom of representation.

9. Limited evidence from other studies confirm our assessment. Werner Patzelt, in a study of German legislators, found some evidence of interest group links with deputies elected in the former East Germany, but noted nonetheless that the system of interest groups had developed from the top down and had not yet taken firm root. The groups that did exist provided a considerable source of political impulses, 'but by no means do they have, thus far, the important position they have in West Germany', W.J. Patzelt, 'Legislators of New Parliaments: The Case of East Germany', in Ágh (ed.), *The Emergence of East Central European Parliaments*, p.278. A similar situation appears to exist in Russia, where groups are often formed in order to oppose other movements and operate in a fairly atomistic manner. O.A. Kolobov, 'Interest Groups in the Legislative Structures of Power: The Case of Russia', in L.D. Longley (ed.), *Working Papers on Comparative Legislative Studies* (Appleton WI: Research Committee of Legislative Specialists of the the IPSA, 1994), pp.109–10.

10. On Hungary see, in addition to Attila Ágh's paper in this volume. D. Judge and G. Ilonszki, 'Member-Constituency Linkages in the Hungarian Parliament', *Legislative Studies Quarterly,* 19, 1994.

11. M.L. Mezey, 'Parliament in the New Europe', in J. Hayward and E.C. Page (eds.), *Governing the New Europe* (Cambridge: Polity Press, 1995), p.213. see also W.J. Patzelt, 'Legislators of New Parliaments: The Case of East Germany', pp.271–3.

12. See M. Shaw, 'Conclusion', in J.D. Lees and M. Shaw (eds.), *Committees in Legislatures* (Oxford: Martin Robertson, 1979), pp.361–434.

13. W. Mishler and R. Rose, 'Support for Parliaments and Regimes in the Transition Toward Democracy in Eastern Europe', *Legislative Studies Quarterly,* 19, 1 (Feb. 1994), pp.14–18.

14. See J.R. Hibbing and S.C. Patterson, 'Public Trust in the New Parliaments of Central and Eastern Europe', in L.D. Longley (ed.), *Working Papers on Comparative Legislative Studies* (Appleton WI: Research Committee of Legislative Specialists of the the IPSA, 1994), p.91.

15. D. Judge, 'East Central European Parliaments: The First Steps', in Ágh (ed.), *The Emergence of East Central European Parliaments*, p.27.

16. G. Pridham, 'Political Parties, Parliaments and Democratic Consolidation in Southern Europe: Empirical and Theoretical Perspectives', in U. Liebert and M. Cotta (eds.), *Parliament and Democratic Consolidation in Southern Europe* (London: Pinter, 1990), p.228.

Index